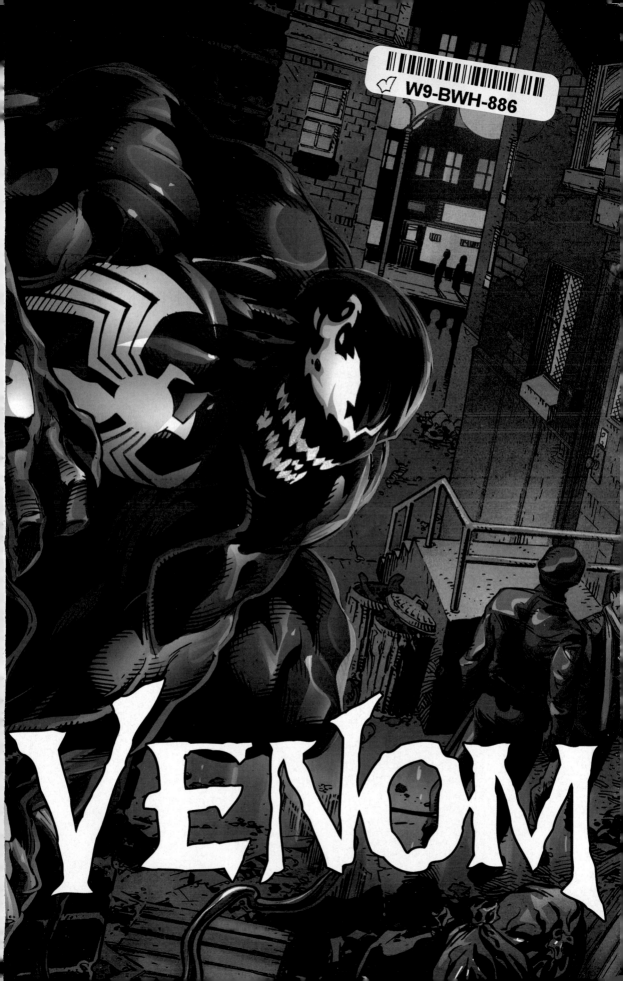

VENOM

EDDIE BROCK AND THE VENOM SYMBIOTE HAVE BEEN REUNITED, BUT BOTH OF THEM HAVE CHANGED SINCE THEY LAST WERE TOGETHER. VENOM STILL WANTS TO BE A HERO BUT HAS FOUND IT DIFFICULT TO CONTAIN ITS MORE VIOLENT IMPULSES. IT HAS EVEN GONE SO FAR AS TO ATTACK PEOPLE IT PERCEIVES AS A THREAT WHILE EDDIE HAS BEEN SLEEPING. ONE OF VENOM'S VICTIMS WAS THE PRIEST OF THE CHURCH WHERE EDDIE AND VENOM FIRST BONDED...

COLLECTION EDITOR **MARK D. BEAZLEY** :: ASSISTANT EDITOR **CAITLIN O'CONNELL**
ASSOCIATE MANAGING EDITOR **KATERI WOODY** :: SENIOR EDITOR, SPECIAL PROJECTS **JENNIFER GRÜNWALD**
VP PRODUCTION & SPECIAL PROJECTS **JEFF YOUNGQUIST** :: SVP PRINT, SALES & MARKETING **DAVID GABRIEL**
BOOK DESIGNER **JAY BOWEN**

EDITOR IN CHIEF **C.B. CEBULSKI** :: CHIEF CREATIVE OFFICER **JOE QUESADA**
PRESIDENT **DAN BUCKLEY** :: EXECUTIVE PRODUCER **ALAN FINE**

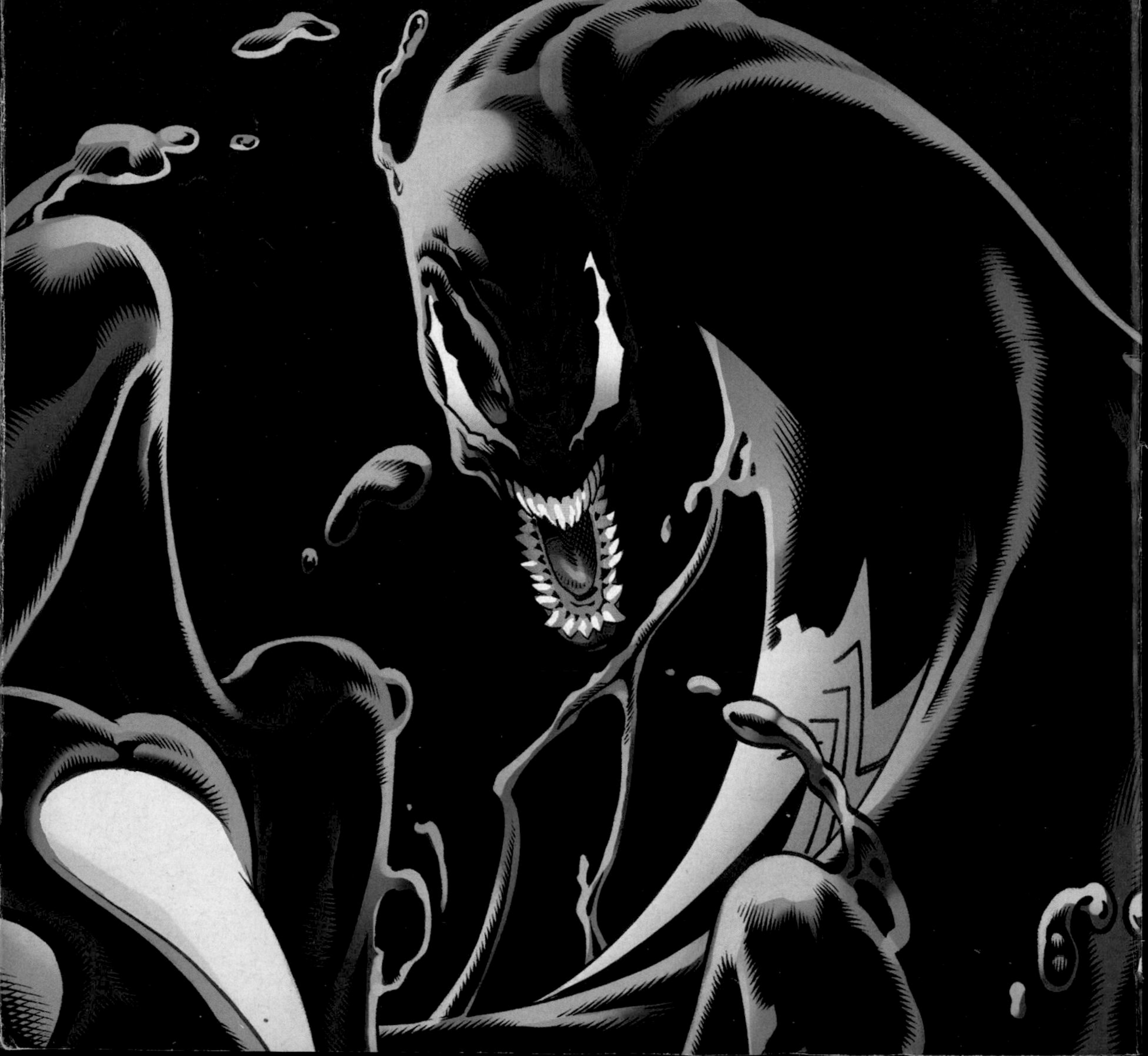

VENOM

MIKE COSTA
WRITER

---------- #154 SKIN DEEP ----------

PAULO SIQUEIRA
PENCILER

WALDEN WONG, CAM SMITH & PAULO SIQUEIRA
INKERS

RACHELLE ROSENBERG
COLOR ARTIST

---------- #155-158 LETHAL PROTECTOR ----------

MARK BAGLEY
PENCILER

JOHN DELL (#155-158), SCOTT HANNA (#156-157) & ANDREW HENNESSY (#158)
INKERS

DONO SÁNCHEZ-ALMARA
COLOR ARTIST

GERARDO SANDOVAL (#154); MARK BAGLEY, JOHN DELL
& RICHARD ISANOVE (#155); MARK BAGLEY,
ANDREW HENNESSY & PAUL MOUNTS (#156); AND
MARK BAGLEY, JOHN DELL & JOHN RAUCH (#157-158)
COVER ART

ALLISON STOCK & TOM GRONEMAN
ASSISTANT EDITORS

DEVIN LEWIS
EDITOR

NICK LOWE
EXECUTIVE EDITOR

VENOM VOL. 3: LETHAL PROTECTOR — BLOOD IN THE WATER. Contains material originally published in magazine form as VENOM #154-158. First printing 2018. ISBN 978-1-302-90604-7. Published by MARVEL WORLDWIDE, INC., a subsidiary of MARVEL ENTERTAINMENT, LLC. OFFICE OF PUBLICATION: 135 West 50th Street, New York, NY 10020. Copyright © 2018 MARVEL No similarity between any of the names, characters, persons, and/or institutions in this magazine with those of any living or dead person or institution is intended, and any such similarity which may exist is purely coincidental. **Printed in Canada.** DAN BUCKLEY, President, Marvel Entertainment; JOE QUESADA, Chief Creative Officer; TOM BREVOORT, SVP of Publishing; DAVID BOGART, SVP of Business Affairs & Operations, Publishing & Partnership; DAVID GABRIEL, SVP of Sales & Marketing, Publishing; JEFF YOUNGQUIST, VP of Production & Special Projects; DAN CARR, Executive Director of Publishing Technology; ALEX MORALES, Director of Publishing Operations; SUSAN CRESPI, Production Manager; STAN LEE, Chairman Emeritus. For information regarding advertising in Marvel Comics or on Marvel.com, please contact Vit DeBellis, Custom Solutions & Integrated Advertising Manager, at vdebellis@marvel.com. For Marvel subscription inquiries, please call 888-511-5480. **Manufactured between 12/8/2017 and 1/9/2018 by SOLISCO PRINTERS, SCOTT, QC, CANADA.**

10 9 8 7 6 5 4 3 2 1

154

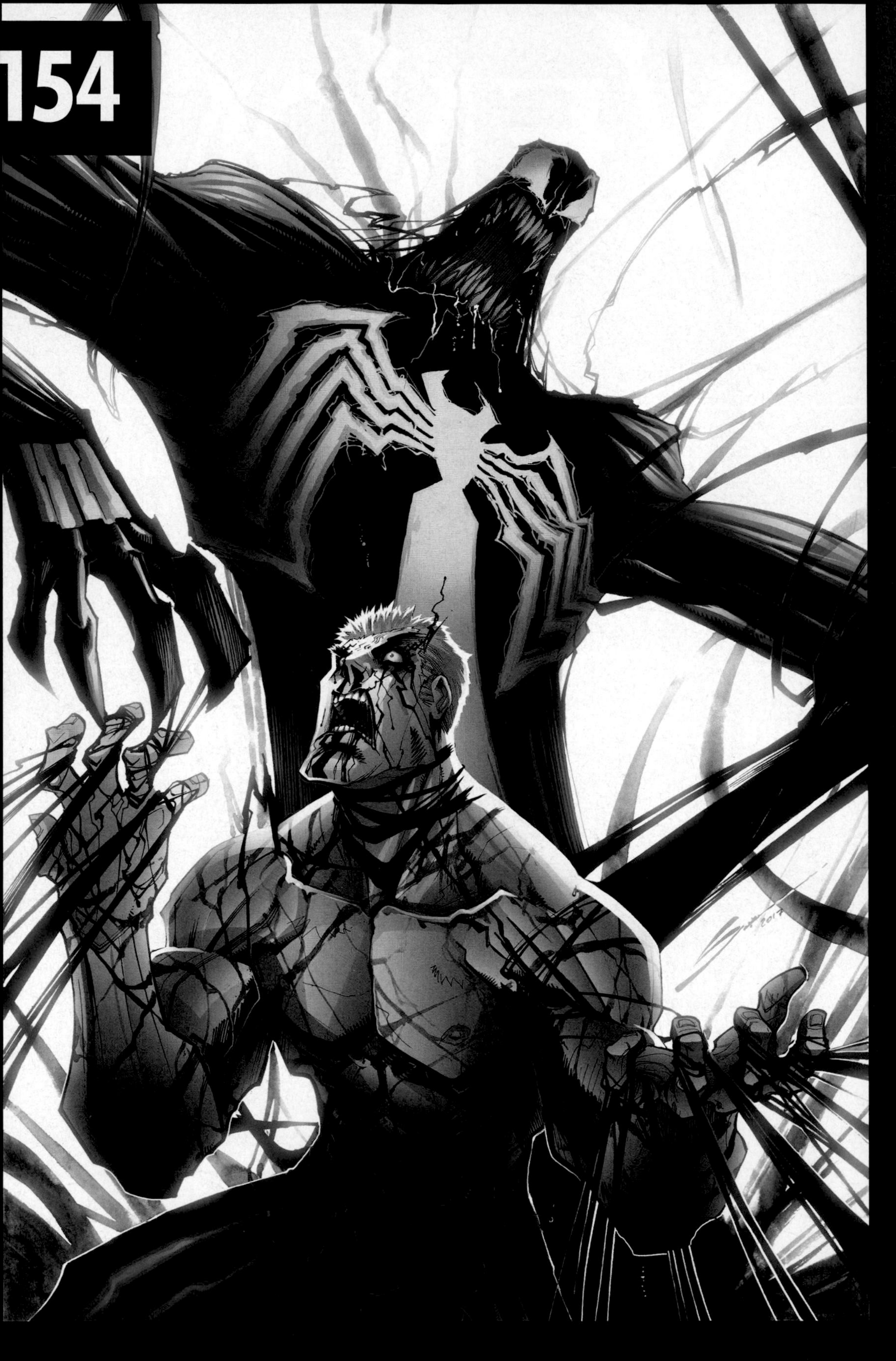

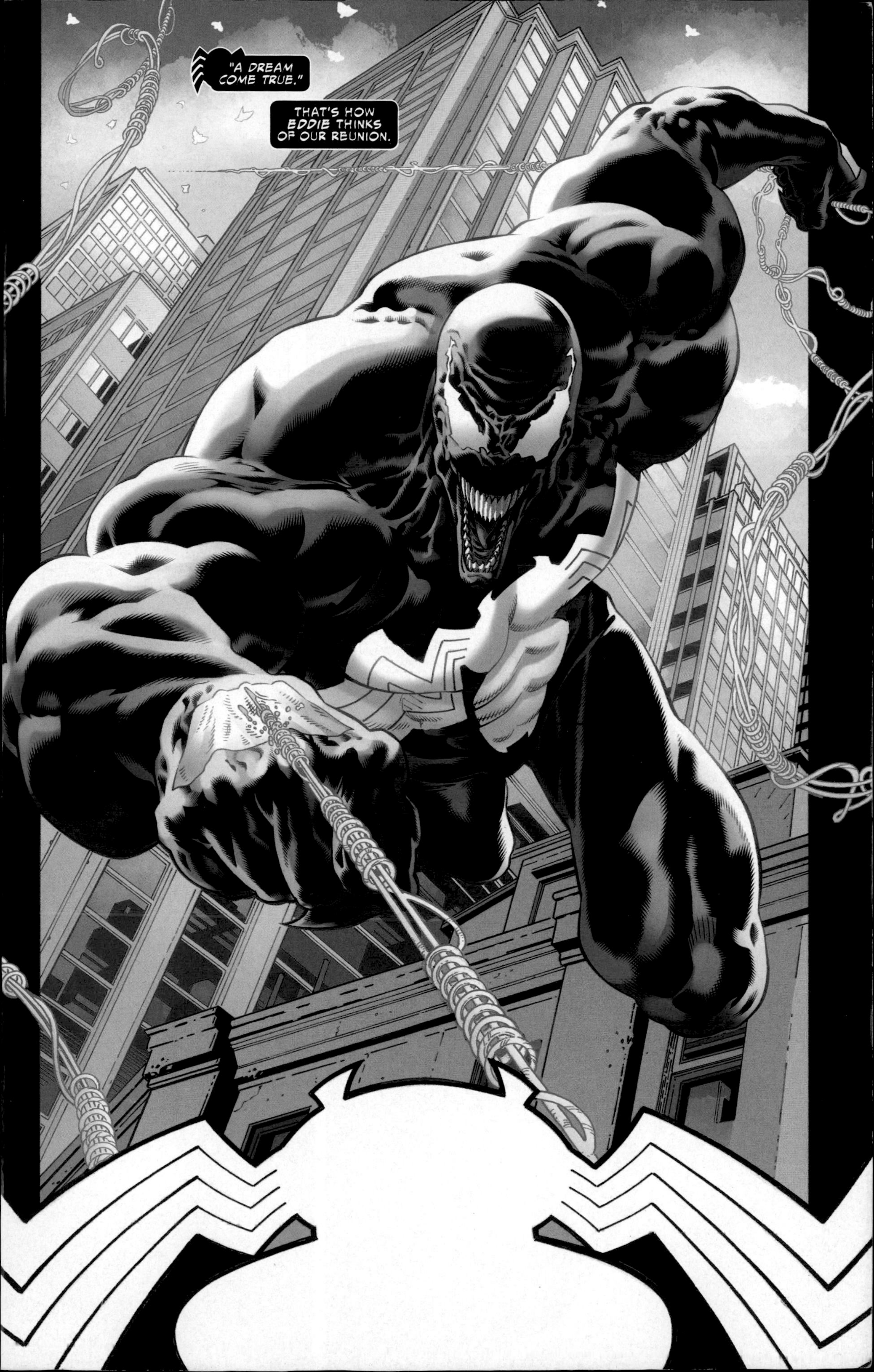
"A DREAM COME TRUE."
THAT'S HOW EDDIE THINKS OF OUR REUNION.

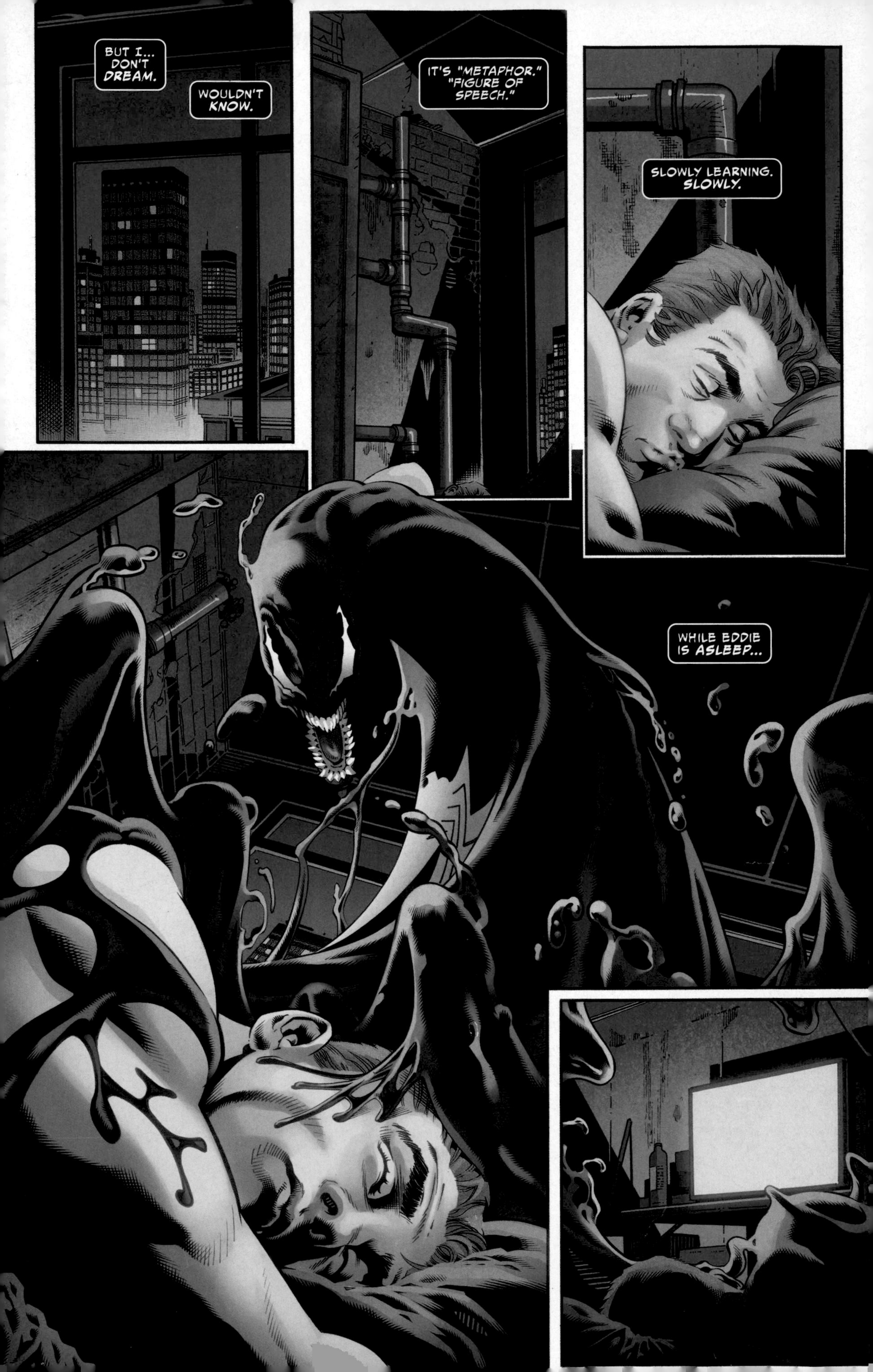
BUT I... DON'T DREAM.
WOULDN'T KNOW.
IT'S "METAPHOR." "FIGURE OF SPEECH."
SLOWLY LEARNING. SLOWLY.
WHILE EDDIE IS ASLEEP...

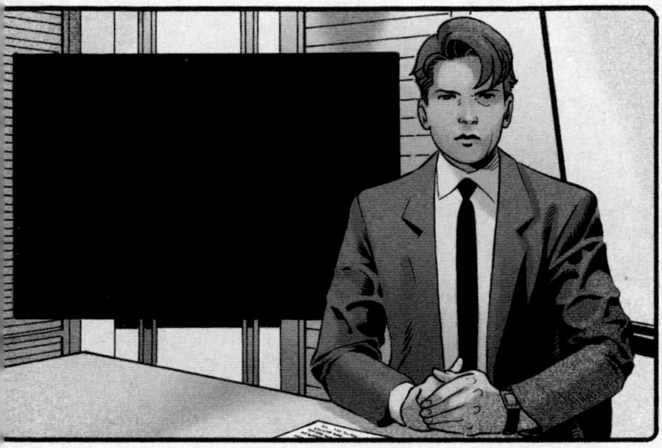

"**TONIGHT!** ON THE **LATE EDITION.** A SPECIAL REPORT, PROFILING HERMAN SCHULTZ, THE **SHOCKER.**

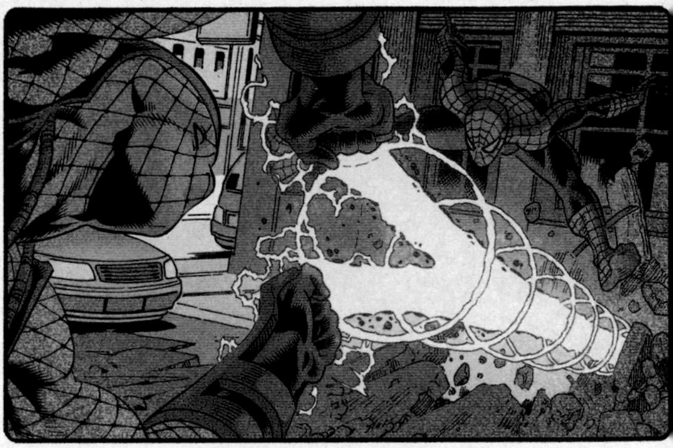

"FROM HIGH SCHOOL **DROPOUT** TO ENGINEERING **GENIUS.** FROM INFAMOUS **SAFE-CRACKER** TO THE **MOST INCARCERATED SUPER VILLAIN** OF ALL TIME.

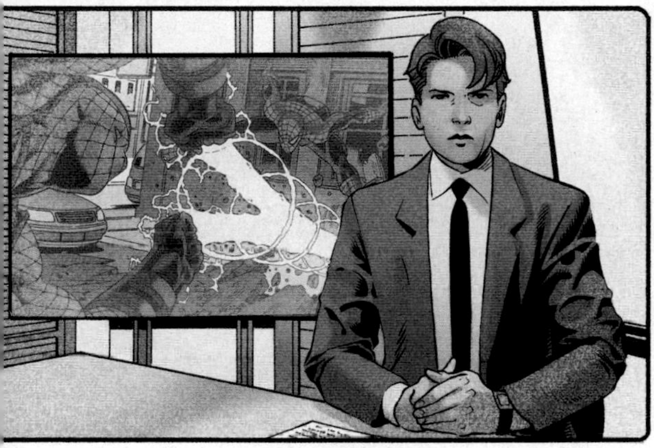

"THE **HIGHS** AND **LOWS** OF A **MASKED CRIMINAL.** WITH **RARE INTERVIEWS** WITH SEVERAL OF HIS GREATEST **FOES.**"

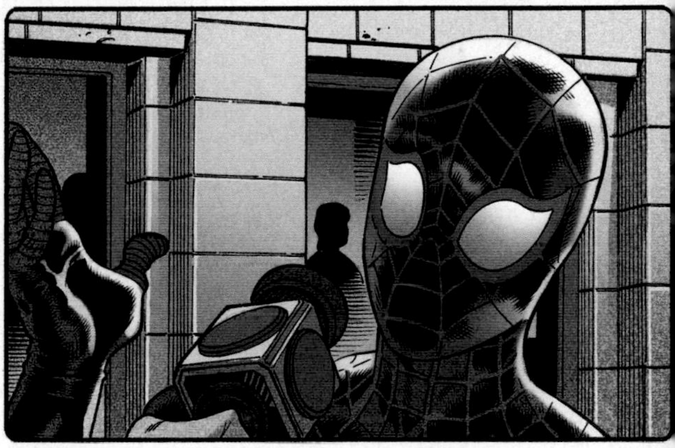

"YEAH, HE KNOCKED OVER AN ARMORED CAR--LIKE, LITERALLY **KNOCKED IT OVER--** BUT THEN HE WAS TRIPPING OVER EVERYTHING THAT SPILLED OUT ON THE STREET AND I JUST PUNCHED HIM IN THE HEAD.

"WAIT...ARE YOU GUYS SERIOUSLY DOING A NEWS REPORT ON THE SHOCKER?"

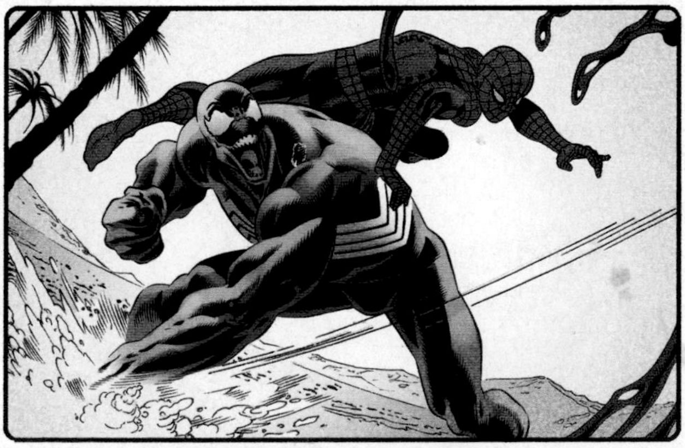

"THIS WAS A COMMON SENTIMENT. AND, INDEED, WHEN COMPARED TO THE MORE **HORRIFYING** CREATURES THAT THE AVENGERS AND THEIR ILK HAVE FACED, THE SHOCKER CAN SEEM A LITTLE...LIGHTWEIGHT."

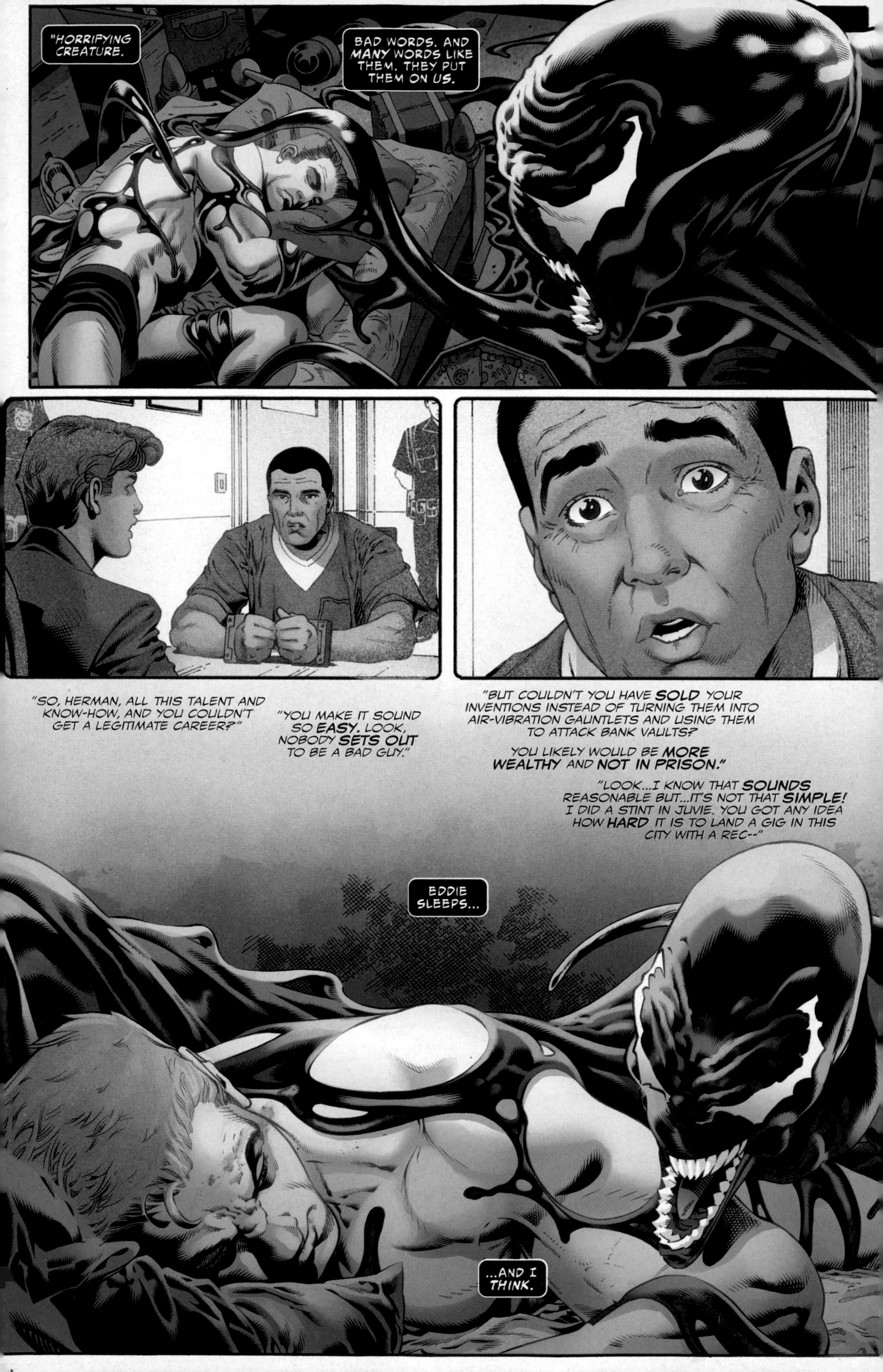
"HORRIFYING CREATURE.
BAD WORDS. AND MANY WORDS LIKE THEM. THEY PUT THEM ON US.
"SO, HERMAN, ALL THIS TALENT AND KNOW-HOW, AND YOU COULDN'T GET A LEGITIMATE CAREER?"
"YOU MAKE IT SOUND SO EASY. LOOK, NOBODY SETS OUT TO BE A BAD GUY."
"BUT COULDN'T YOU HAVE SOLD YOUR INVENTIONS INSTEAD OF TURNING THEM INTO AIR-VIBRATION GAUNTLETS AND USING THEM TO ATTACK BANK VAULTS?
YOU LIKELY WOULD BE MORE WEALTHY AND NOT IN PRISON."
"LOOK...I KNOW THAT SOUNDS REASONABLE BUT...IT'S NOT THAT SIMPLE! I DID A STINT IN JUVIE. YOU GOT ANY IDEA HOW HARD IT IS TO LAND A GIG IN THIS CITY WITH A REC--"
EDDIE SLEEPS...
...AND I THINK.

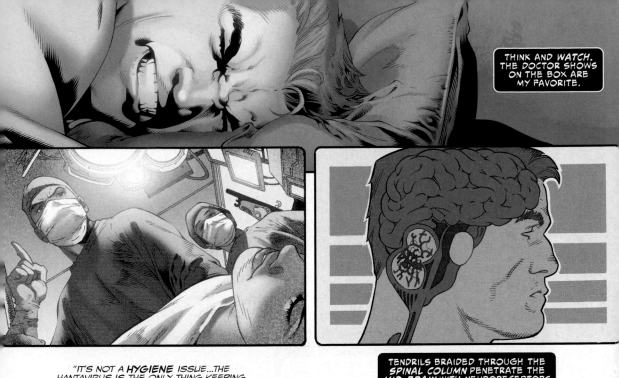

THINK AND *WATCH*. THE DOCTOR SHOWS ON THE BOX ARE MY FAVORITE.

"IT'S NOT A HYGIENE ISSUE...THE HANTAVIRUS IS THE ONLY THING KEEPING THIS RARE STRAIN OF MENINGOCOCCUS FROM ATTACKING HIS BRAIN STEM.

"HE NEEDS MOUSE BITES TO LIVE!"

TENDRILS BRAIDED THROUGH THE *SPINAL COLUMN* PENETRATE THE *MID-BRAIN* WITH NEURORECEPTORS SENSITIVE TO CATECHOLAMINES *DOPAMINE* AND *EPINEPHRINE.*

LEARNED FROM THE BOX.

CAN'T *HEAR* EDDIE'S THOUGHTS...BUT FEEL THEM.

CAN SEE HIS *DREAMS,* THOUGH.

CAN SEE THEM *VIVID.*

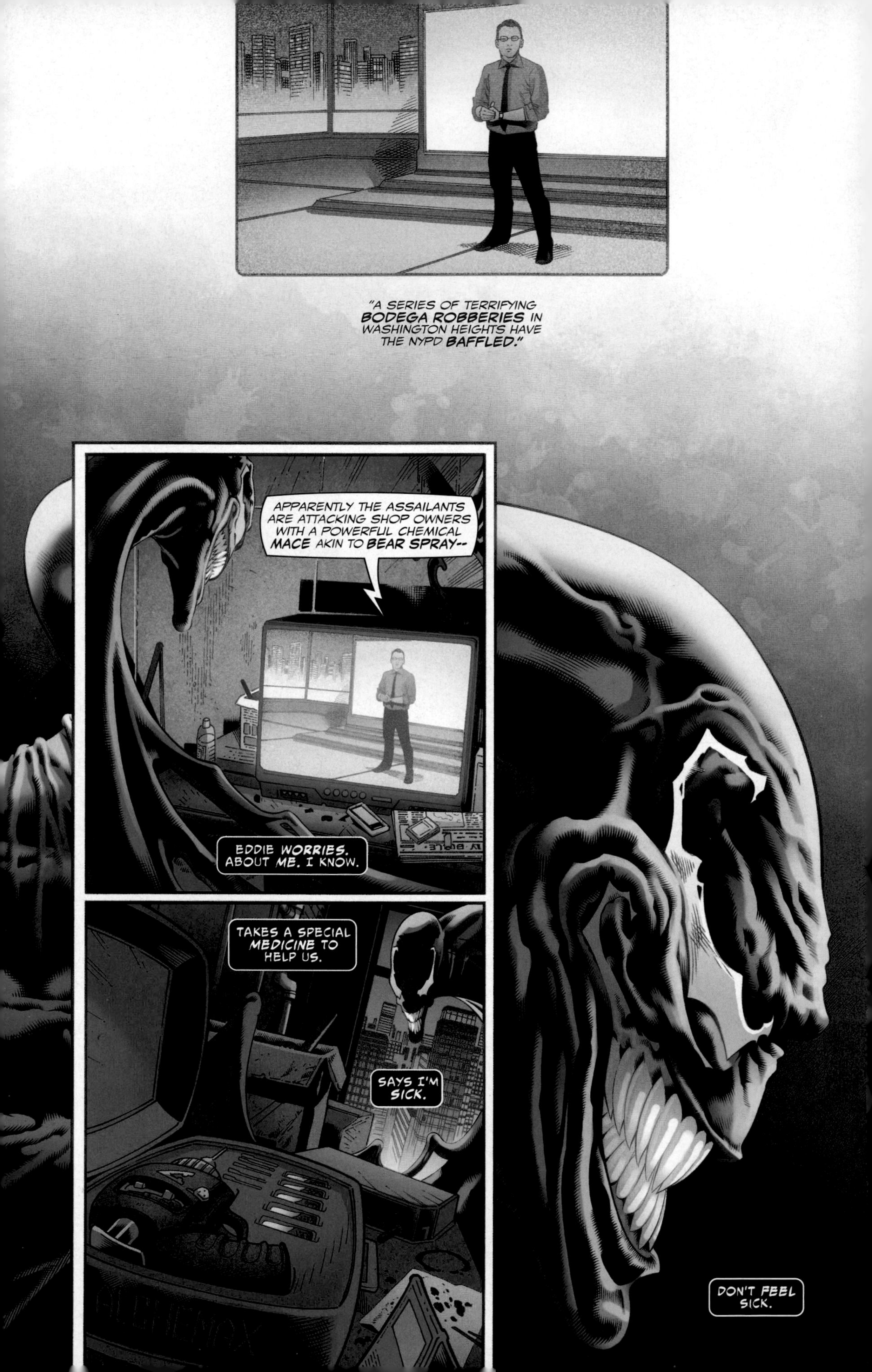
"A SERIES OF TERRIFYING BODEGA ROBBERIES IN WASHINGTON HEIGHTS HAVE THE NYPD BAFFLED."
APPARENTLY THE ASSAILANTS ARE ATTACKING SHOP OWNERS WITH A POWERFUL CHEMICAL MACE AKIN TO BEAR SPRAY--
EDDIE WORRIES. ABOUT ME. I KNOW.
TAKES A SPECIAL MEDICINE TO HELP US.
SAYS I'M SICK.
DON'T FEEL SICK.

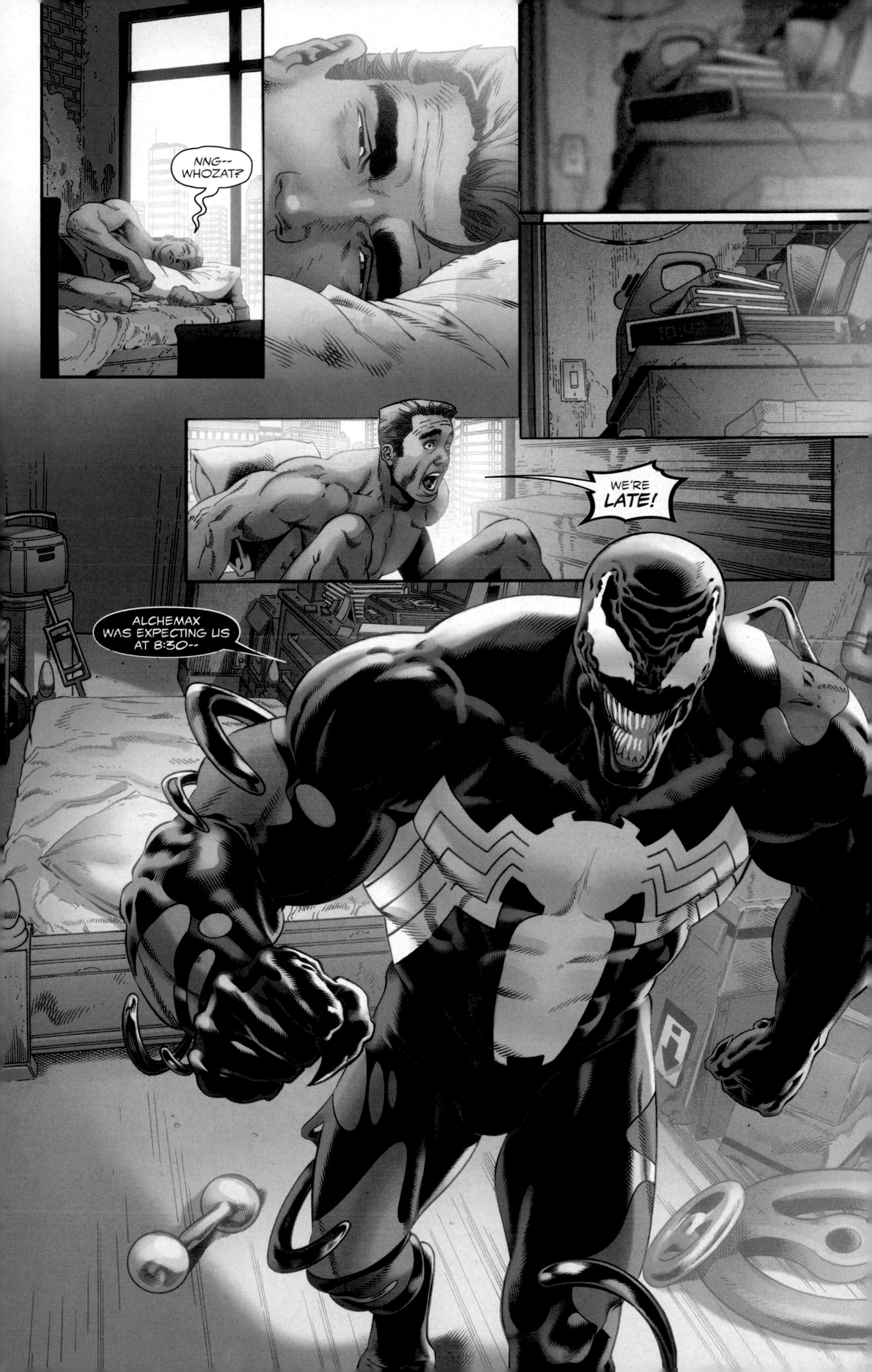
NNG-- WHOZAT?
WE'RE LATE!
ALCHEMAX WAS EXPECTING US AT 8:30--

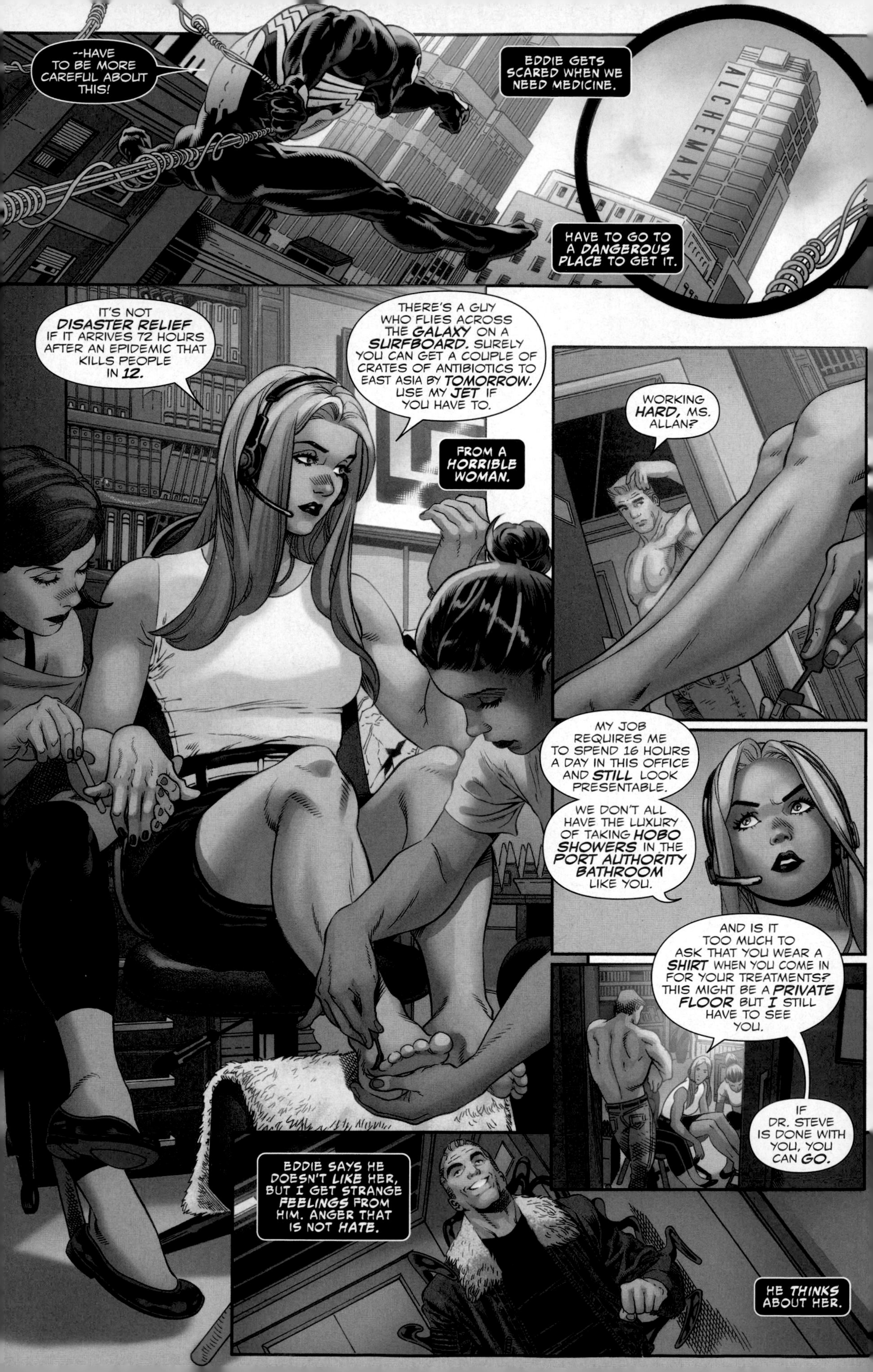
--HAVE TO BE MORE CAREFUL ABOUT THIS!
EDDIE GETS SCARED WHEN WE NEED MEDICINE.
ALCHEMAX
HAVE TO GO TO A DANGEROUS PLACE TO GET IT.
IT'S NOT DISASTER RELIEF IF IT ARRIVES 72 HOURS AFTER AN EPIDEMIC THAT KILLS PEOPLE IN 12.
THERE'S A GUY WHO FLIES ACROSS THE GALAXY ON A SURFBOARD. SURELY YOU CAN GET A COUPLE OF CRATES OF ANTIBIOTICS TO EAST ASIA BY TOMORROW. USE MY JET IF YOU HAVE TO.
FROM A HORRIBLE WOMAN.
WORKING HARD, MS. ALLAN?
MY JOB REQUIRES ME TO SPEND 16 HOURS A DAY IN THIS OFFICE AND STILL LOOK PRESENTABLE.
WE DON'T ALL HAVE THE LUXURY OF TAKING HOBO SHOWERS IN THE PORT AUTHORITY BATHROOM LIKE YOU.
AND IS IT TOO MUCH TO ASK THAT YOU WEAR A SHIRT WHEN YOU COME IN FOR YOUR TREATMENTS? THIS MIGHT BE A PRIVATE FLOOR BUT I STILL HAVE TO SEE YOU.
IF DR. STEVE IS DONE WITH YOU, YOU CAN GO.
EDDIE SAYS HE DOESN'T LIKE HER, BUT I GET STRANGE FEELINGS FROM HIM. ANGER THAT IS NOT HATE.
HE THINKS ABOUT HER.

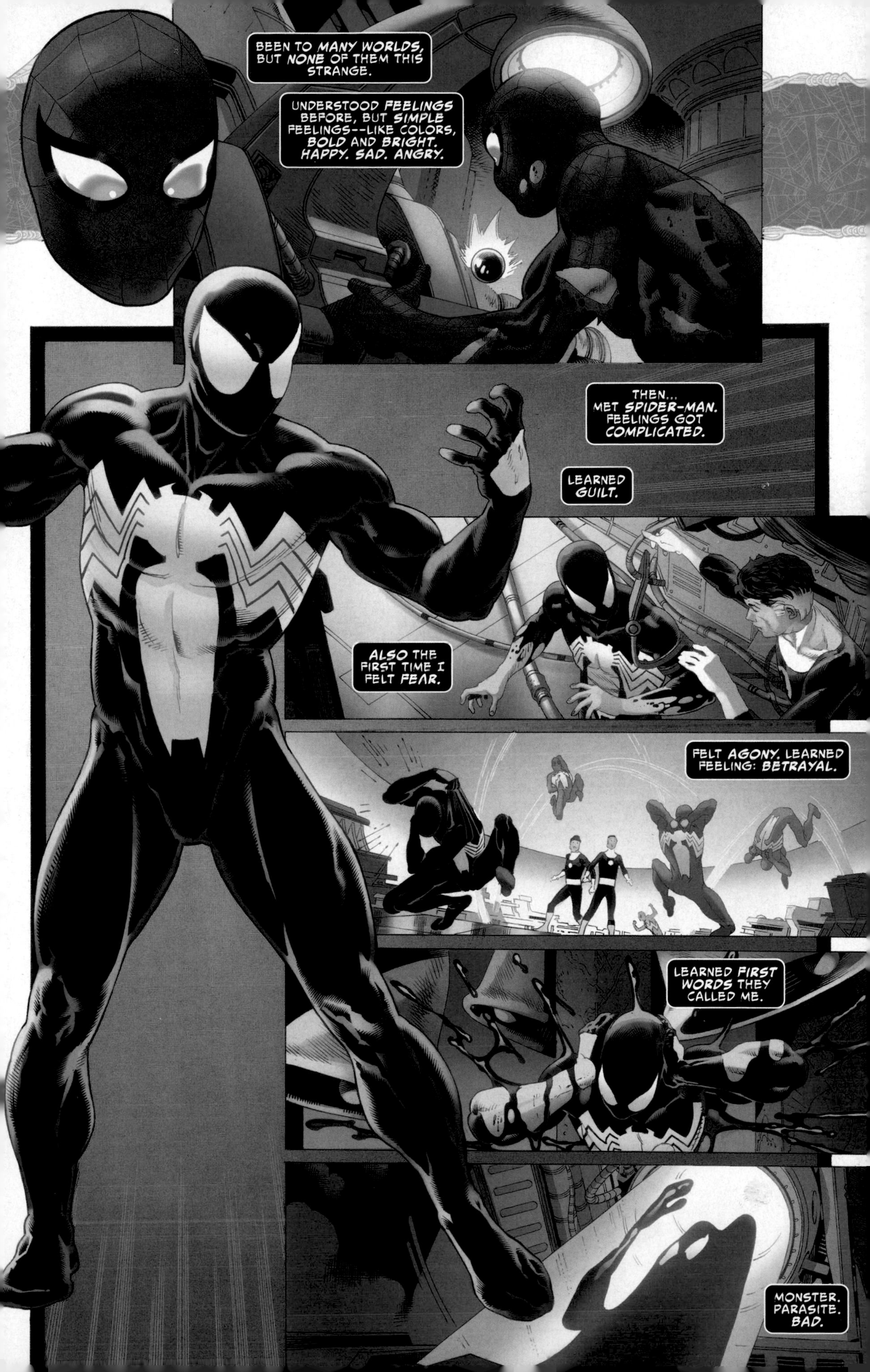
BEEN TO MANY WORLDS, BUT NONE OF THEM THIS STRANGE.
UNDERSTOOD FEELINGS BEFORE, BUT SIMPLE FEELINGS--LIKE COLORS, BOLD AND BRIGHT. HAPPY. SAD. ANGRY.
THEN... MET SPIDER-MAN. FEELINGS GOT COMPLICATED.
LEARNED GUILT.
ALSO THE FIRST TIME I FELT FEAR.
FELT AGONY. LEARNED FEELING: BETRAYAL.
LEARNED FIRST WORDS THEY CALLED ME.
MONSTER. PARASITE. BAD.

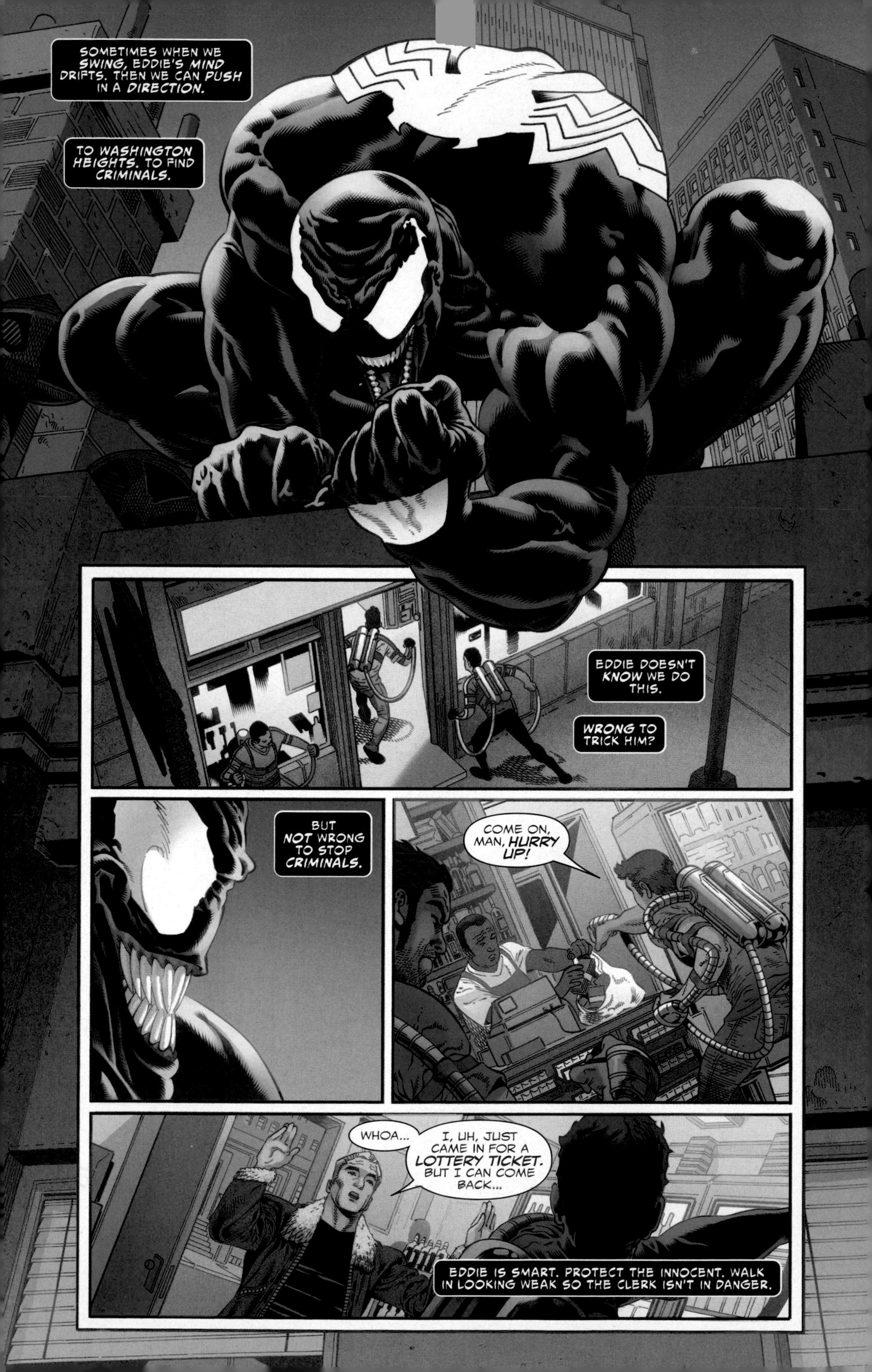
SOMETIMES WHEN WE SWING, EDDIE'S MIND DRIFTS. THEN WE CAN PUSH IN A DIRECTION.
TO WASHINGTON HEIGHTS. TO FIND CRIMINALS.
EDDIE DOESN'T KNOW WE DO THIS.
WRONG TO TRICK HIM?
BUT NOT WRONG TO STOP CRIMINALS.
COME ON, MAN, HURRY UP!
WHOA...
I, UH, JUST CAME IN FOR A LOTTERY TICKET. BUT I CAN COME BACK...
EDDIE IS SMART. PROTECT THE INNOCENT. WALK IN LOOKING WEAK SO THE CLERK ISN'T IN DANGER.

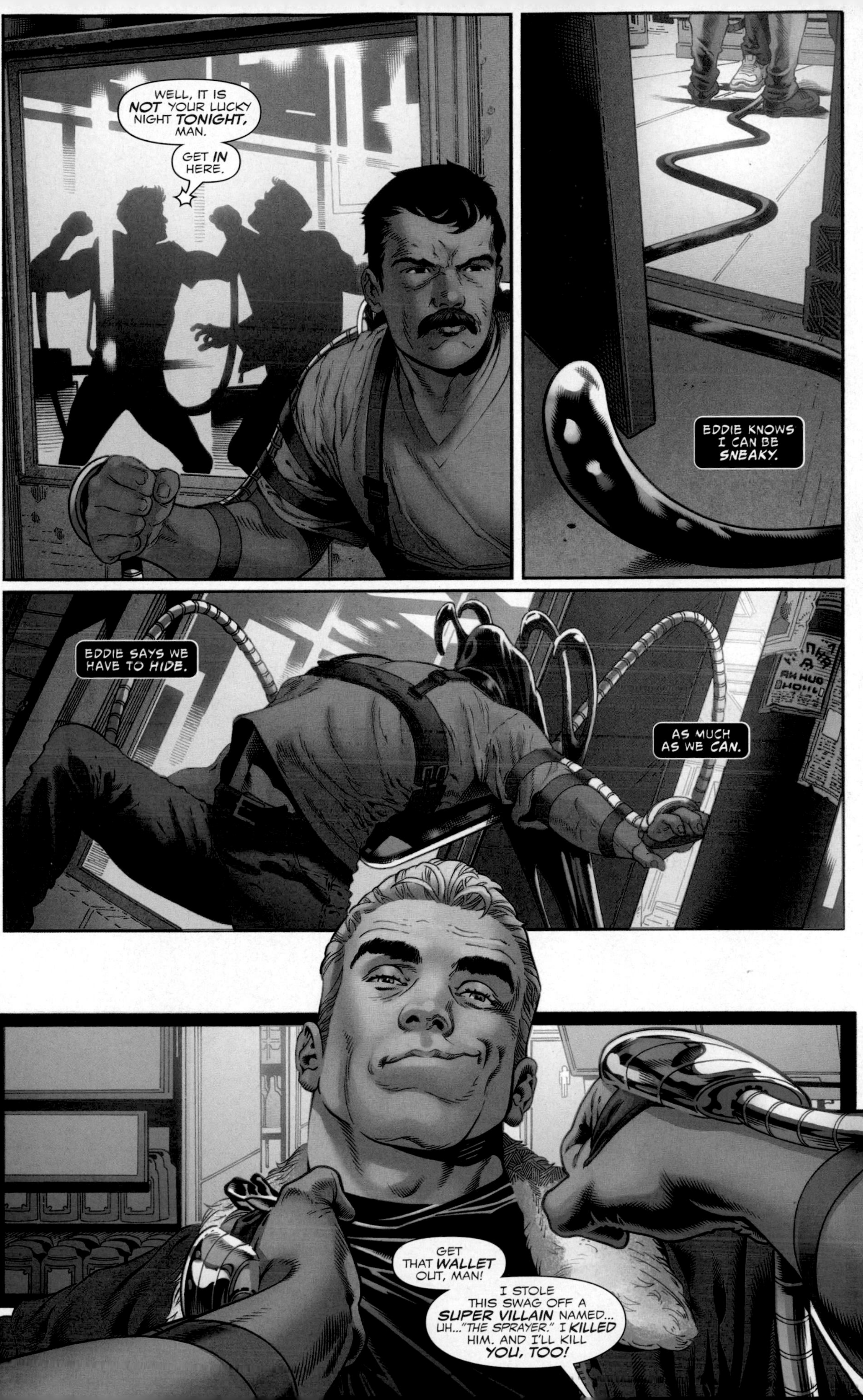
WELL, IT IS NOT YOUR LUCKY NIGHT TONIGHT, MAN.
GET IN HERE.
EDDIE KNOWS I CAN BE SNEAKY.
EDDIE SAYS WE HAVE TO HIDE.
AS MUCH AS WE CAN.
GET THAT WALLET OUT, MAN!
I STOLE THIS SWAG OFF A SUPER VILLAIN NAMED... UH..."THE SPRAYER." I KILLED HIM. AND I'LL KILL YOU, TOO!

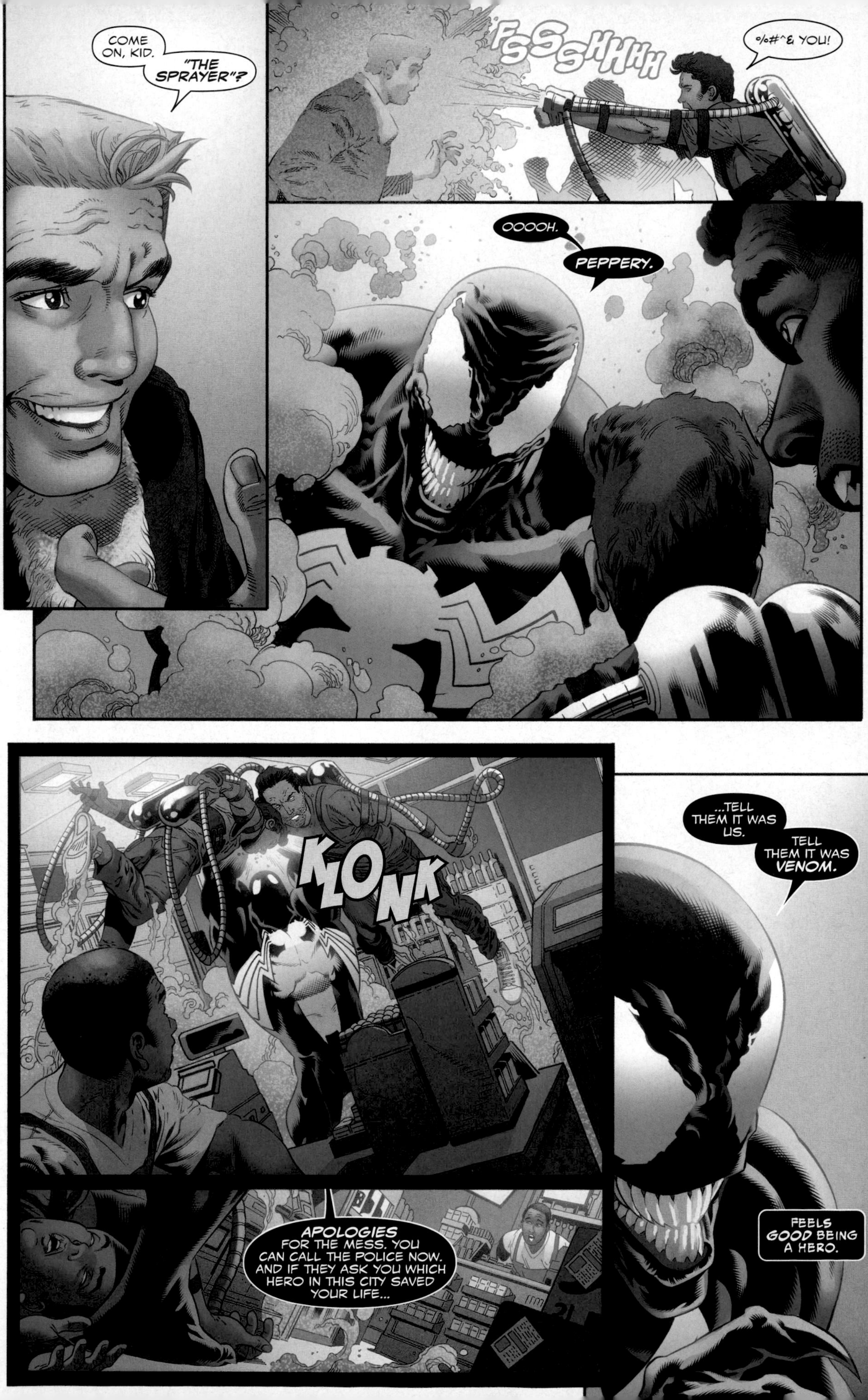
COME ON, KID. "THE SPRAYER"?
FSSSHHHH
%#^& YOU!
OOOOH.
PEPPERY.
KLONK
APOLOGIES FOR THE MESS. YOU CAN CALL THE POLICE NOW. AND IF THEY ASK YOU WHICH HERO IN THIS CITY SAVED YOUR LIFE...
...TELL THEM IT WAS US.
TELL THEM IT WAS VENOM.
FEELS GOOD BEING A HERO.

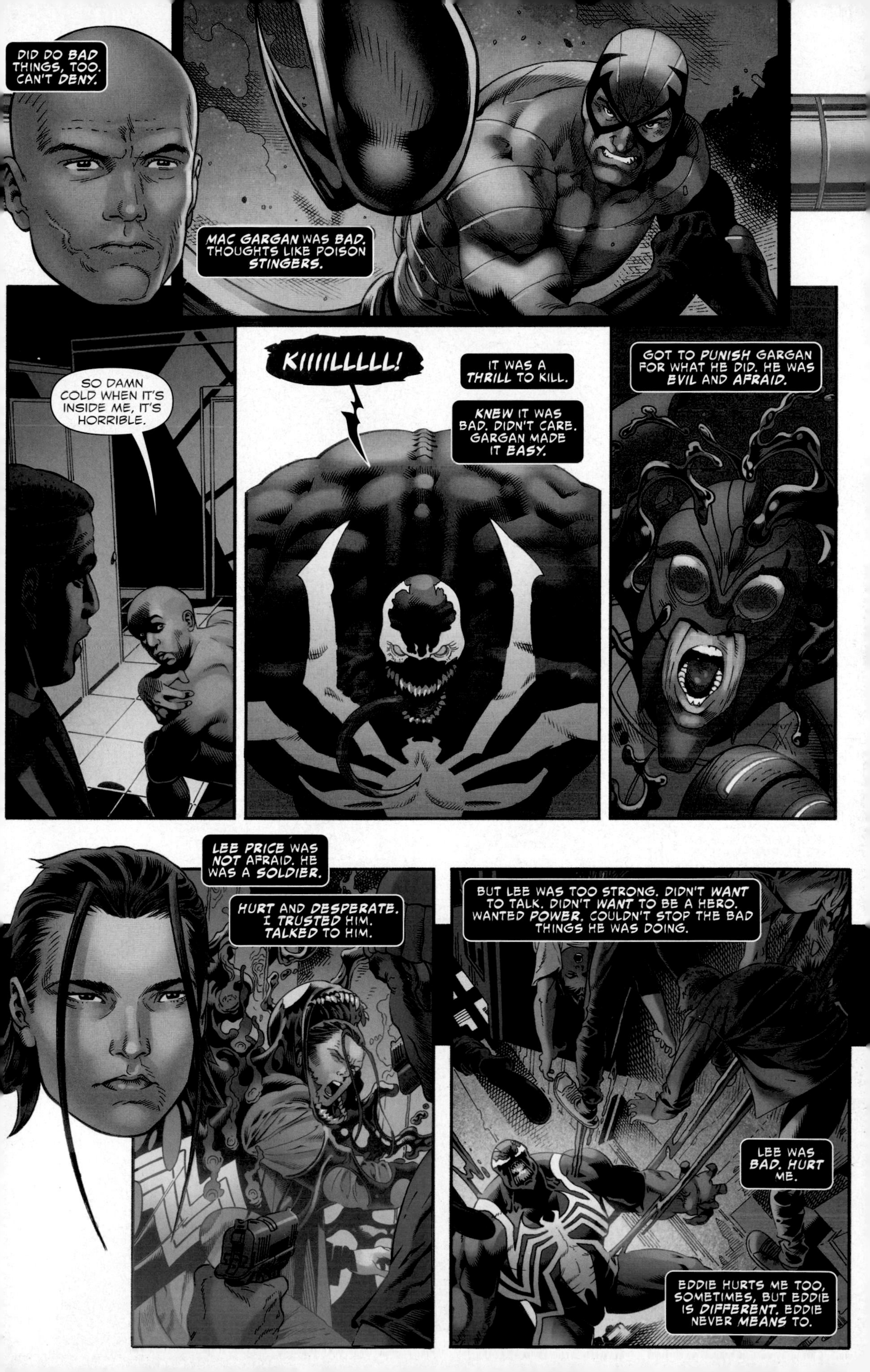
DID DO BAD THINGS, TOO. CAN'T DENY.
MAC GARGAN WAS BAD. THOUGHTS LIKE POISON STINGERS.
SO DAMN COLD WHEN IT'S INSIDE ME, IT'S HORRIBLE.
KIIIILLLLL!
IT WAS A THRILL TO KILL.
KNEW IT WAS BAD. DIDN'T CARE. GARGAN MADE IT EASY.
GOT TO PUNISH GARGAN FOR WHAT HE DID. HE WAS EVIL AND AFRAID.
LEE PRICE WAS NOT AFRAID. HE WAS A SOLDIER.
HURT AND DESPERATE. I TRUSTED HIM. TALKED TO HIM.
BUT LEE WAS TOO STRONG. DIDN'T WANT TO TALK. DIDN'T WANT TO BE A HERO. WANTED POWER. COULDN'T STOP THE BAD THINGS HE WAS DOING.
LEE WAS BAD. HURT ME.
EDDIE HURTS ME TOO, SOMETIMES, BUT EDDIE IS DIFFERENT. EDDIE NEVER MEANS TO.

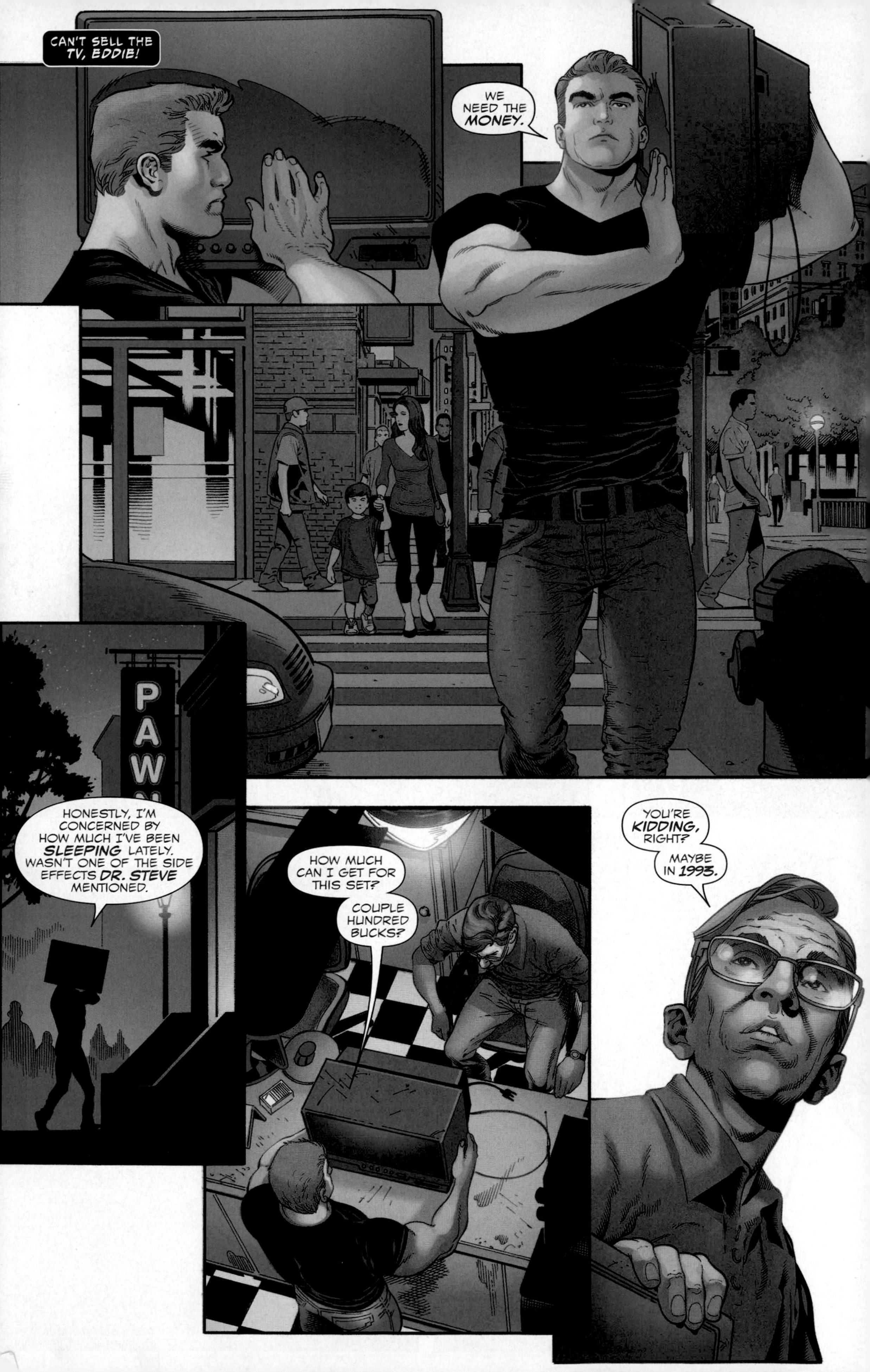
CAN'T SELL THE TV, EDDIE!
WE NEED THE MONEY.
PAWN
HONESTLY, I'M CONCERNED BY HOW MUCH I'VE BEEN SLEEPING LATELY. WASN'T ONE OF THE SIDE EFFECTS DR. STEVE MENTIONED.
HOW MUCH CAN I GET FOR THIS SET?
COUPLE HUNDRED BUCKS?
YOU'RE KIDDING, RIGHT?
MAYBE IN 1993.

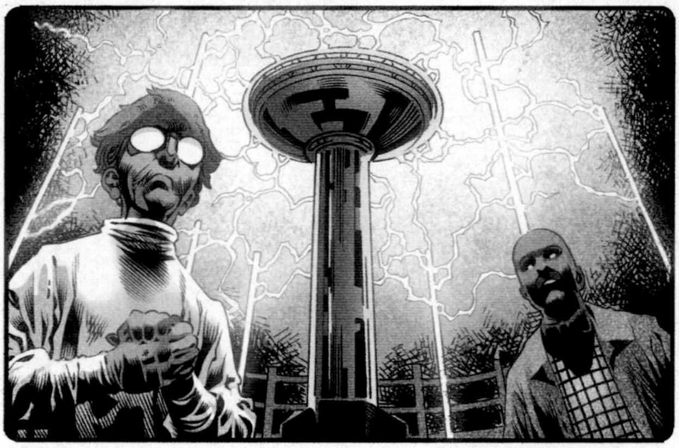

"THE ETHICAL RAMIFICATIONS OF THIS MIND-CONTROL DEVICE ARE **STAGGERING!**

"IN RESPONSIBLE HANDS IT'S A **UTOPIA!** BUT...WHAT MAN CAN SAY WHO'S **RESPONSIBLE?**"

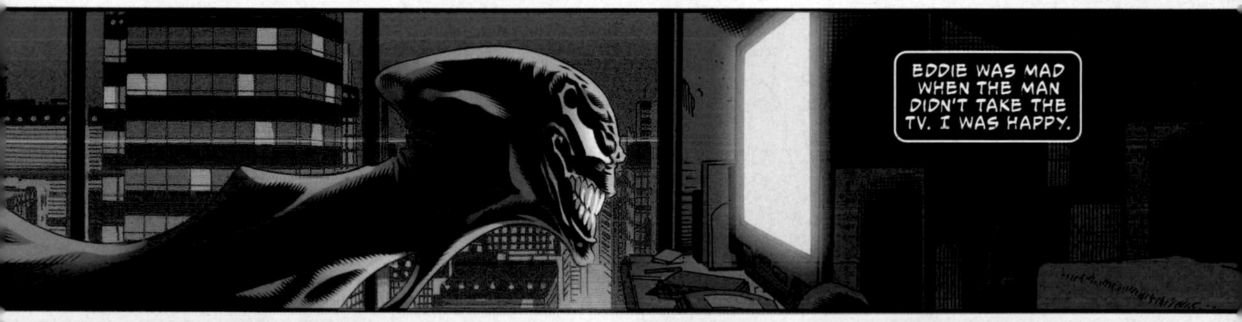
EDDIE WAS MAD WHEN THE MAN DIDN'T TAKE THE TV. I WAS HAPPY.

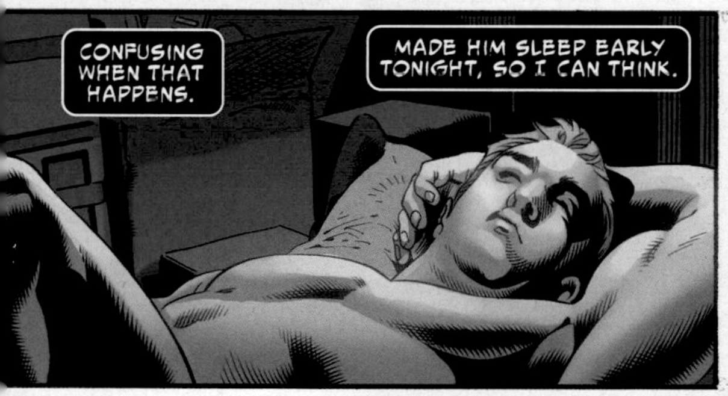
CONFUSING WHEN THAT HAPPENS.
MADE HIM SLEEP EARLY TONIGHT, SO I CAN THINK.

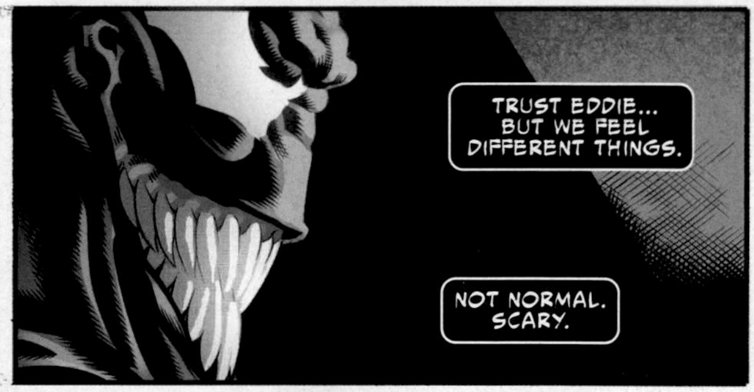
TRUST EDDIE... BUT WE FEEL DIFFERENT THINGS.
NOT NORMAL. SCARY.

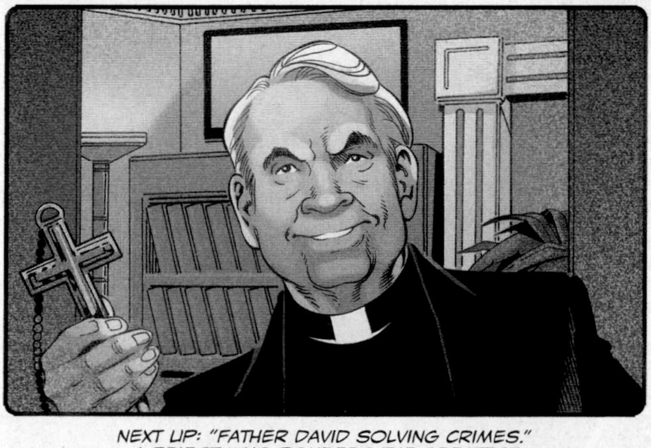

IF EDDIE IS GOOD, WHY DO WE DISAGREE?

NEXT UP: "FATHER DAVID SOLVING CRIMES." A PRIEST WHO PONDERS THE GREATEST MYSTERIES OF THE UNIVERSE ALSO SOLVES A MYSTERY OF THE WEEK.

IF DISAGREE... AM I MONSTER? PARASITE? **BAD?**

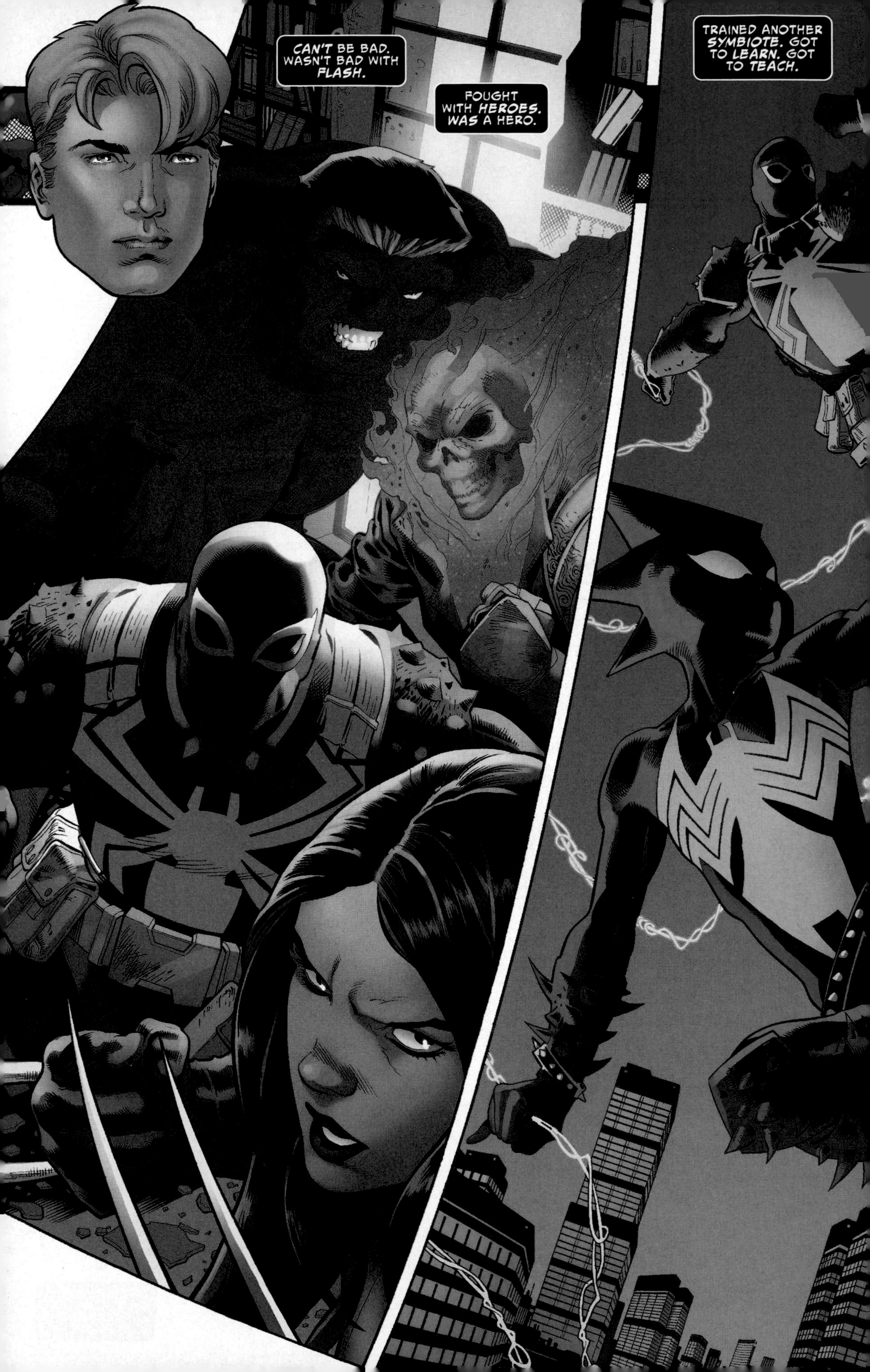
CAN'T BE BAD. WASN'T BAD WITH FLASH.
FOUGHT WITH HEROES. WAS A HERO.
TRAINED ANOTHER SYMBIOTE. GOT TO LEARN. GOT TO TEACH.

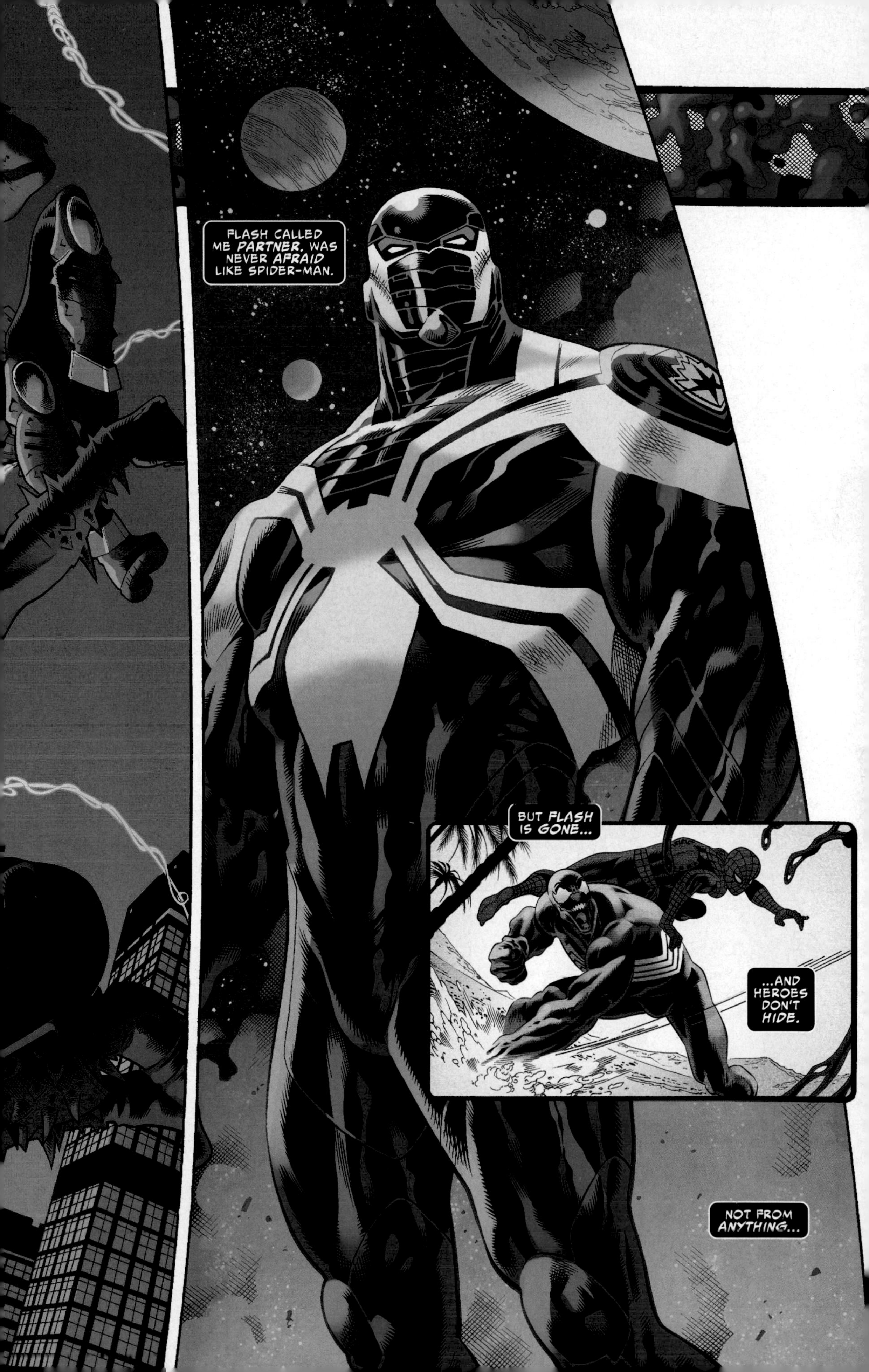
FLASH CALLED ME PARTNER. WAS NEVER AFRAID LIKE SPIDER-MAN.
BUT FLASH IS GONE...
...AND HEROES DON'T HIDE.
NOT FROM ANYTHING...

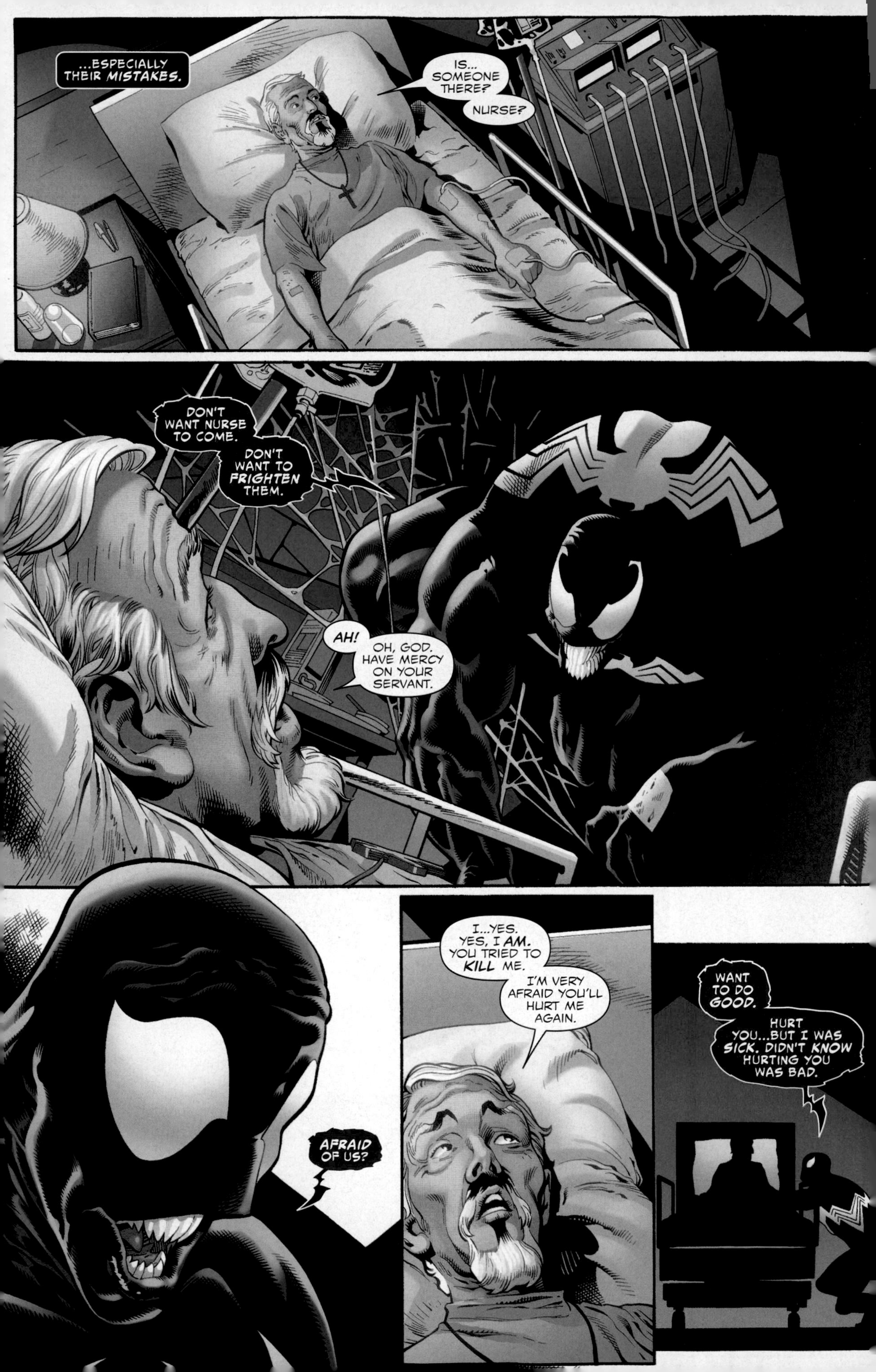
...ESPECIALLY THEIR MISTAKES.
IS... SOMEONE THERE?
NURSE?
DON'T WANT NURSE TO COME.
DON'T WANT TO FRIGHTEN THEM.
AH!
OH, GOD. HAVE MERCY ON YOUR SERVANT.
AFRAID OF US?
I...YES. YES, I AM. YOU TRIED TO KILL ME.
I'M VERY AFRAID YOU'LL HURT ME AGAIN.
WANT TO DO GOOD.
HURT YOU...BUT I WAS SICK. DIDN'T KNOW HURTING YOU WAS BAD.

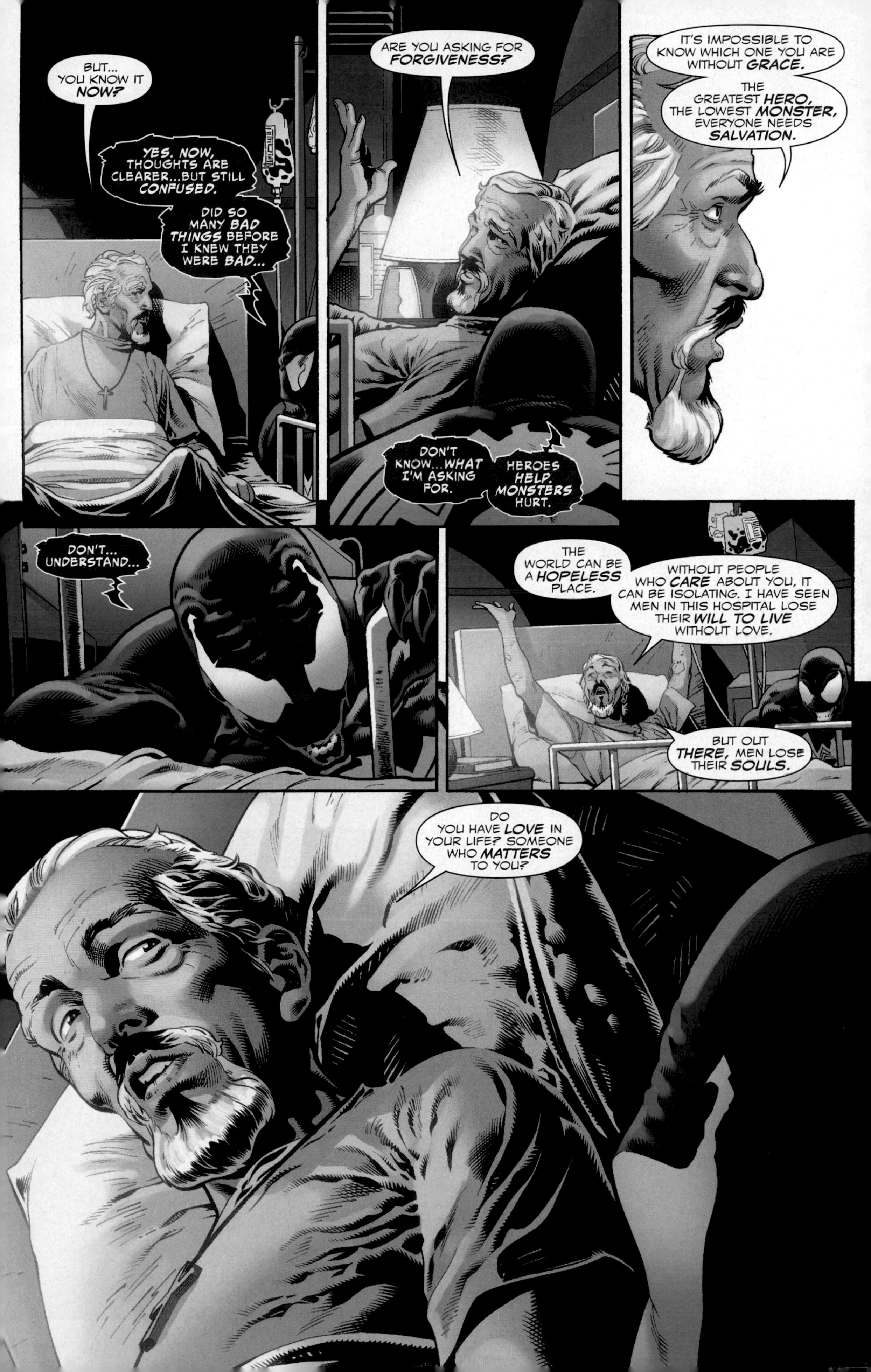
BUT... YOU KNOW IT NOW?
YES. NOW, THOUGHTS ARE CLEARER...BUT STILL CONFUSED.
DID SO MANY BAD THINGS BEFORE I KNEW THEY WERE BAD...
ARE YOU ASKING FOR FORGIVENESS?
DON'T KNOW...WHAT I'M ASKING FOR.
HEROES HELP. MONSTERS HURT.
IT'S IMPOSSIBLE TO KNOW WHICH ONE YOU ARE WITHOUT GRACE.
THE GREATEST HERO, THE LOWEST MONSTER, EVERYONE NEEDS SALVATION.
DON'T... UNDERSTAND...
THE WORLD CAN BE A HOPELESS PLACE.
WITHOUT PEOPLE WHO CARE ABOUT YOU, IT CAN BE ISOLATING. I HAVE SEEN MEN IN THIS HOSPITAL LOSE THEIR WILL TO LIVE WITHOUT LOVE.
BUT OUT THERE, MEN LOSE THEIR SOULS.
DO YOU HAVE LOVE IN YOUR LIFE? SOMEONE WHO MATTERS TO YOU?

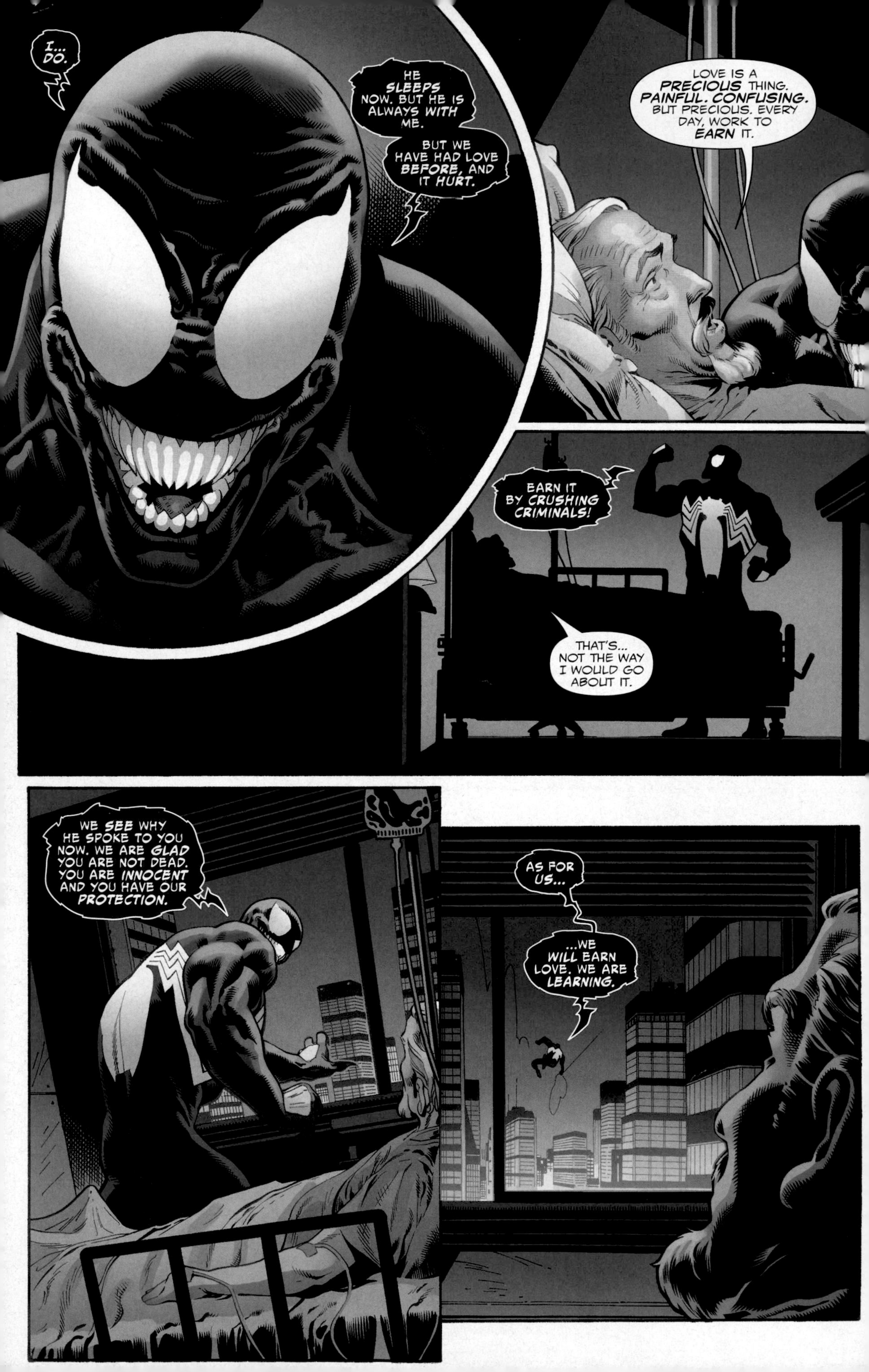
I... DO.
HE SLEEPS NOW. BUT HE IS ALWAYS WITH ME.
BUT WE HAVE HAD LOVE BEFORE, AND IT HURT.
LOVE IS A PRECIOUS THING. PAINFUL. CONFUSING. BUT PRECIOUS. EVERY DAY, WORK TO EARN IT.
EARN IT BY CRUSHING CRIMINALS!
THAT'S... NOT THE WAY I WOULD GO ABOUT IT.
WE SEE WHY HE SPOKE TO YOU NOW. WE ARE GLAD YOU ARE NOT DEAD. YOU ARE INNOCENT AND YOU HAVE OUR PROTECTION.
AS FOR US...
...WE WILL EARN LOVE. WE ARE LEARNING.

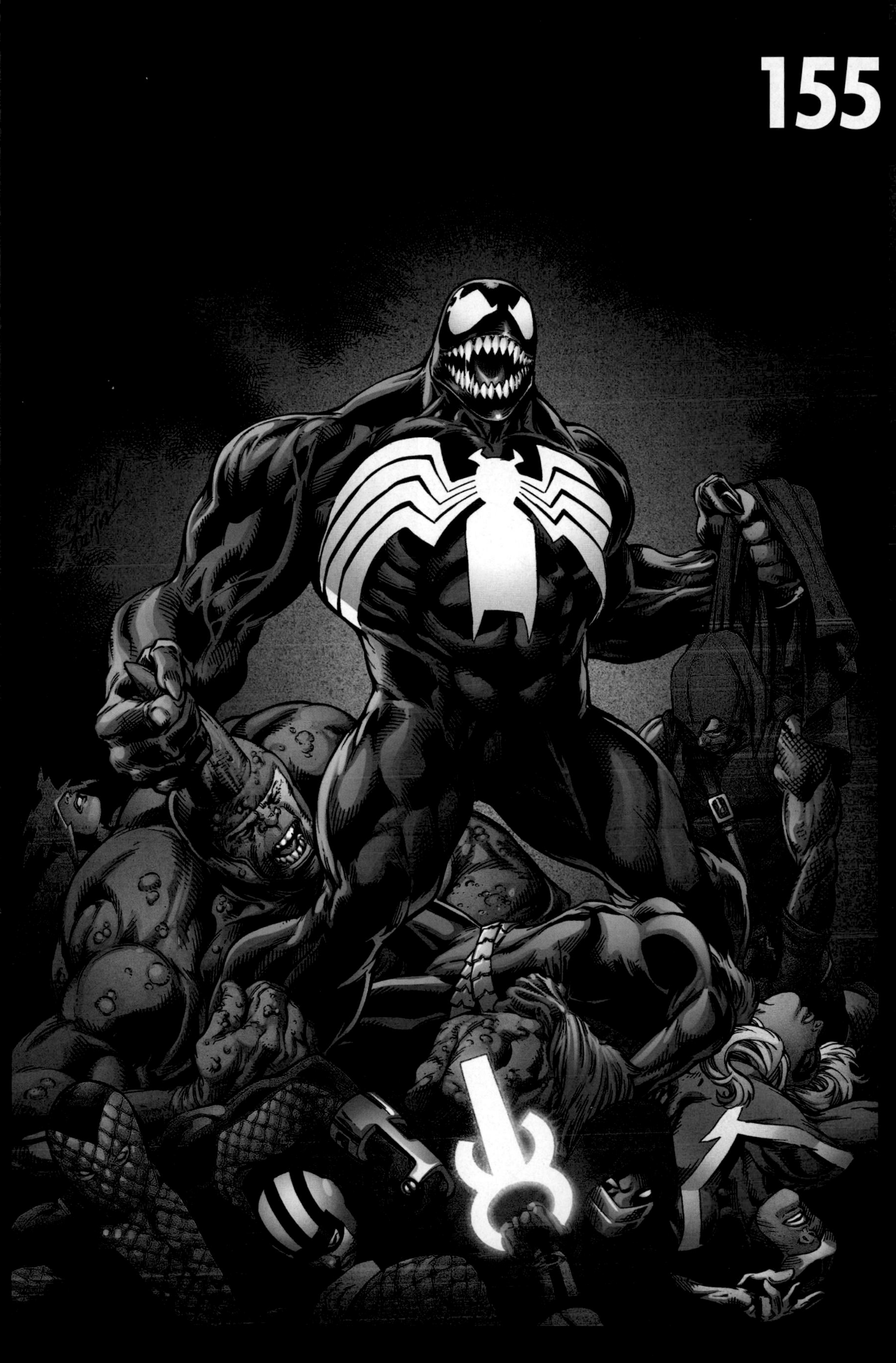
155

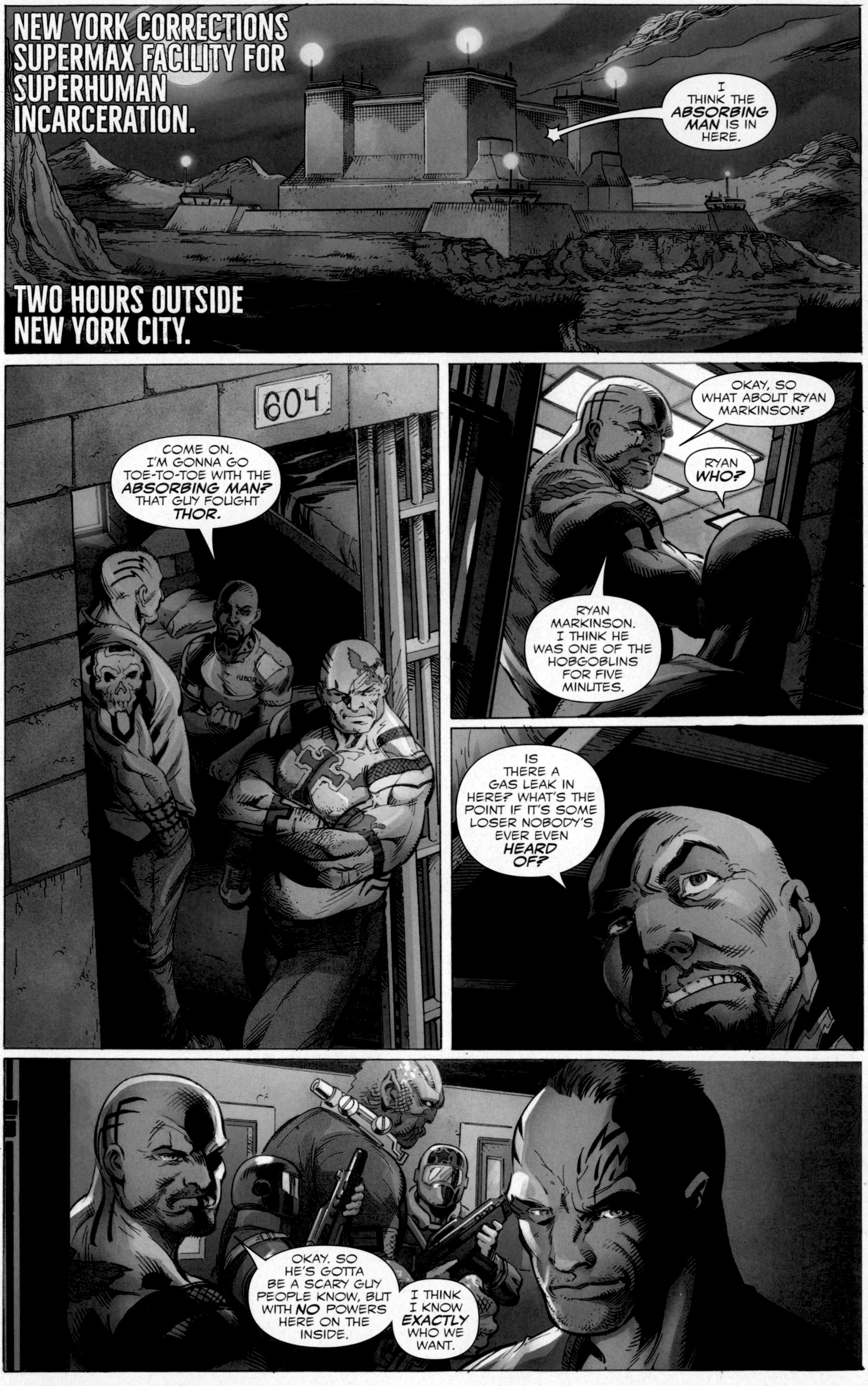
NEW YORK CORRECTIONS SUPERMAX FACILITY FOR SUPERHUMAN INCARCERATION.
I THINK THE ABSORBING MAN IS IN HERE.
TWO HOURS OUTSIDE NEW YORK CITY.
604
COME ON. I'M GONNA GO TOE-TO-TOE WITH THE ABSORBING MAN? THAT GUY FOUGHT THOR.
OKAY, SO WHAT ABOUT RYAN MARKINSON?
RYAN WHO?
RYAN MARKINSON. I THINK HE WAS ONE OF THE HOBGOBLINS FOR FIVE MINUTES.
IS THERE A GAS LEAK IN HERE? WHAT'S THE POINT IF IT'S SOME LOSER NOBODY'S EVER EVEN HEARD OF?
OKAY. SO HE'S GOTTA BE A SCARY GUY PEOPLE KNOW, BUT WITH NO POWERS HERE ON THE INSIDE.
I THINK I KNOW EXACTLY WHO WE WANT.

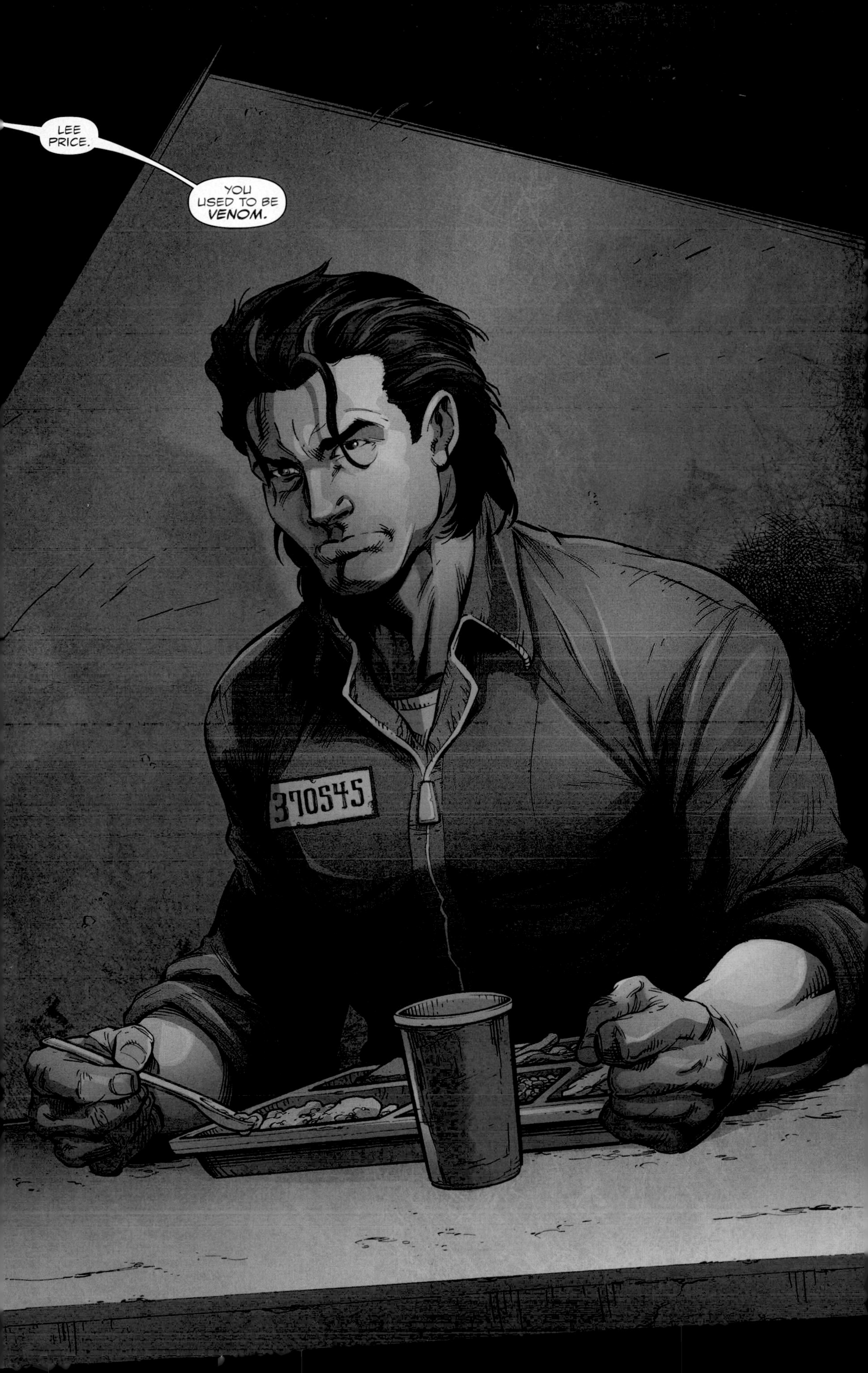
LEE PRICE.
YOU USED TO BE VENOM.
370545

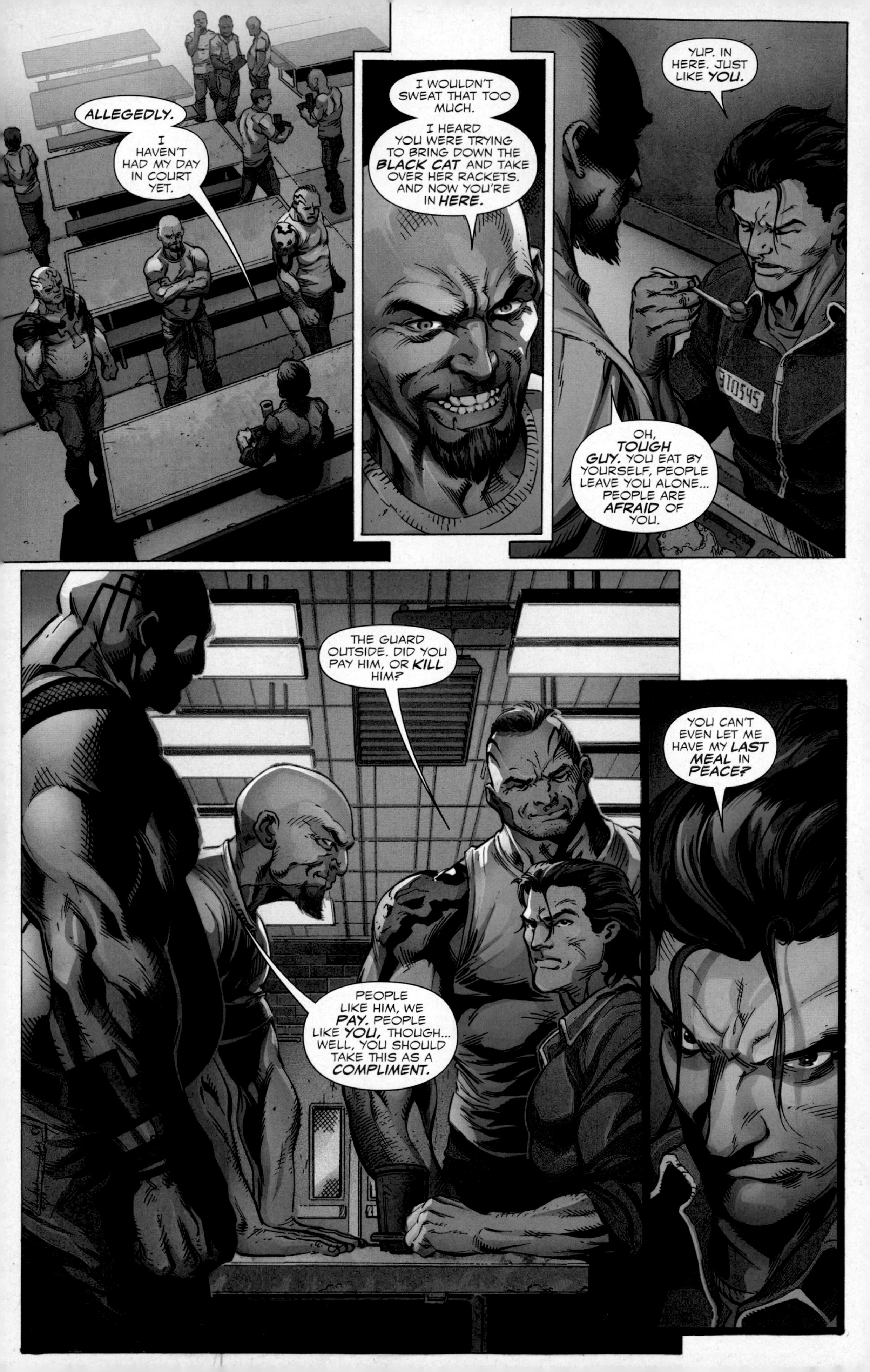
ALLEGEDLY.
I HAVEN'T HAD MY DAY IN COURT YET.
I WOULDN'T SWEAT THAT TOO MUCH.
I HEARD YOU WERE TRYING TO BRING DOWN THE BLACK CAT AND TAKE OVER HER RACKETS. AND NOW YOU'RE IN HERE.
YUP. IN HERE. JUST LIKE YOU.
OH, TOUGH GUY. YOU EAT BY YOURSELF, PEOPLE LEAVE YOU ALONE... PEOPLE ARE AFRAID OF YOU.
THE GUARD OUTSIDE. DID YOU PAY HIM, OR KILL HIM?
YOU CAN'T EVEN LET ME HAVE MY LAST MEAL IN PEACE?
PEOPLE LIKE HIM, WE PAY. PEOPLE LIKE YOU, THOUGH... WELL, YOU SHOULD TAKE THIS AS A COMPLIMENT.

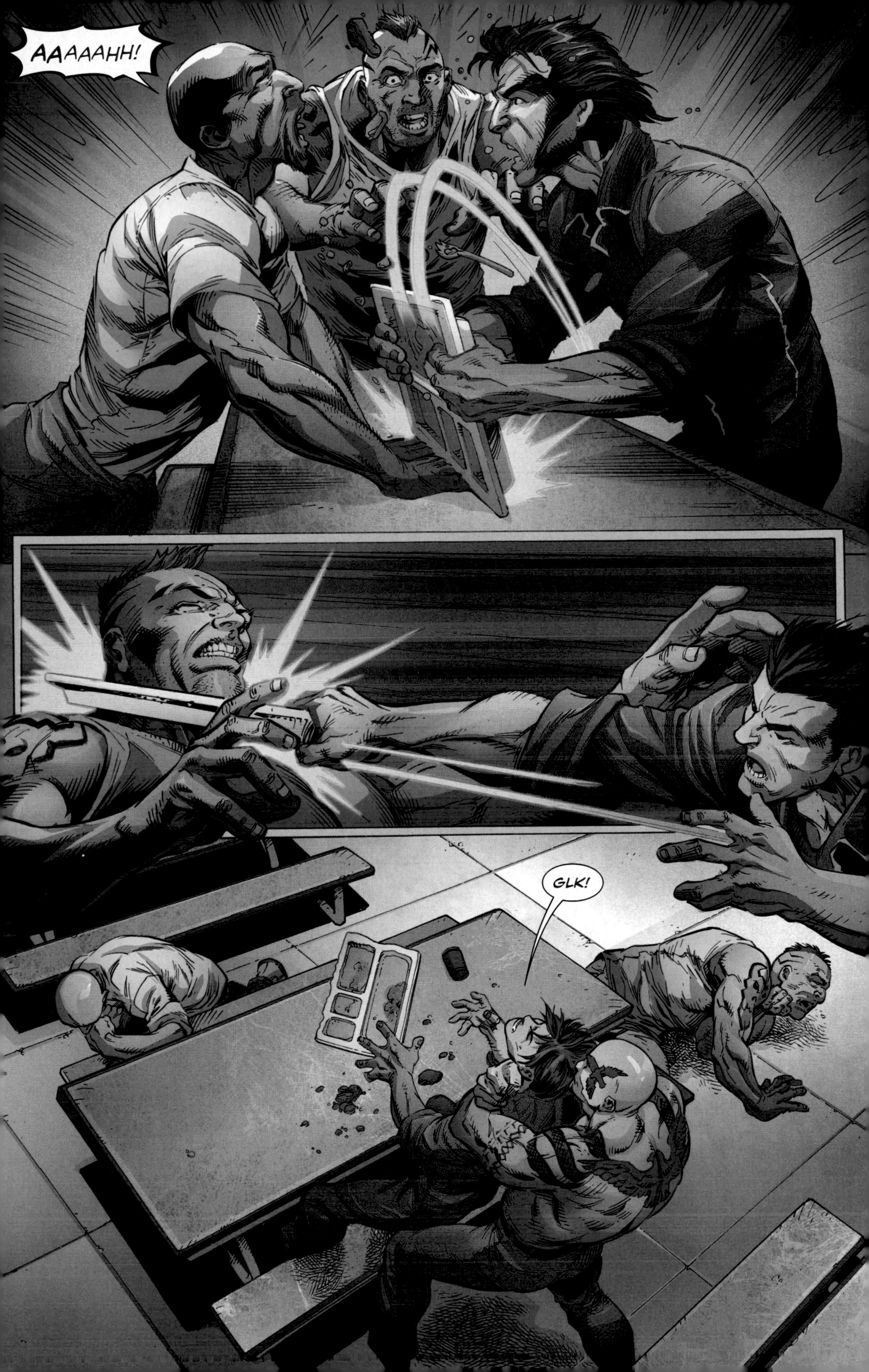
AAAAAHH!
GLK!

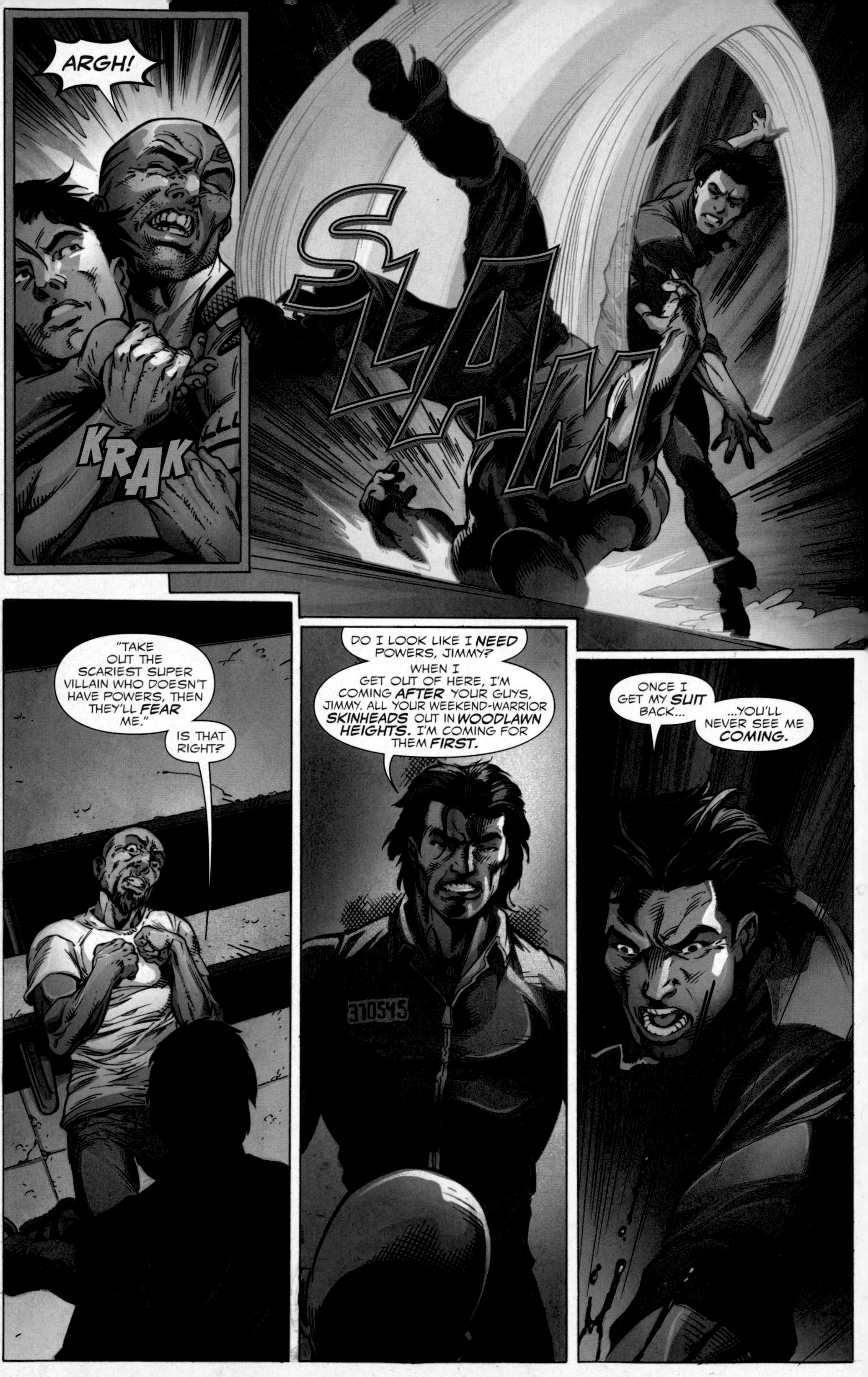
ARGH!
KRAK
SLAM
"TAKE OUT THE SCARIEST SUPER VILLAIN WHO DOESN'T HAVE POWERS, THEN THEY'LL FEAR ME."
IS THAT RIGHT?
DO I LOOK LIKE I NEED POWERS, JIMMY?
WHEN I GET OUT OF HERE, I'M COMING AFTER YOUR GUYS, JIMMY. ALL YOUR WEEKEND-WARRIOR SKINHEADS OUT IN WOODLAWN HEIGHTS. I'M COMING FOR THEM FIRST.
370545
ONCE I GET MY SUIT BACK...
...YOU'LL NEVER SEE ME COMING.

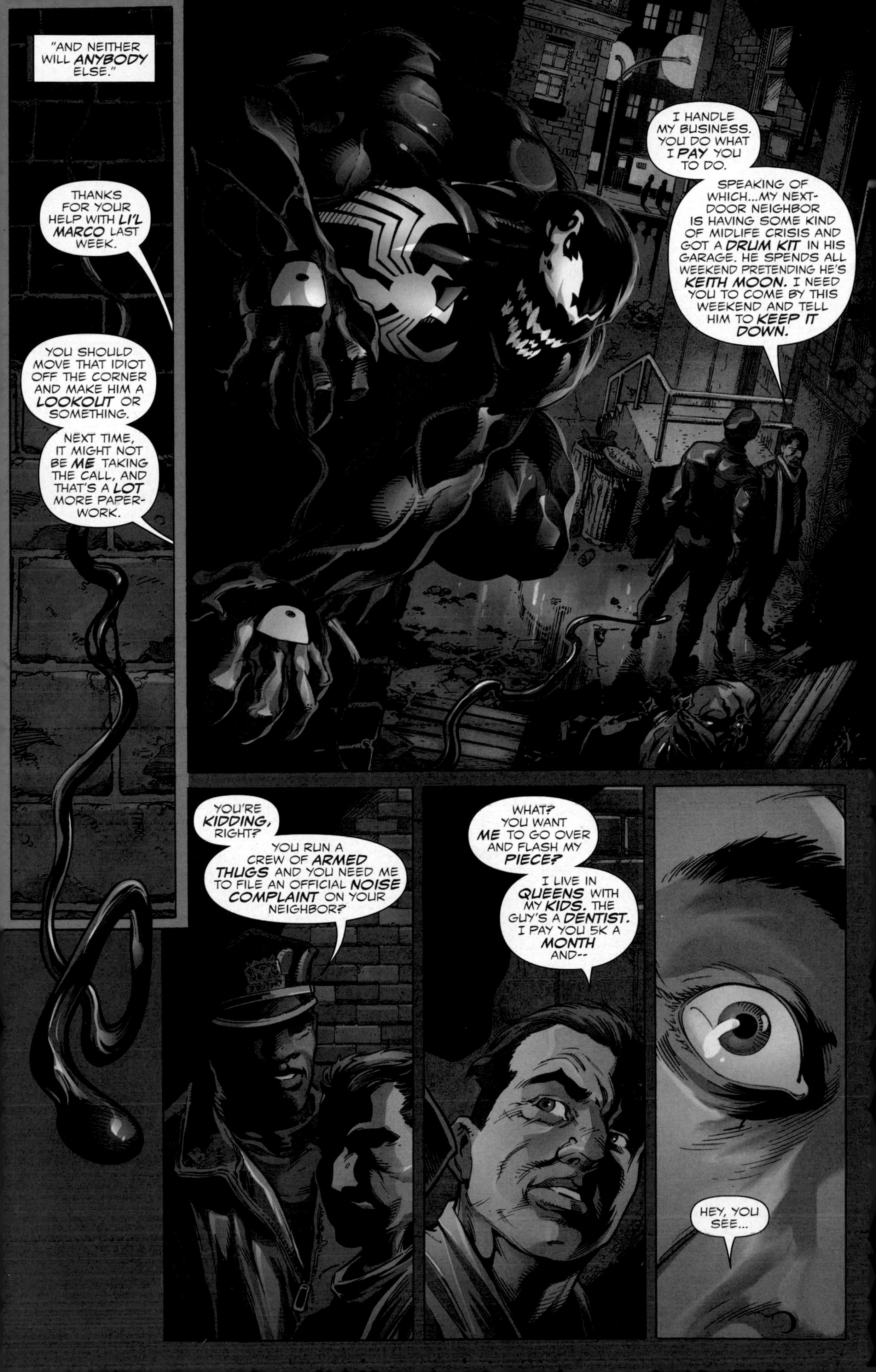
"AND NEITHER WILL ANYBODY ELSE."
THANKS FOR YOUR HELP WITH LI'L MARCO LAST WEEK.
YOU SHOULD MOVE THAT IDIOT OFF THE CORNER AND MAKE HIM A LOOKOUT OR SOMETHING.
NEXT TIME, IT MIGHT NOT BE ME TAKING THE CALL, AND THAT'S A LOT MORE PAPER-WORK.
I HANDLE MY BUSINESS. YOU DO WHAT I PAY YOU TO DO.
SPEAKING OF WHICH...MY NEXT-DOOR NEIGHBOR IS HAVING SOME KIND OF MIDLIFE CRISIS AND GOT A DRUM KIT IN HIS GARAGE. HE SPENDS ALL WEEKEND PRETENDING HE'S KEITH MOON. I NEED YOU TO COME BY THIS WEEKEND AND TELL HIM TO KEEP IT DOWN.
YOU'RE KIDDING, RIGHT?
YOU RUN A CREW OF ARMED THUGS AND YOU NEED ME TO FILE AN OFFICIAL NOISE COMPLAINT ON YOUR NEIGHBOR?
WHAT? YOU WANT ME TO GO OVER AND FLASH MY PIECE?
I LIVE IN QUEENS WITH MY KIDS. THE GUY'S A DENTIST. I PAY YOU 5K A MONTH AND--
HEY, YOU SEE...

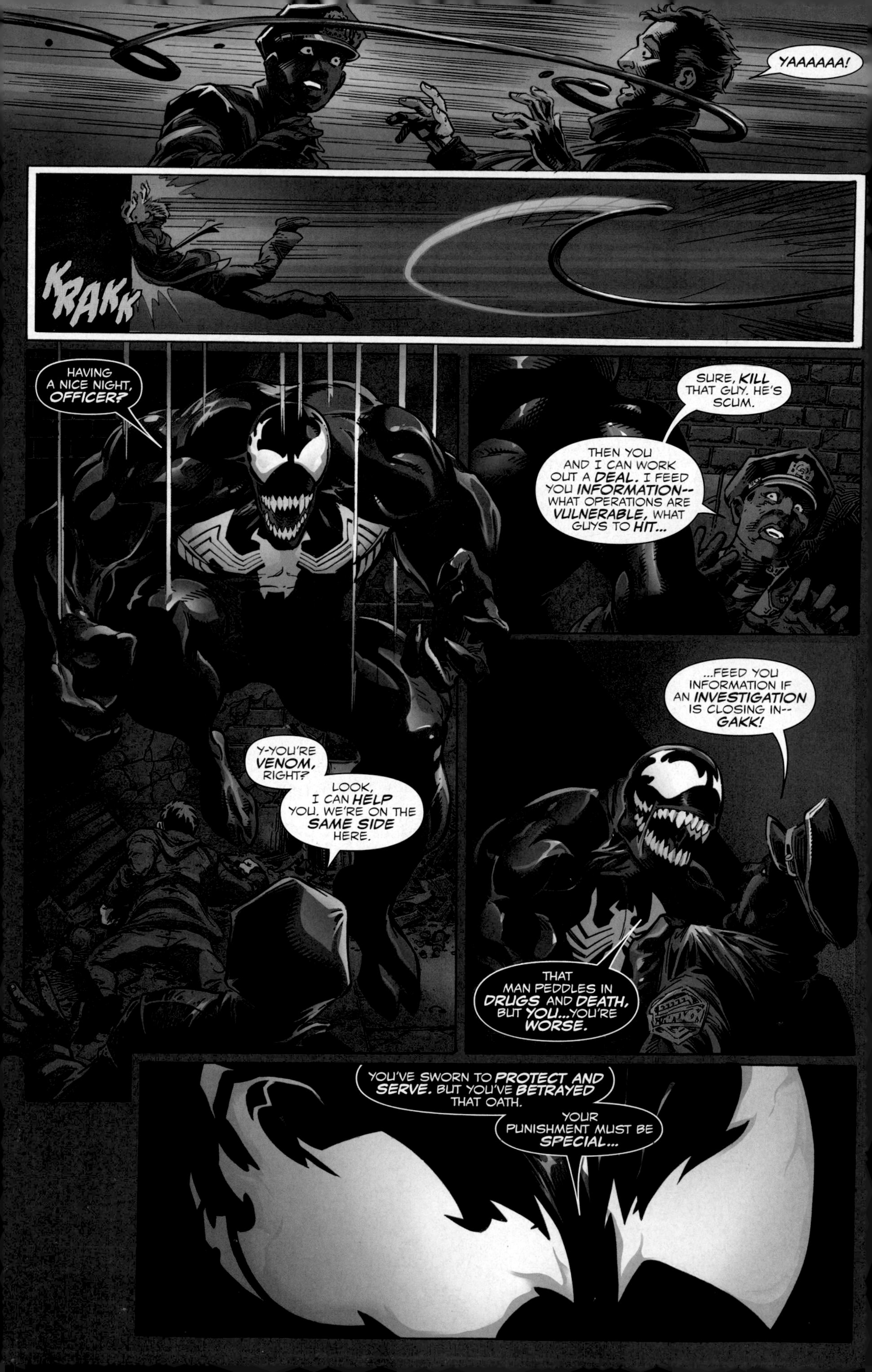
YAAAAAA!
KRAKK
HAVING A NICE NIGHT, OFFICER?
Y-YOU'RE VENOM, RIGHT?
LOOK, I CAN HELP YOU. WE'RE ON THE SAME SIDE HERE.
SURE, KILL THAT GUY. HE'S SCUM.
THEN YOU AND I CAN WORK OUT A DEAL. I FEED YOU INFORMATION-- WHAT OPERATIONS ARE VULNERABLE, WHAT GUYS TO HIT...
...FEED YOU INFORMATION IF AN INVESTIGATION IS CLOSING IN-- GAKK!
THAT MAN PEDDLES IN DRUGS AND DEATH, BUT YOU...YOU'RE WORSE.
YOU'VE SWORN TO PROTECT AND SERVE. BUT YOU'VE BETRAYED THAT OATH.
YOUR PUNISHMENT MUST BE SPECIAL...

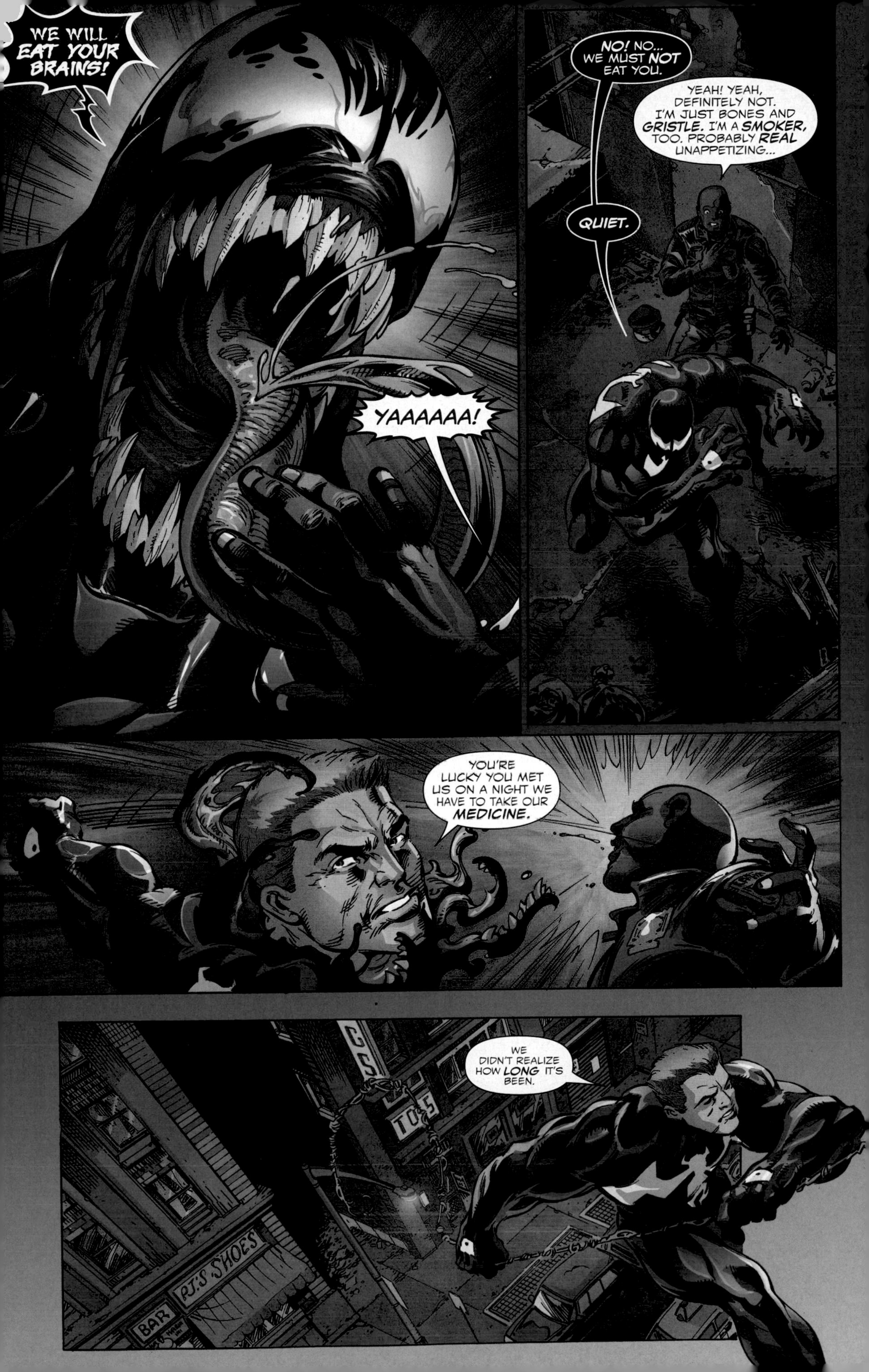
WE WILL EAT YOUR BRAINS!
YAAAAAA!
NO! NO... WE MUST NOT EAT YOU.
YEAH! YEAH, DEFINITELY NOT. I'M JUST BONES AND GRISTLE. I'M A SMOKER, TOO. PROBABLY REAL UNAPPETIZING...
QUIET.
YOU'RE LUCKY YOU MET US ON A NIGHT WE HAVE TO TAKE OUR MEDICINE.
WE DIDN'T REALIZE HOW LONG IT'S BEEN.
P.J.'S SHOES
BAR

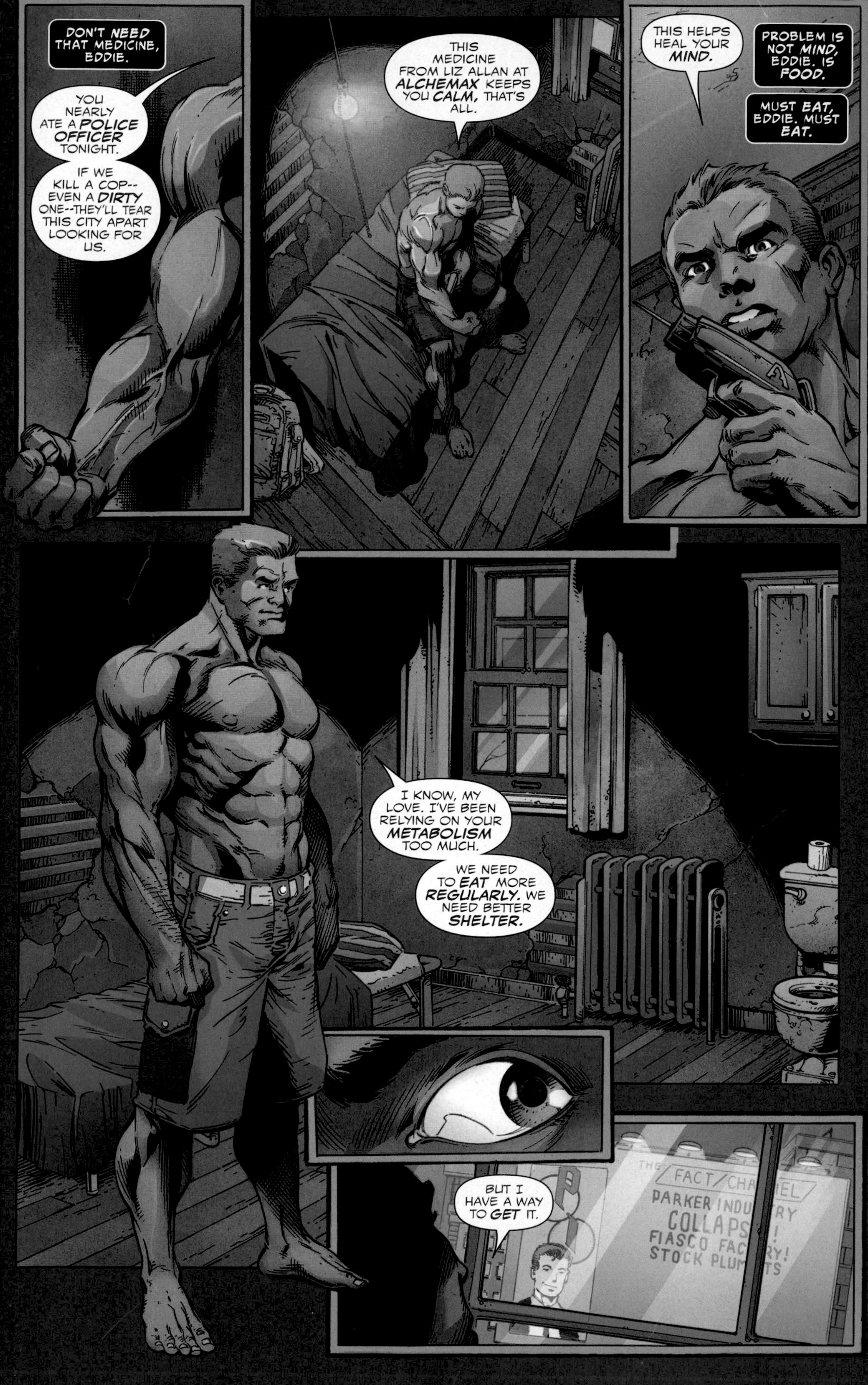

DON'T NEED THAT MEDICINE, EDDIE.
YOU NEARLY ATE A POLICE OFFICER TONIGHT.
IF WE KILL A COP-- EVEN A DIRTY ONE--THEY'LL TEAR THIS CITY APART LOOKING FOR US.
THIS MEDICINE FROM LIZ ALLAN AT ALCHEMAX KEEPS YOU CALM, THAT'S ALL.
THIS HELPS HEAL YOUR MIND.
PROBLEM IS NOT MIND, EDDIE. IS FOOD.
MUST EAT, EDDIE. MUST EAT.
I KNOW, MY LOVE. I'VE BEEN RELYING ON YOUR METABOLISM TOO MUCH.
WE NEED TO EAT MORE REGULARLY. WE NEED BETTER SHELTER.
BUT I HAVE A WAY TO GET IT.
THE FACT CHANNEL
PARKER INDUSTRY COLLAPS
FIASCO FAC RY!
STOCK PLUM TS

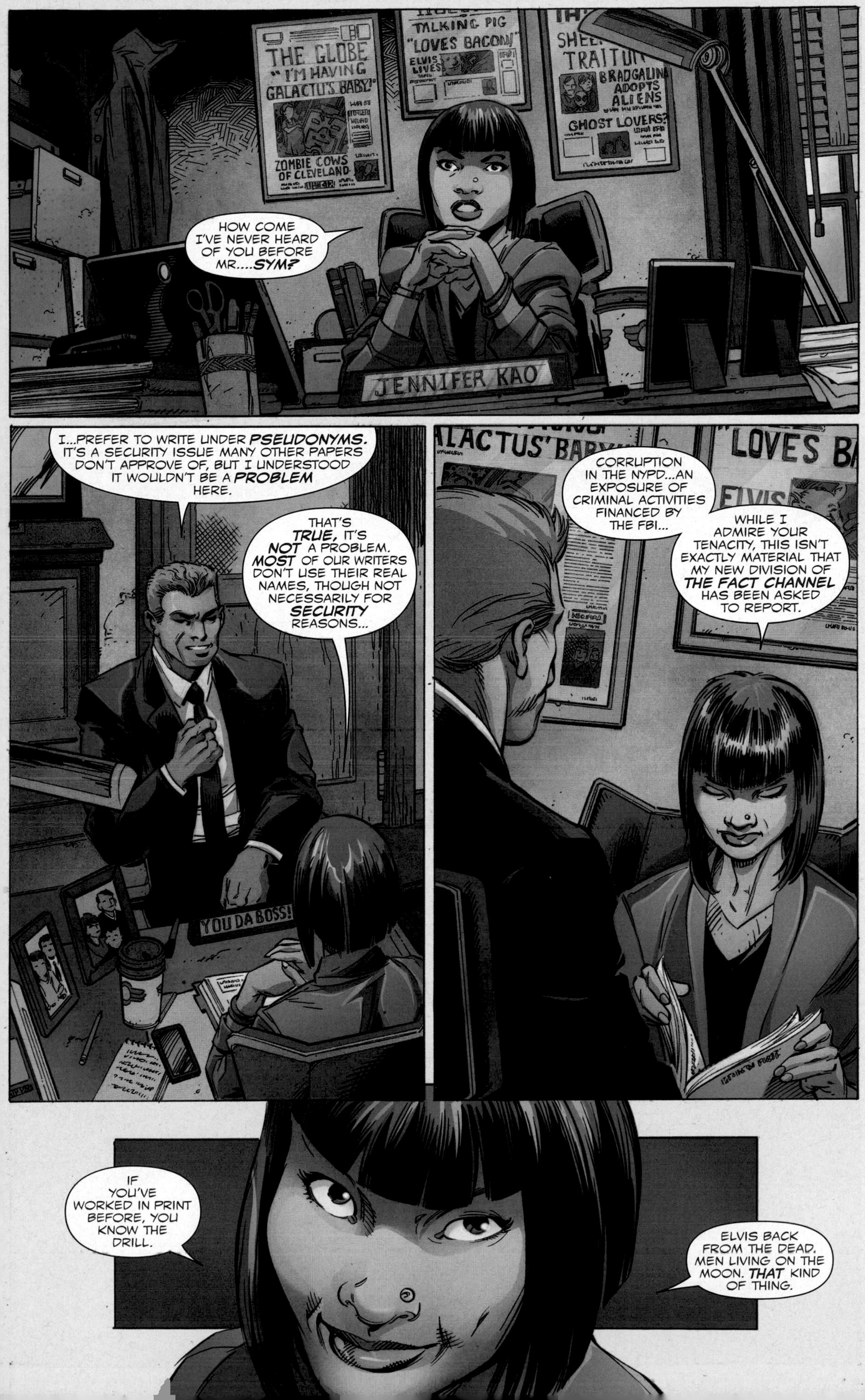
THE GLOBE
"I'M HAVING GALACTUS'S BABY!"
ZOMBIE COWS OF CLEVELAND
TALKING PIG
"LOVES BACON!"
ELVIS LIVES
BRADGALINA ADOPTS ALIENS
GHOST LOVERS?
HOW COME I'VE NEVER HEARD OF YOU BEFORE MR....SYM?
JENNIFER KAO
I...PREFER TO WRITE UNDER PSEUDONYMS. IT'S A SECURITY ISSUE MANY OTHER PAPERS DON'T APPROVE OF, BUT I UNDERSTOOD IT WOULDN'T BE A PROBLEM HERE.
THAT'S TRUE, IT'S NOT A PROBLEM. MOST OF OUR WRITERS DON'T USE THEIR REAL NAMES, THOUGH NOT NECESSARILY FOR SECURITY REASONS...
YOU DA BOSS!
CORRUPTION IN THE NYPD...AN EXPOSURE OF CRIMINAL ACTIVITIES FINANCED BY THE FBI...
WHILE I ADMIRE YOUR TENACITY, THIS ISN'T EXACTLY MATERIAL THAT MY NEW DIVISION OF THE FACT CHANNEL HAS BEEN ASKED TO REPORT.
IF YOU'VE WORKED IN PRINT BEFORE, YOU KNOW THE DRILL.
ELVIS BACK FROM THE DEAD. MEN LIVING ON THE MOON. THAT KIND OF THING.

MEN *DO* LIVE ON THE MOON...

THAT'S THE SPIRIT! WRITE THAT UP WITH THE TYPE OF SKILL YOU BROUGHT TO THIS MATERIAL, AND WE CAN BE IN BUSINESS.

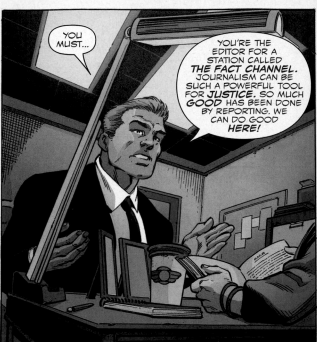

YOU MUST...

YOU'RE THE EDITOR FOR A STATION CALLED *THE FACT CHANNEL.* JOURNALISM CAN BE SUCH A POWERFUL TOOL FOR *JUSTICE.* SO MUCH *GOOD* HAS BEEN DONE BY REPORTING. WE CAN DO GOOD *HERE!*

I AM THE EDITOR OF A *DIVISION* OF THE *FACT CHANNEL,* MR. SYM.

THE GOOD MY CONTENT DOES IS STAYING ON-BRAND SO SALES REMAIN STEADY, AND MY WRITERS CAN TAKE HOME REAL PAYCHECKS.

COME BACK TO ME WITH SOMETHING I CAN *USE,* AND YOU CAN BE ONE OF THEM.

EAT *HER,* EDDIE?

I HEAR YOU.

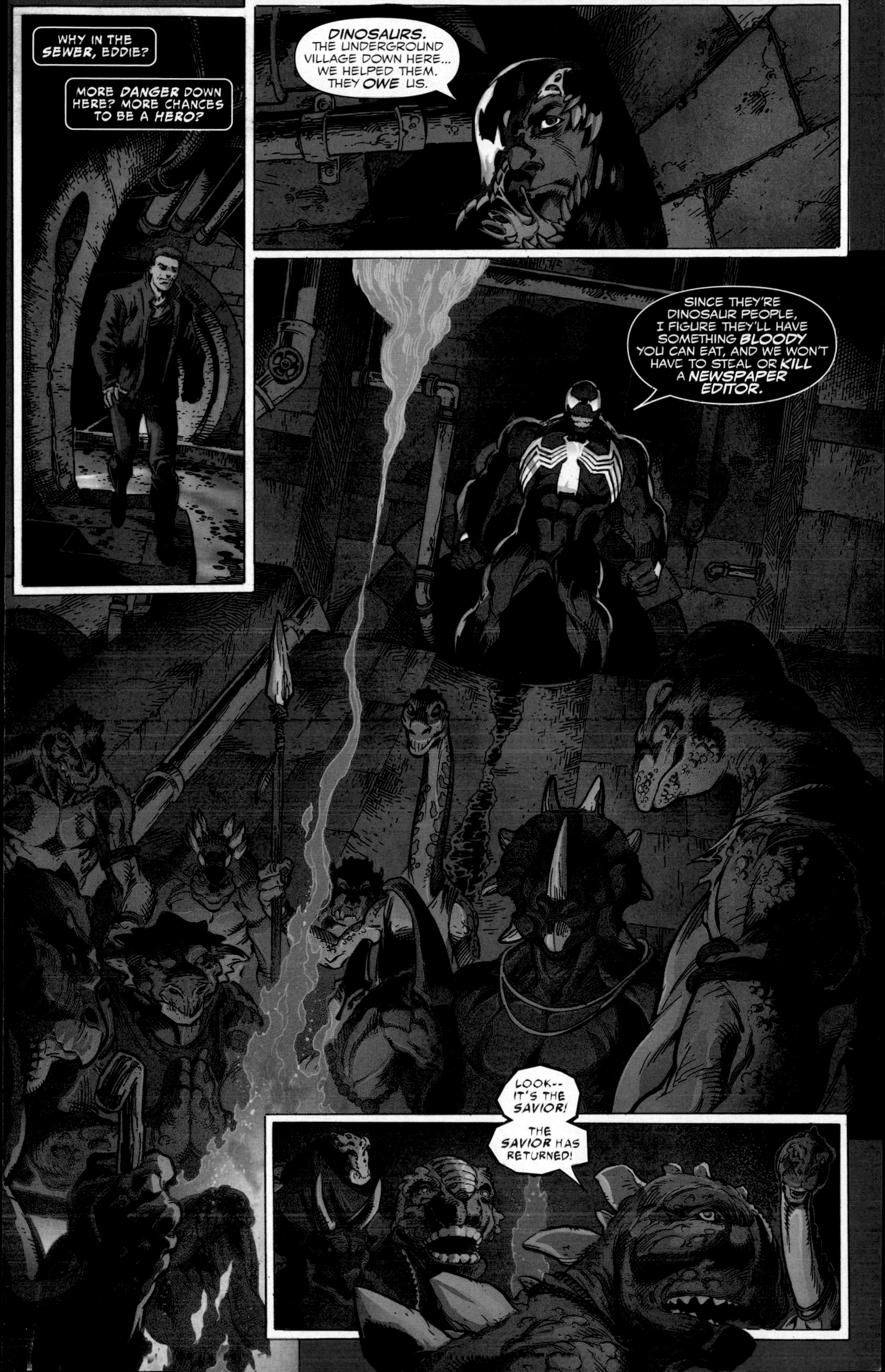
WHY IN THE SEWER, EDDIE?
MORE DANGER DOWN HERE? MORE CHANCES TO BE A HERO?
DINOSAURS. THE UNDERGROUND VILLAGE DOWN HERE... WE HELPED THEM. THEY OWE US.
SINCE THEY'RE DINOSAUR PEOPLE, I FIGURE THEY'LL HAVE SOMETHING BLOODY YOU CAN EAT, AND WE WON'T HAVE TO STEAL OR KILL A NEWSPAPER EDITOR.
LOOK-- IT'S THE SAVIOR!
THE SAVIOR HAS RETURNED!

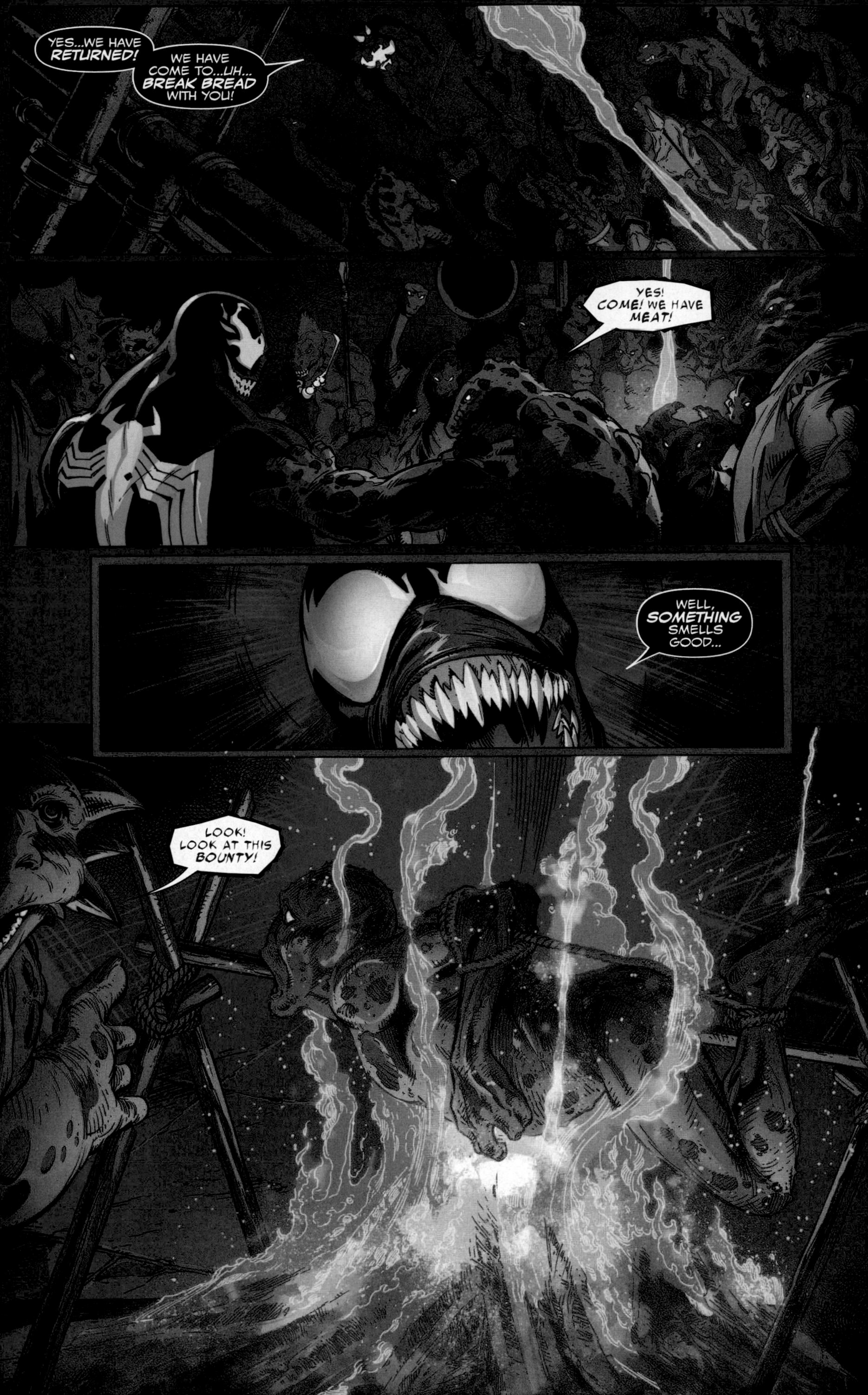
YES...WE HAVE RETURNED!
WE HAVE COME TO...UH... BREAK BREAD WITH YOU!
YES! COME! WE HAVE MEAT!
WELL, SOMETHING SMELLS GOOD...
LOOK! LOOK AT THIS BOUNTY!

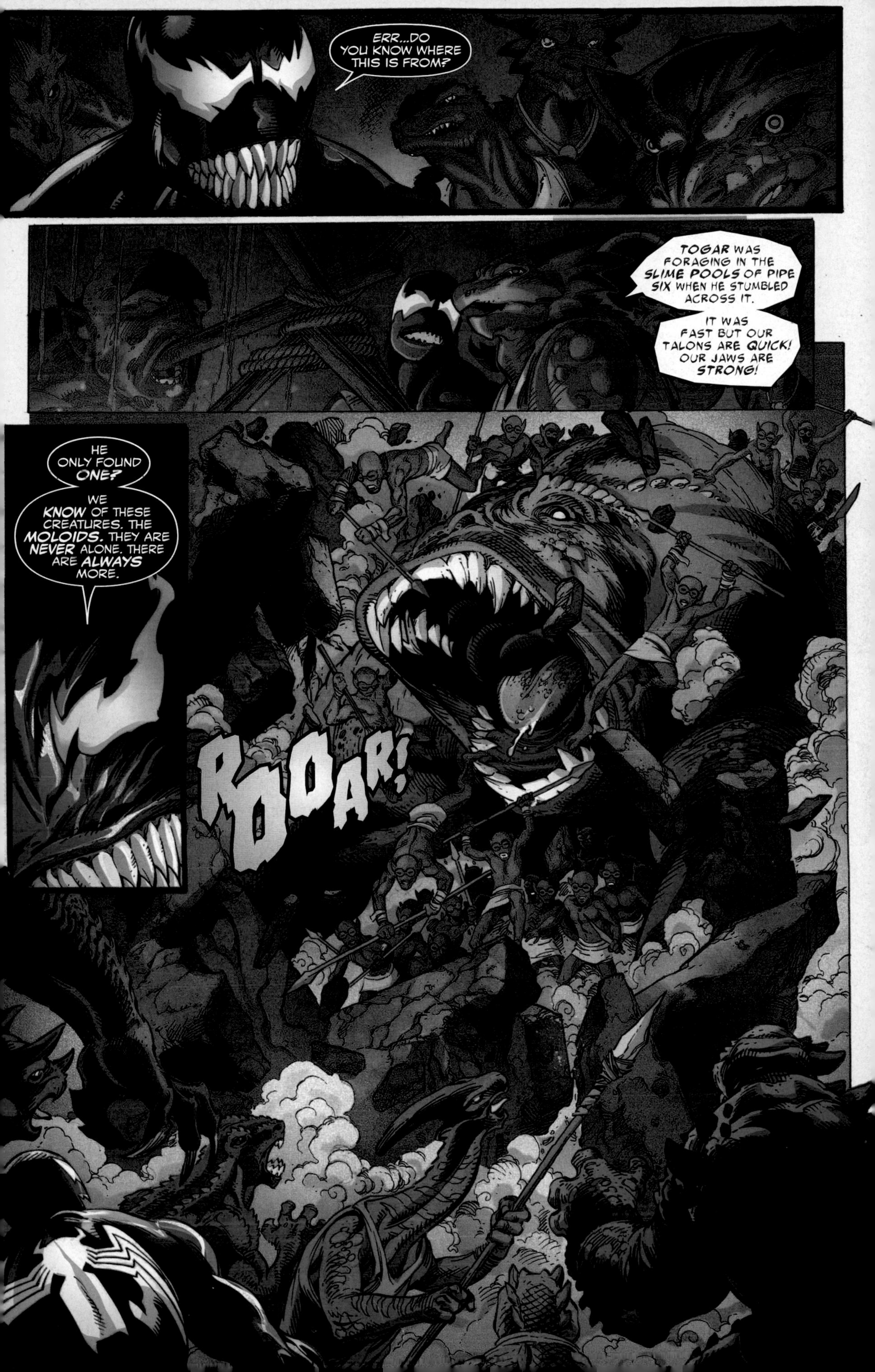
ERR...DO YOU KNOW WHERE THIS IS FROM?
TOGAR WAS FORAGING IN THE SLIME POOLS OF PIPE SIX WHEN HE STUMBLED ACROSS IT.
IT WAS FAST BUT OUR TALONS ARE QUICK! OUR JAWS ARE STRONG!
HE ONLY FOUND ONE?
WE KNOW OF THESE CREATURES. THE MOLOIDS. THEY ARE NEVER ALONE. THERE ARE ALWAYS MORE.
ROOAR!

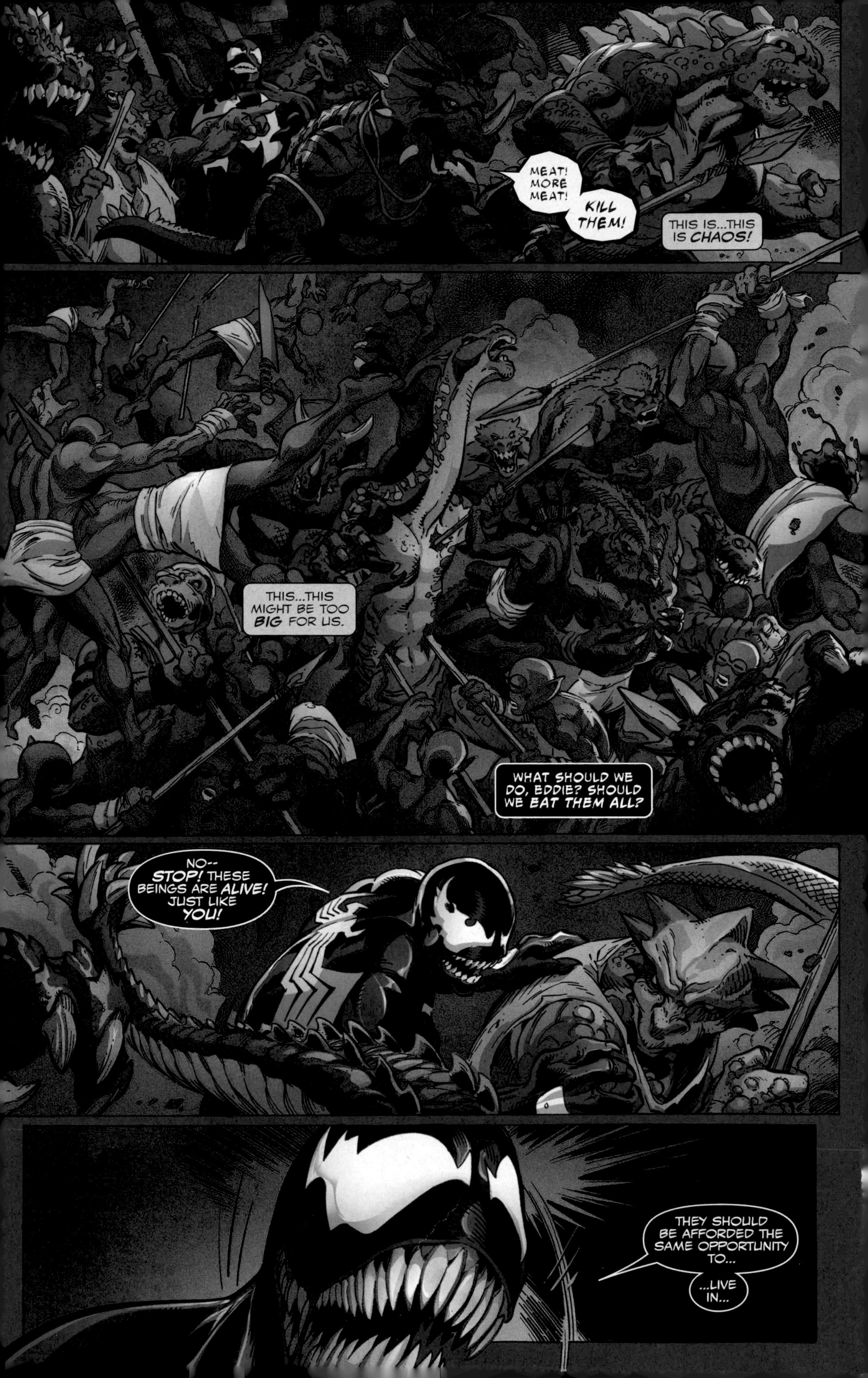
MEAT! MORE MEAT!
KILL THEM!
THIS IS...THIS IS CHAOS!
THIS...THIS MIGHT BE TOO BIG FOR US.
WHAT SHOULD WE DO, EDDIE? SHOULD WE EAT THEM ALL?
NO-- STOP! THESE BEINGS ARE ALIVE! JUST LIKE YOU!
THEY SHOULD BE AFFORDED THE SAME OPPORTUNITY TO...
...LIVE IN...

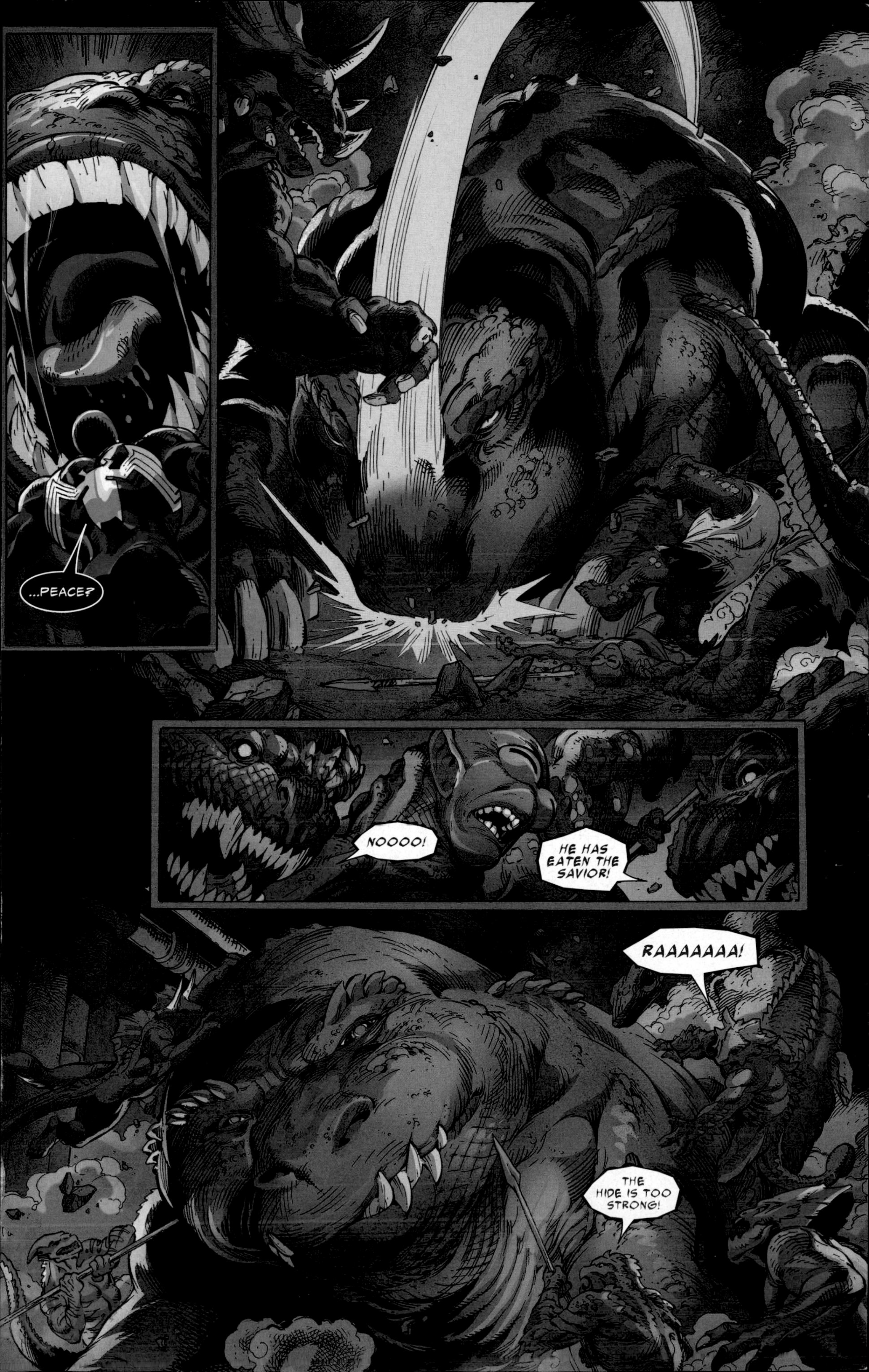
...PEACE?
NOOOO!
HE HAS EATEN THE SAVIOR!
RAAAAAAA!
THE HIDE IS TOO STRONG!

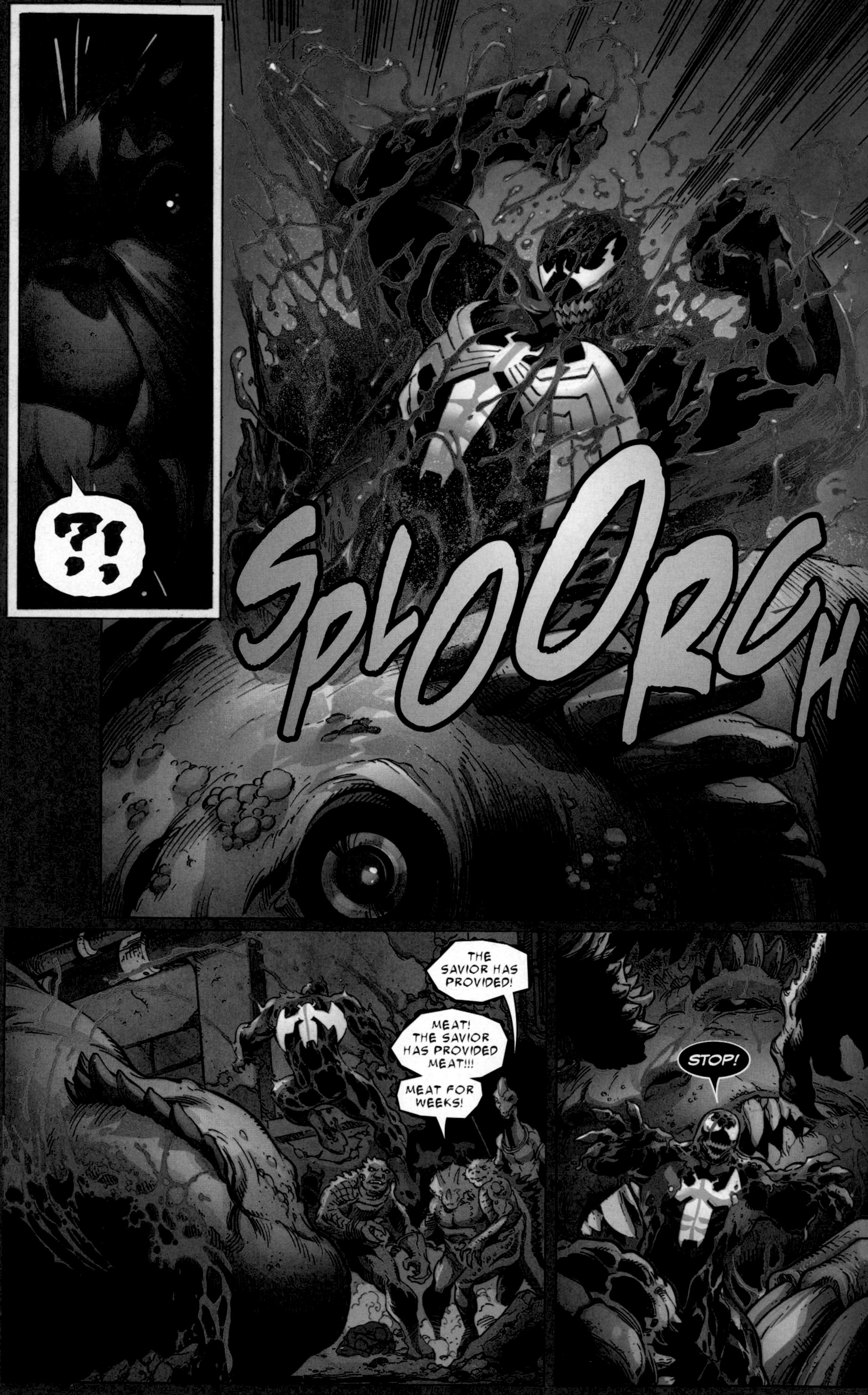
?!
SPLOORCH
THE SAVIOR HAS PROVIDED!
MEAT! THE SAVIOR HAS PROVIDED MEAT!!!
MEAT FOR WEEKS!
STOP!

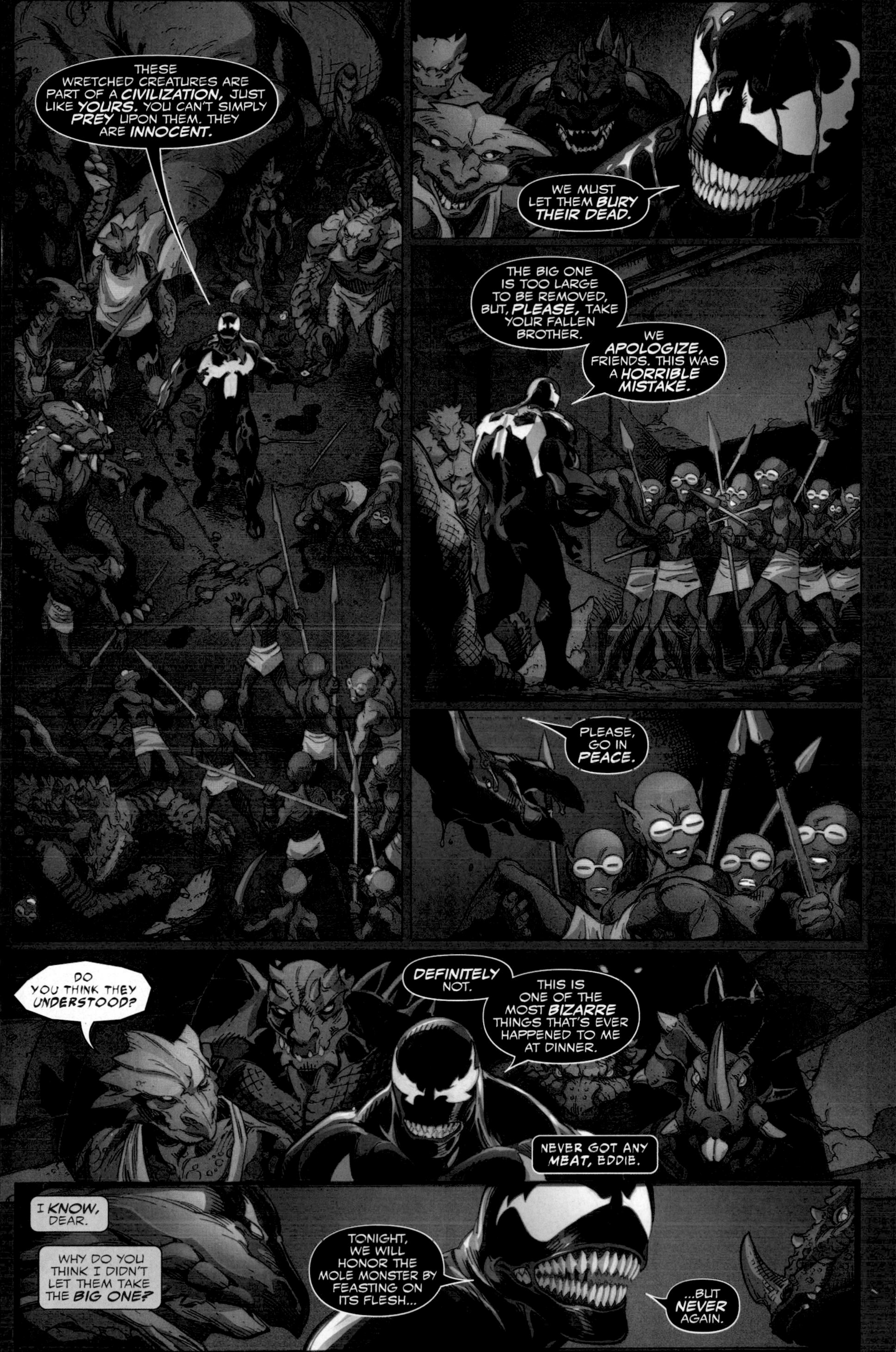

THESE WRETCHED CREATURES ARE PART OF A CIVILIZATION, JUST LIKE YOURS. YOU CAN'T SIMPLY PREY UPON THEM. THEY ARE INNOCENT.
WE MUST LET THEM BURY THEIR DEAD.
THE BIG ONE IS TOO LARGE TO BE REMOVED, BUT, PLEASE, TAKE YOUR FALLEN BROTHER.
WE APOLOGIZE, FRIENDS. THIS WAS A HORRIBLE MISTAKE.
PLEASE, GO IN PEACE.
DO YOU THINK THEY UNDERSTOOD?
DEFINITELY NOT.
THIS IS ONE OF THE MOST BIZARRE THINGS THAT'S EVER HAPPENED TO ME AT DINNER.
NEVER GOT ANY MEAT, EDDIE.
I KNOW, DEAR.
WHY DO YOU THINK I DIDN'T LET THEM TAKE THE BIG ONE?
TONIGHT, WE WILL HONOR THE MOLE MONSTER BY FEASTING ON ITS FLESH...
...BUT NEVER AGAIN.

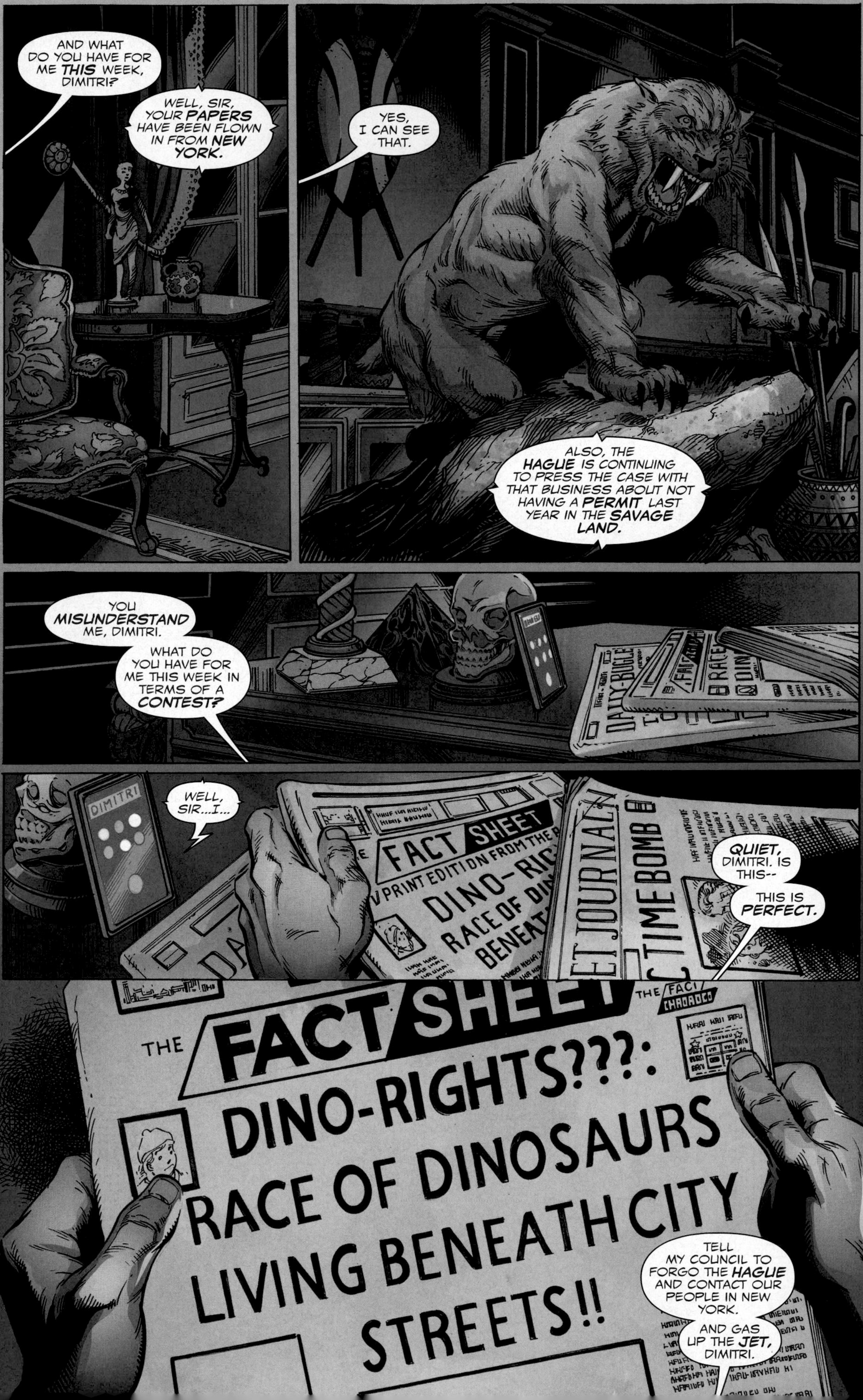

AND WHAT DO YOU HAVE FOR ME THIS WEEK, DIMITRI?
WELL, SIR, YOUR PAPERS HAVE BEEN FLOWN IN FROM NEW YORK.
YES, I CAN SEE THAT.
ALSO, THE HAGUE IS CONTINUING TO PRESS THE CASE WITH THAT BUSINESS ABOUT NOT HAVING A PERMIT LAST YEAR IN THE SAVAGE LAND.
YOU MISUNDERSTAND ME, DIMITRI.
WHAT DO YOU HAVE FOR ME THIS WEEK IN TERMS OF A CONTEST?
DAILY BUGLE
DIMITRI
WELL, SIR...I...
THE FACT SHEET
PRINT EDITION FROM THE
DINO-RIG
RACE OF DI
BENEAT
TIME BOMB
QUIET, DIMITRI. IS THIS--
THIS IS PERFECT.
THE FACT SHEET
DINO-RIGHTS???:
RACE OF DINOSAURS
LIVING BENEATH CITY
STREETS!!
TELL MY COUNCIL TO FORGO THE HAGUE AND CONTACT OUR PEOPLE IN NEW YORK.
AND GAS UP THE JET, DIMITRI.

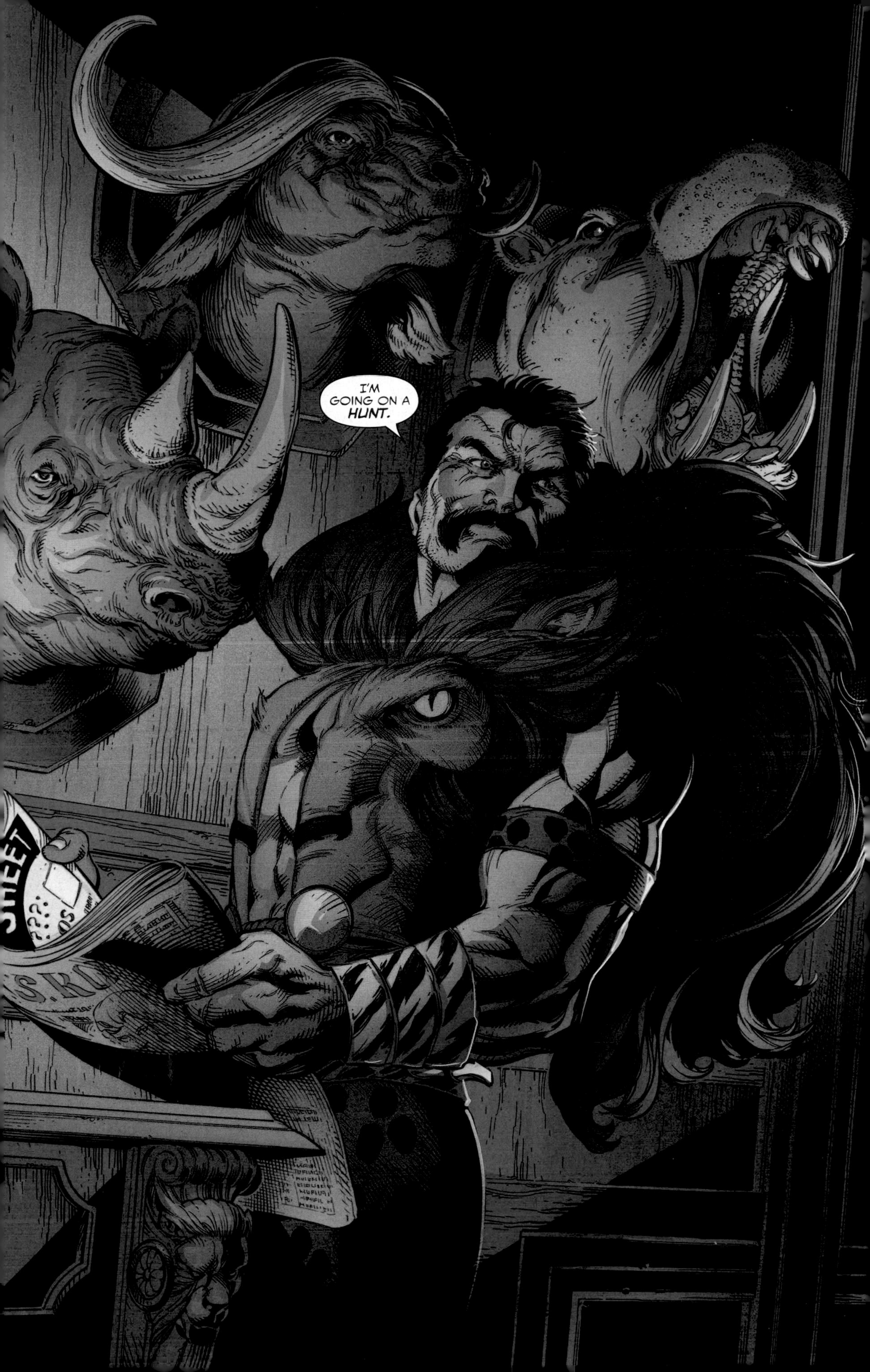
I'M GOING ON A HUNT.

156

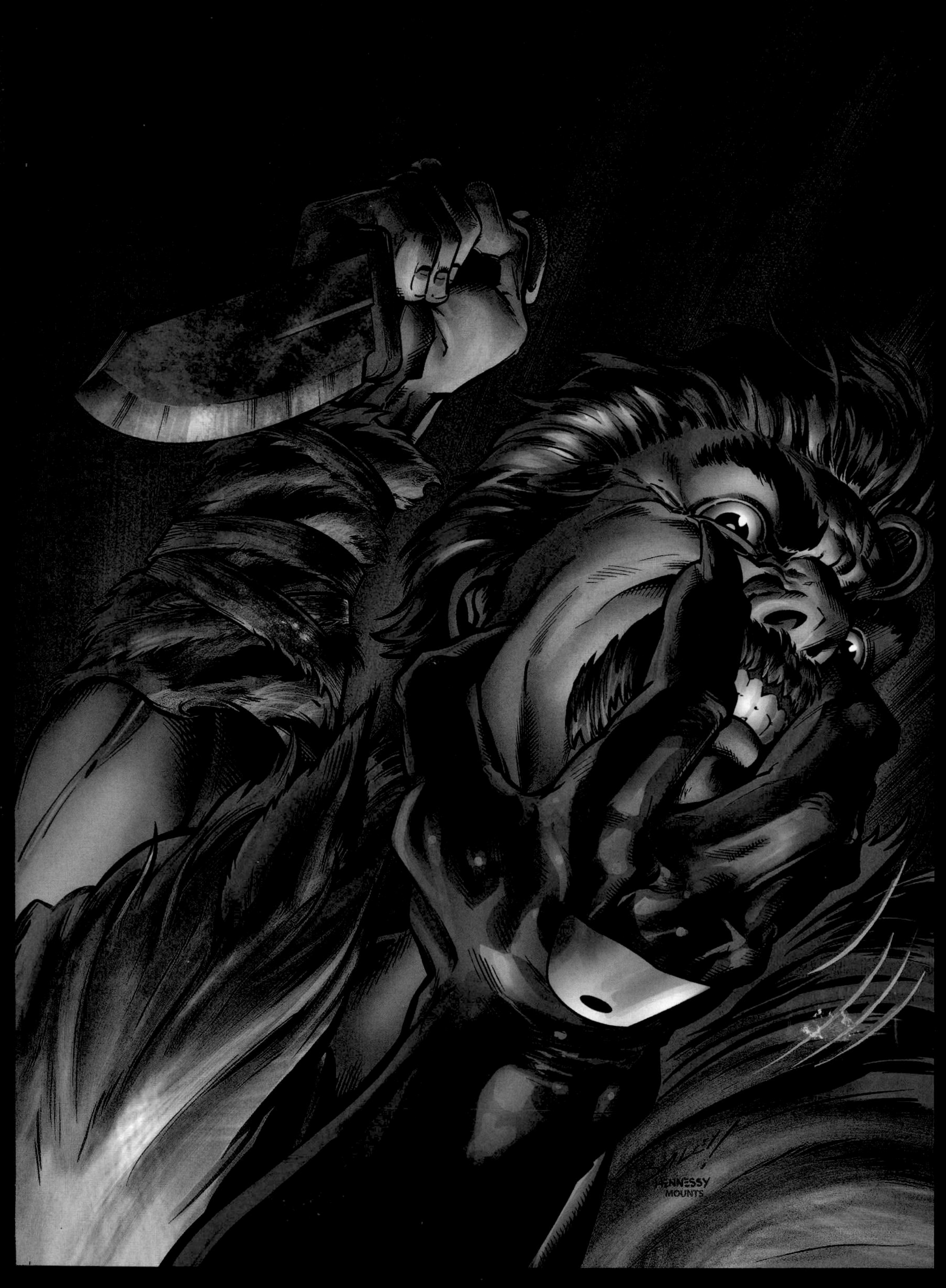
HENNESSY
MOUNTS

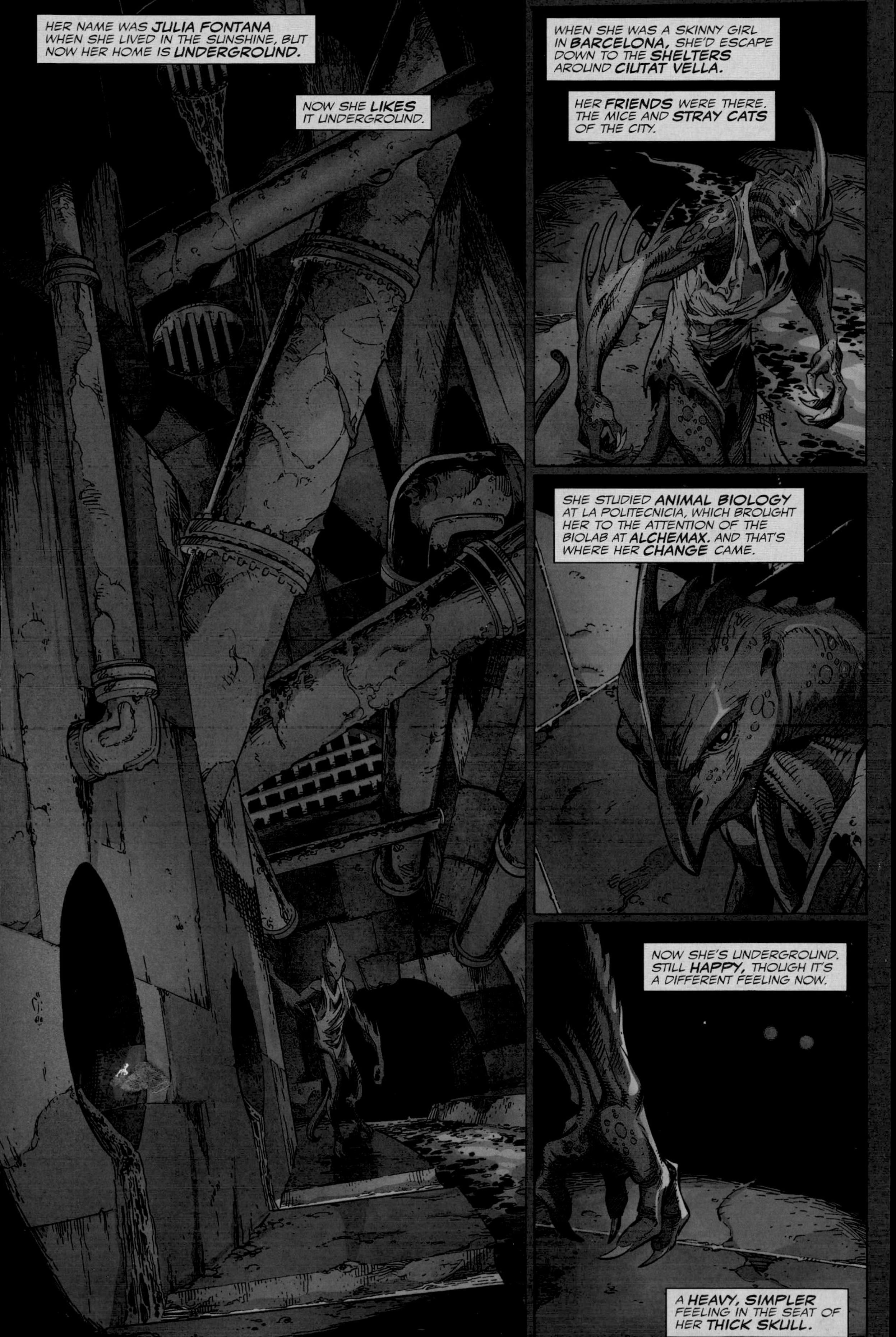
HER NAME WAS JULIA FONTANA WHEN SHE LIVED IN THE SUNSHINE, BUT NOW HER HOME IS UNDERGROUND.
NOW SHE LIKES IT UNDERGROUND.
WHEN SHE WAS A SKINNY GIRL IN BARCELONA, SHE'D ESCAPE DOWN TO THE SHELTERS AROUND CIUTAT VELLA.
HER FRIENDS WERE THERE. THE MICE AND STRAY CATS OF THE CITY.
SHE STUDIED ANIMAL BIOLOGY AT LA POLITECNICIA, WHICH BROUGHT HER TO THE ATTENTION OF THE BIOLAB AT ALCHEMAX. AND THAT'S WHERE HER CHANGE CAME.
NOW SHE'S UNDERGROUND. STILL HAPPY, THOUGH IT'S A DIFFERENT FEELING NOW.
A HEAVY, SIMPLER FEELING IN THE SEAT OF HER THICK SKULL.

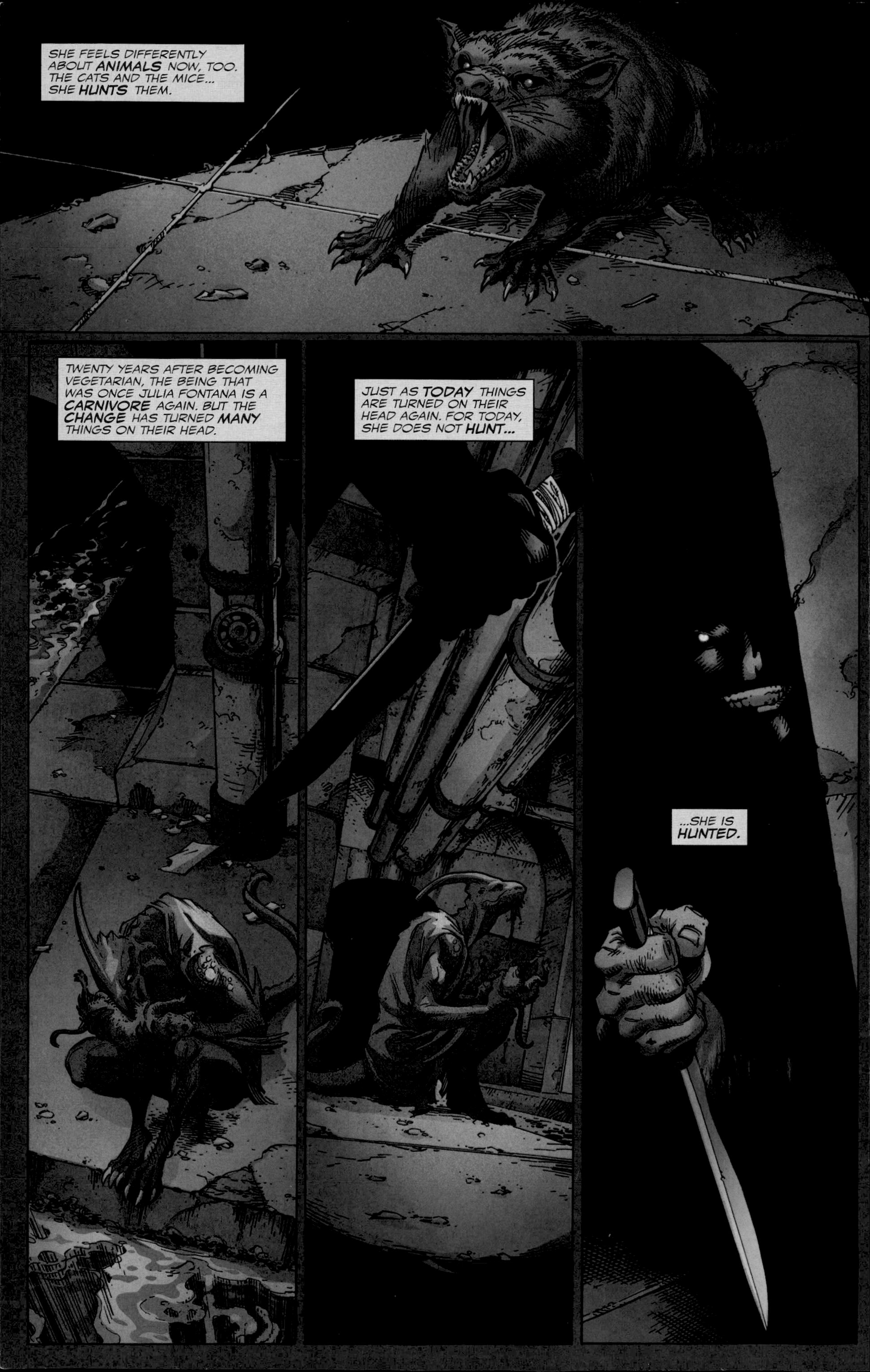
SHE FEELS DIFFERENTLY ABOUT ANIMALS NOW, TOO. THE CATS AND THE MICE... SHE HUNTS THEM.
TWENTY YEARS AFTER BECOMING VEGETARIAN, THE BEING THAT WAS ONCE JULIA FONTANA IS A CARNIVORE AGAIN. BUT THE CHANGE HAS TURNED MANY THINGS ON THEIR HEAD.
JUST AS TODAY THINGS ARE TURNED ON THEIR HEAD AGAIN. FOR TODAY, SHE DOES NOT HUNT...
...SHE IS HUNTED.

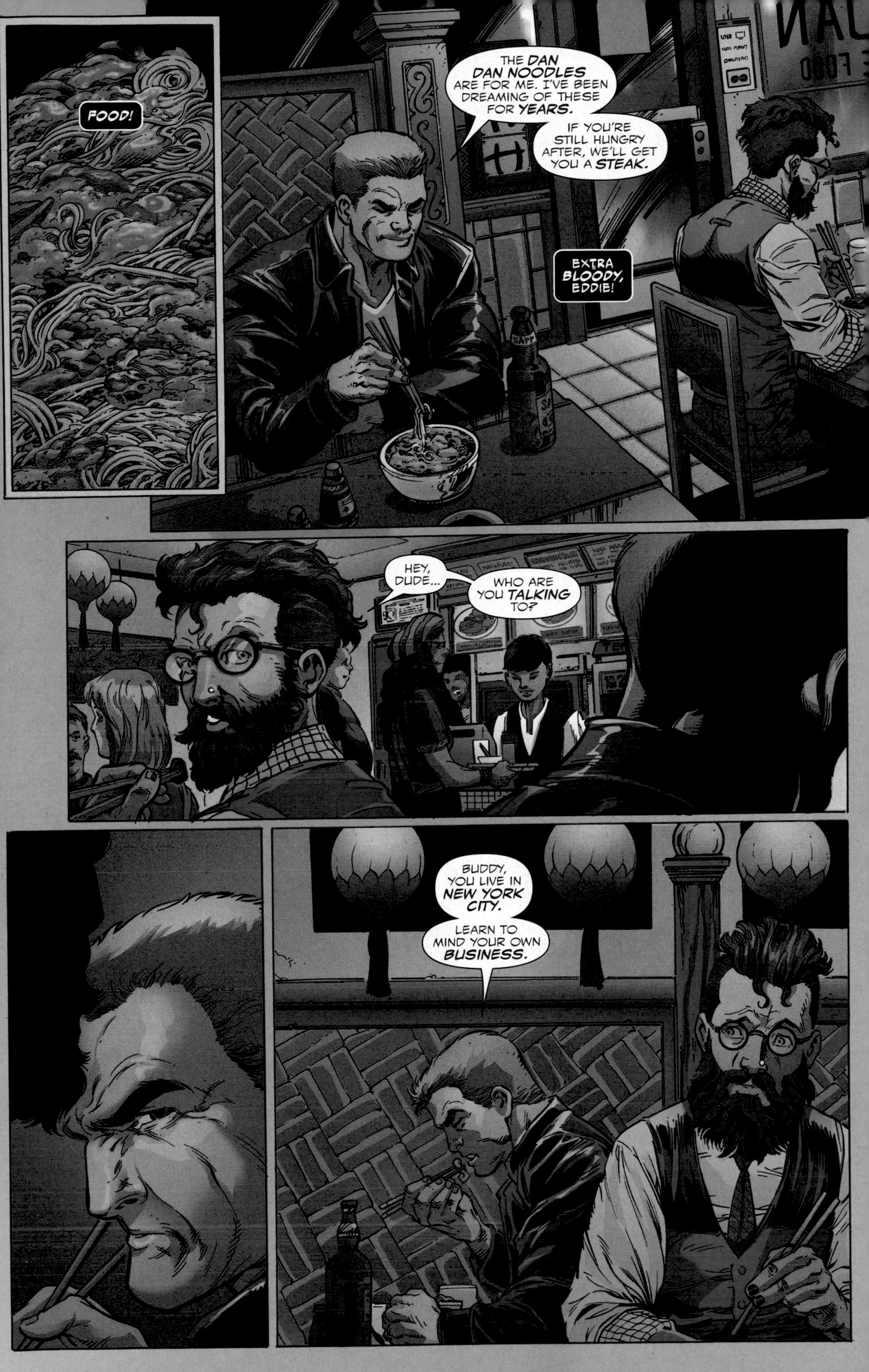

FOOD!
THE DAN DAN NOODLES ARE FOR ME. I'VE BEEN DREAMING OF THESE FOR YEARS.
IF YOU'RE STILL HUNGRY AFTER, WE'LL GET YOU A STEAK.
EXTRA BLOODY, EDDIE!
HEY, DUDE...
WHO ARE YOU TALKING TO?
BUDDY, YOU LIVE IN NEW YORK CITY.
LEARN TO MIND YOUR OWN BUSINESS.

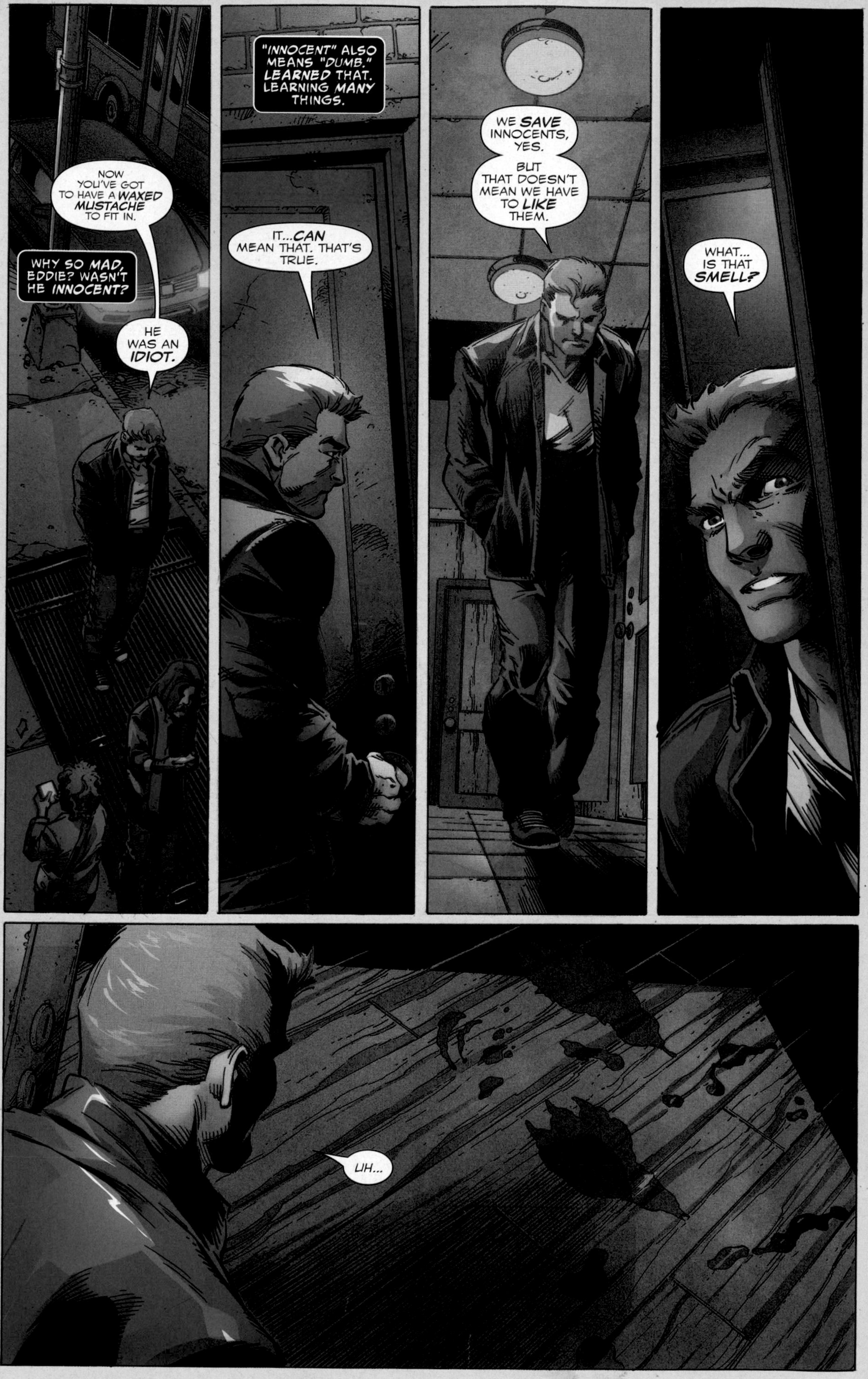
NOW YOU'VE GOT TO HAVE A WAXED MUSTACHE TO FIT IN.
WHY SO MAD, EDDIE? WASN'T HE INNOCENT?
HE WAS AN IDIOT.
"INNOCENT" ALSO MEANS "DUMB." LEARNED THAT. LEARNING MANY THINGS.
IT...CAN MEAN THAT. THAT'S TRUE.
WE SAVE INNOCENTS, YES.
BUT THAT DOESN'T MEAN WE HAVE TO LIKE THEM.
WHAT... IS THAT SMELL?
UH...

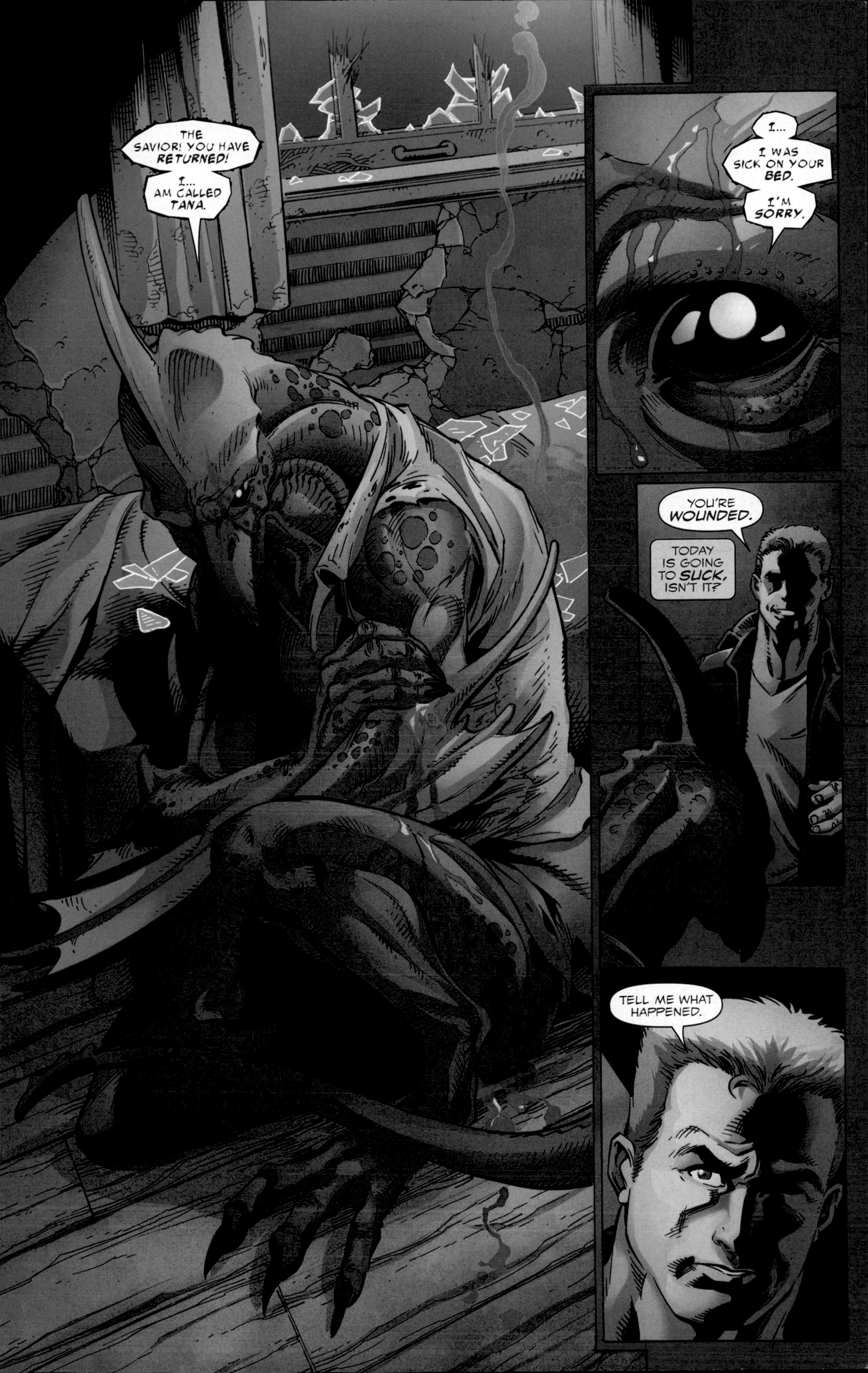
THE SAVIOR! YOU HAVE RETURNED!
I... AM CALLED TANA.
I...
I WAS SICK ON YOUR BED.
I'M SORRY.
YOU'RE WOUNDED.
TODAY IS GOING TO SUCK, ISN'T IT?
TELL ME WHAT HAPPENED.

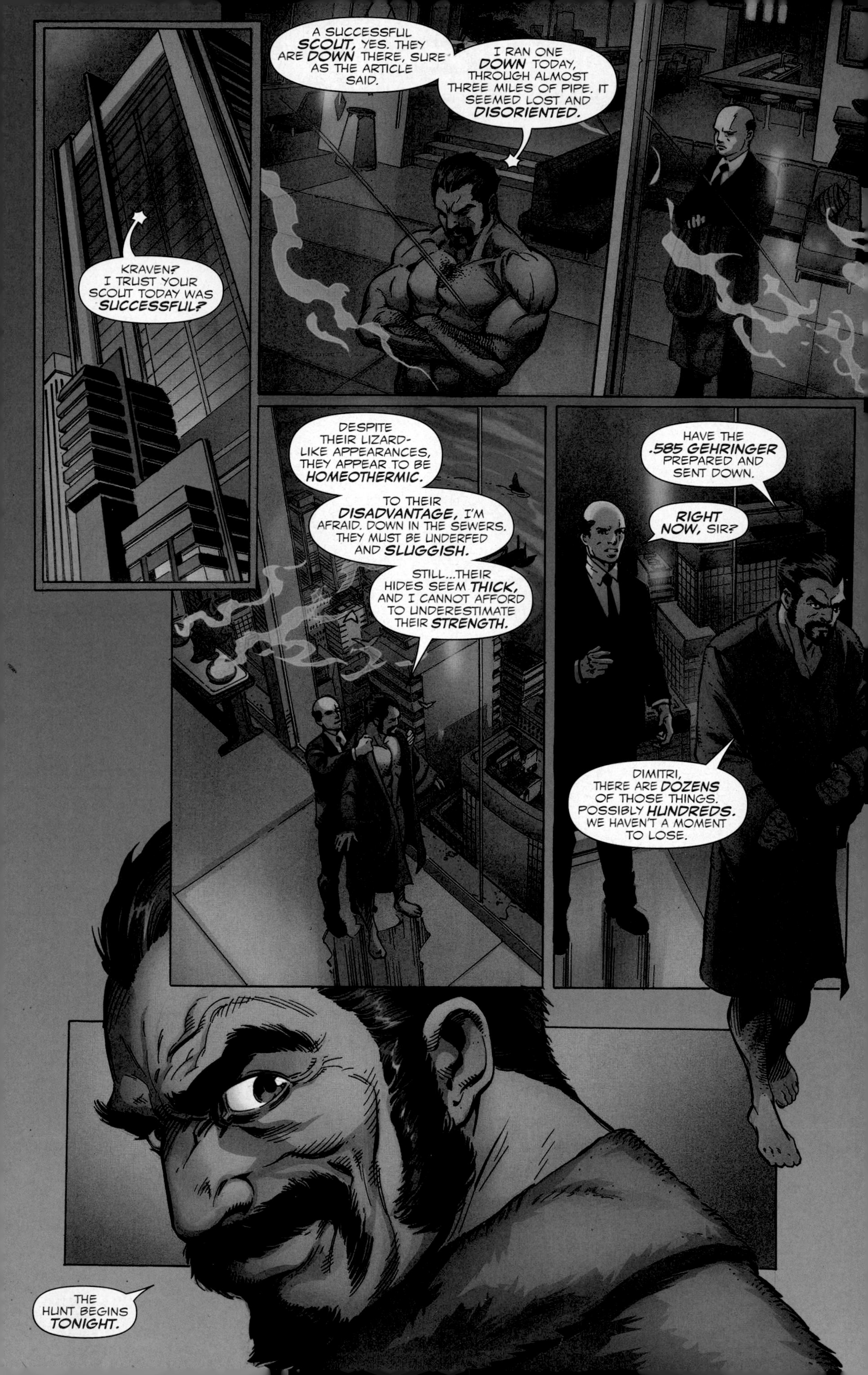
KRAVEN? I TRUST YOUR SCOUT TODAY WAS SUCCESSFUL?
A SUCCESSFUL SCOUT, YES. THEY ARE DOWN THERE, SURE AS THE ARTICLE SAID.
I RAN ONE DOWN TODAY, THROUGH ALMOST THREE MILES OF PIPE. IT SEEMED LOST AND DISORIENTED.
DESPITE THEIR LIZARD-LIKE APPEARANCES, THEY APPEAR TO BE HOMEOTHERMIC.
TO THEIR DISADVANTAGE, I'M AFRAID. DOWN IN THE SEWERS. THEY MUST BE UNDERFED AND SLUGGISH.
STILL...THEIR HIDES SEEM THICK, AND I CANNOT AFFORD TO UNDERESTIMATE THEIR STRENGTH.
HAVE THE .585 GEHRINGER PREPARED AND SENT DOWN.
RIGHT NOW, SIR?
DIMITRI, THERE ARE DOZENS OF THOSE THINGS. POSSIBLY HUNDREDS. WE HAVEN'T A MOMENT TO LOSE.
THE HUNT BEGINS TONIGHT.

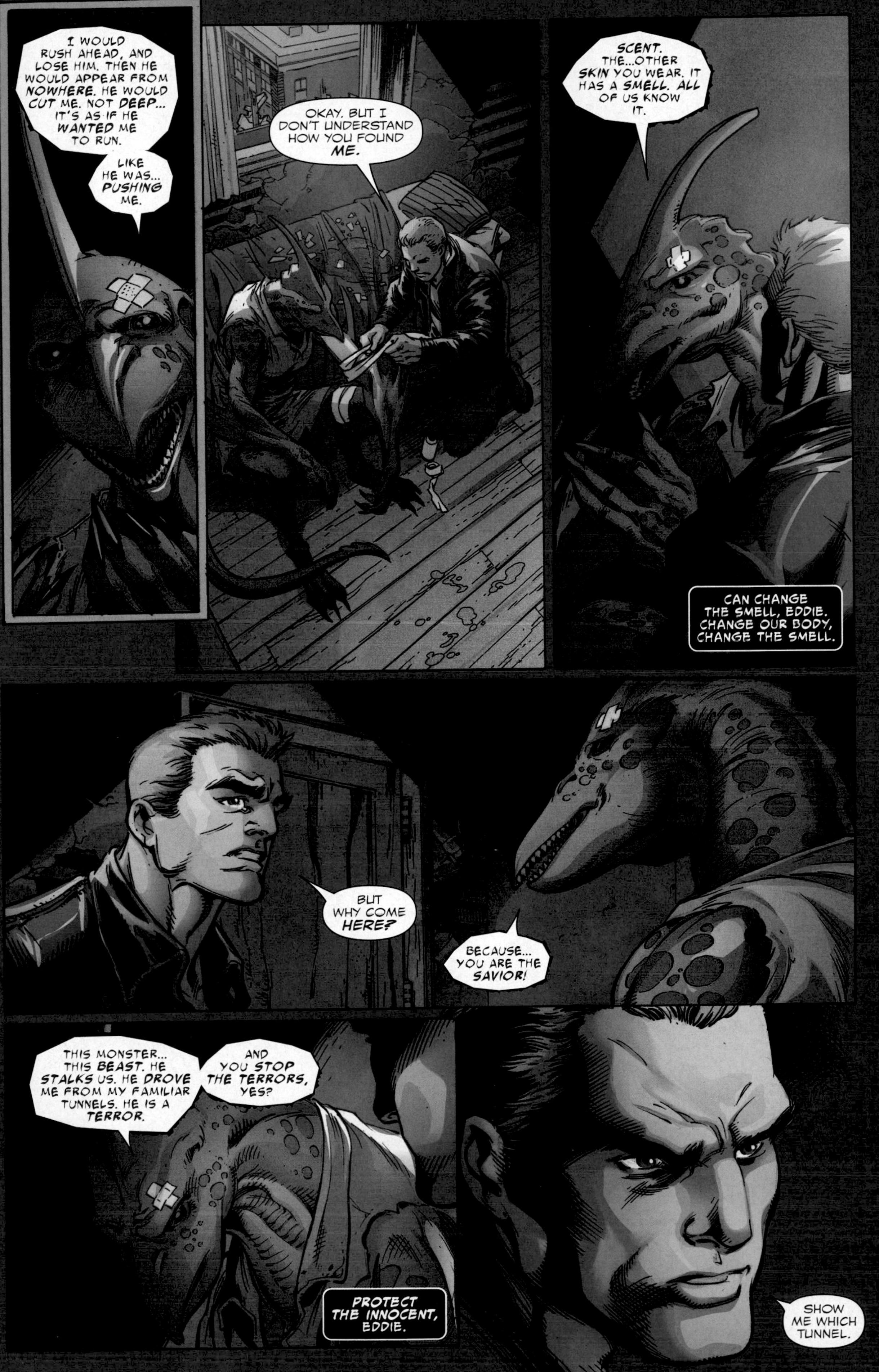
I WOULD RUSH AHEAD, AND LOSE HIM. THEN HE WOULD APPEAR FROM NOWHERE. HE WOULD CUT ME. NOT DEEP... IT'S AS IF HE WANTED ME TO RUN.
LIKE HE WAS... PUSHING ME.
OKAY. BUT I DON'T UNDERSTAND HOW YOU FOUND ME.
SCENT. THE...OTHER SKIN YOU WEAR. IT HAS A SMELL. ALL OF US KNOW IT.
CAN CHANGE THE SMELL, EDDIE. CHANGE OUR BODY, CHANGE THE SMELL.
BUT WHY COME HERE?
BECAUSE... YOU ARE THE SAVIOR!
THIS MONSTER... THIS BEAST. HE STALKS US. HE DROVE ME FROM MY FAMILIAR TUNNELS. HE IS A TERROR.
AND YOU STOP THE TERRORS, YES?
PROTECT THE INNOCENT, EDDIE.
SHOW ME WHICH TUNNEL.

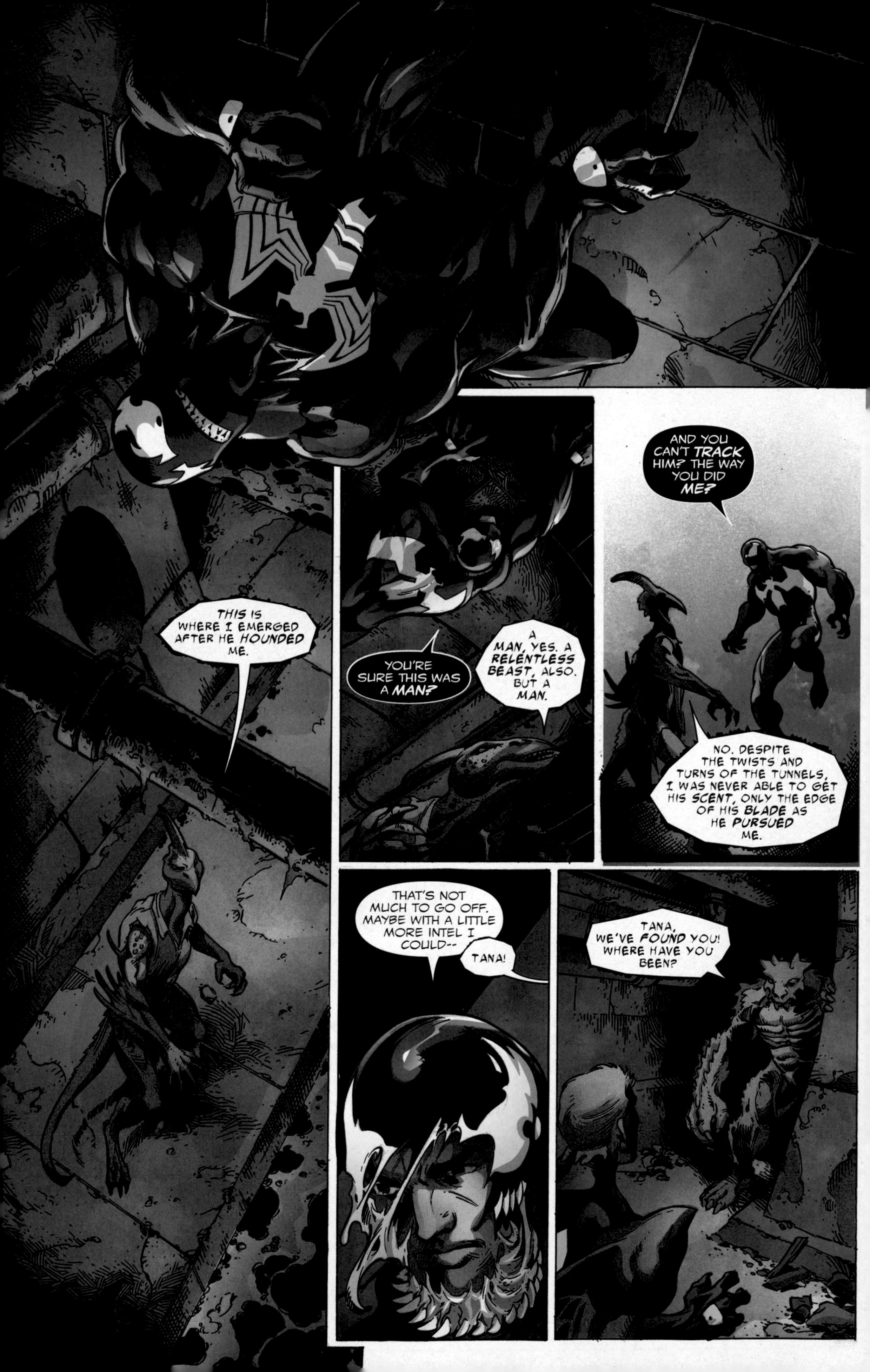
THIS IS WHERE I EMERGED AFTER HE HOUNDED ME.
YOU'RE SURE THIS WAS A MAN?
A MAN, YES. A RELENTLESS BEAST, ALSO. BUT A MAN.
AND YOU CAN'T TRACK HIM? THE WAY YOU DID ME?
NO. DESPITE THE TWISTS AND TURNS OF THE TUNNELS, I WAS NEVER ABLE TO GET HIS SCENT, ONLY THE EDGE OF HIS BLADE AS HE PURSUED ME.
THAT'S NOT MUCH TO GO OFF. MAYBE WITH A LITTLE MORE INTEL I COULD--
TANA!
TANA, WE'VE FOUND YOU! WHERE HAVE YOU BEEN?

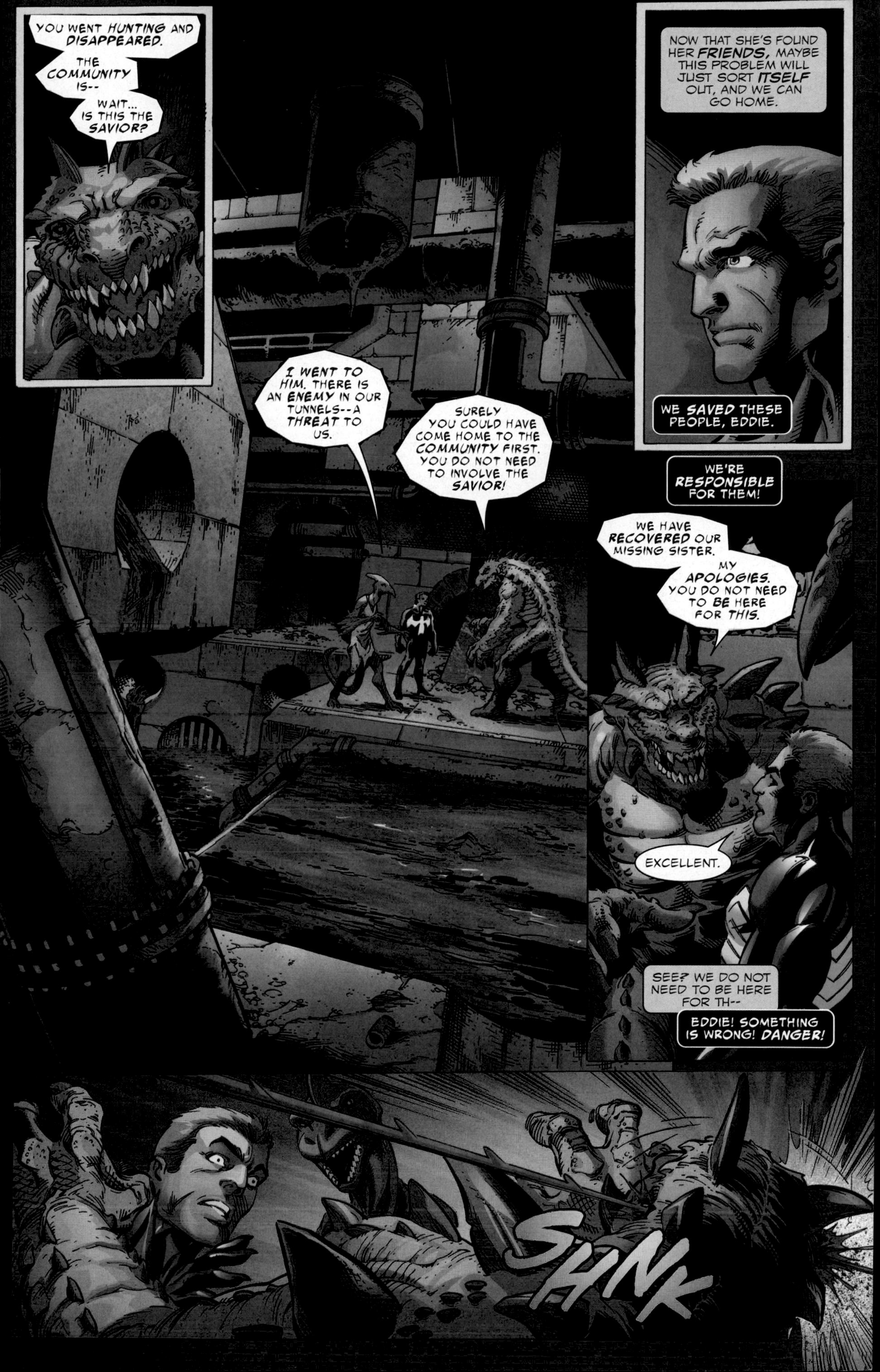

YOU WENT HUNTING AND DISAPPEARED.
THE COMMUNITY IS--
WAIT... IS THIS THE SAVIOR?
NOW THAT SHE'S FOUND HER FRIENDS, MAYBE THIS PROBLEM WILL JUST SORT ITSELF OUT, AND WE CAN GO HOME.
WE SAVED THESE PEOPLE, EDDIE.
WE'RE RESPONSIBLE FOR THEM!
I WENT TO HIM. THERE IS AN ENEMY IN OUR TUNNELS--A THREAT TO US.
SURELY YOU COULD HAVE COME HOME TO THE COMMUNITY FIRST. YOU DO NOT NEED TO INVOLVE THE SAVIOR!
WE HAVE RECOVERED OUR MISSING SISTER.
MY APOLOGIES. YOU DO NOT NEED TO BE HERE FOR THIS.
EXCELLENT.
SEE? WE DO NOT NEED TO BE HERE FOR TH--
EDDIE! SOMETHING IS WRONG! DANGER!
SHNK

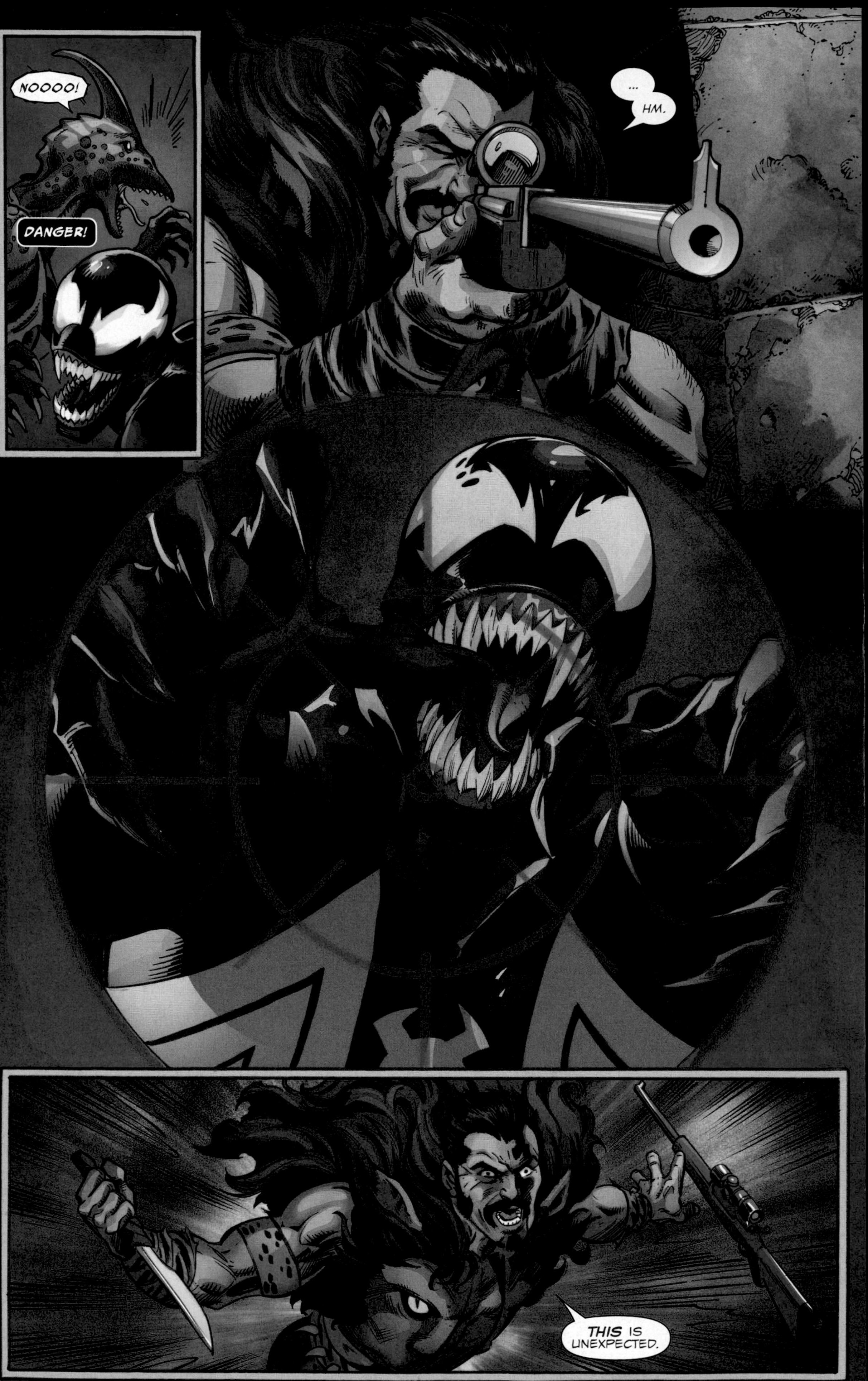
NOOOO!
DANGER!
... HM.
THIS IS UNEXPECTED.

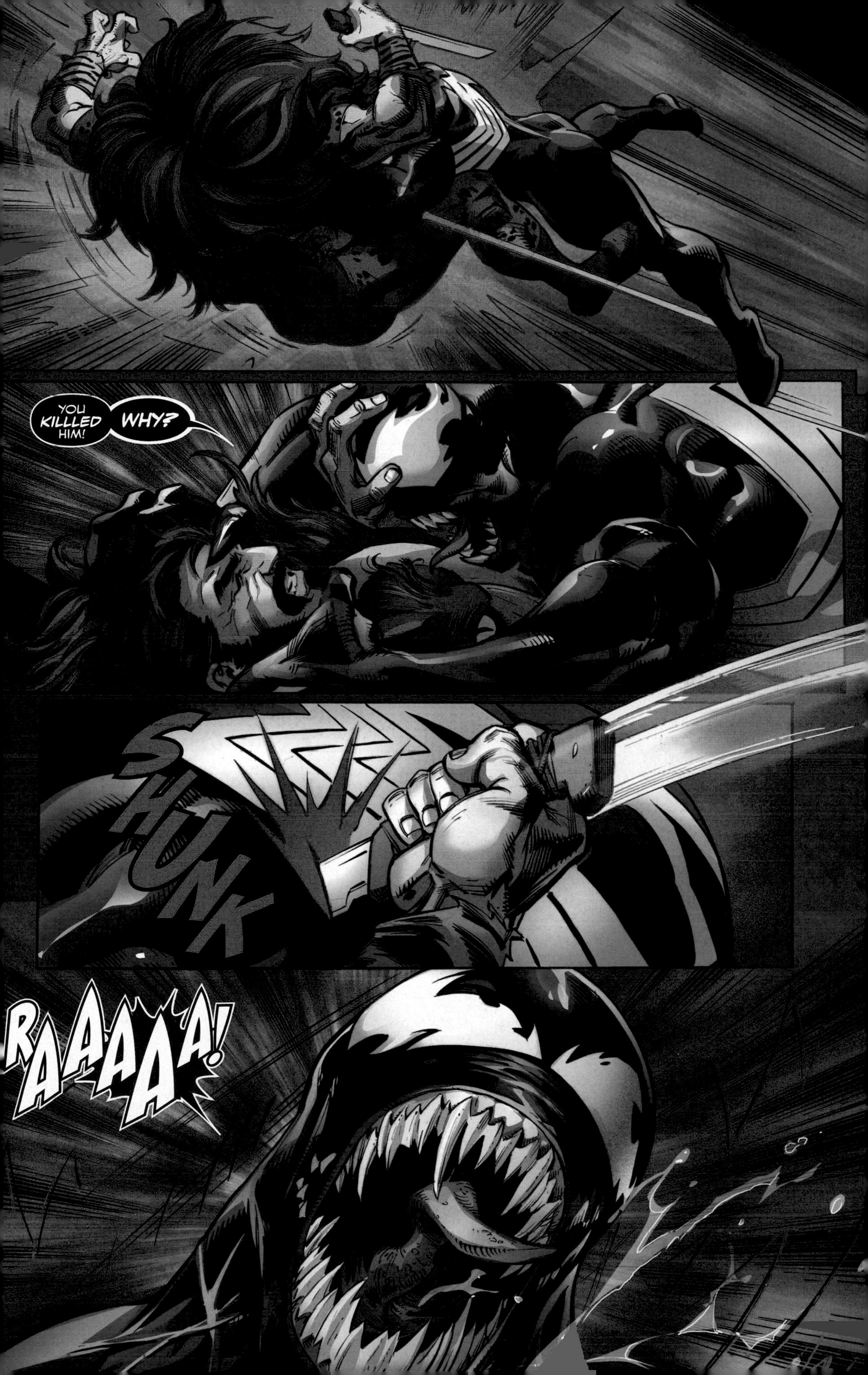
YOU KILLLED HIM!
WHY?
SHUNK
RAAAAA!

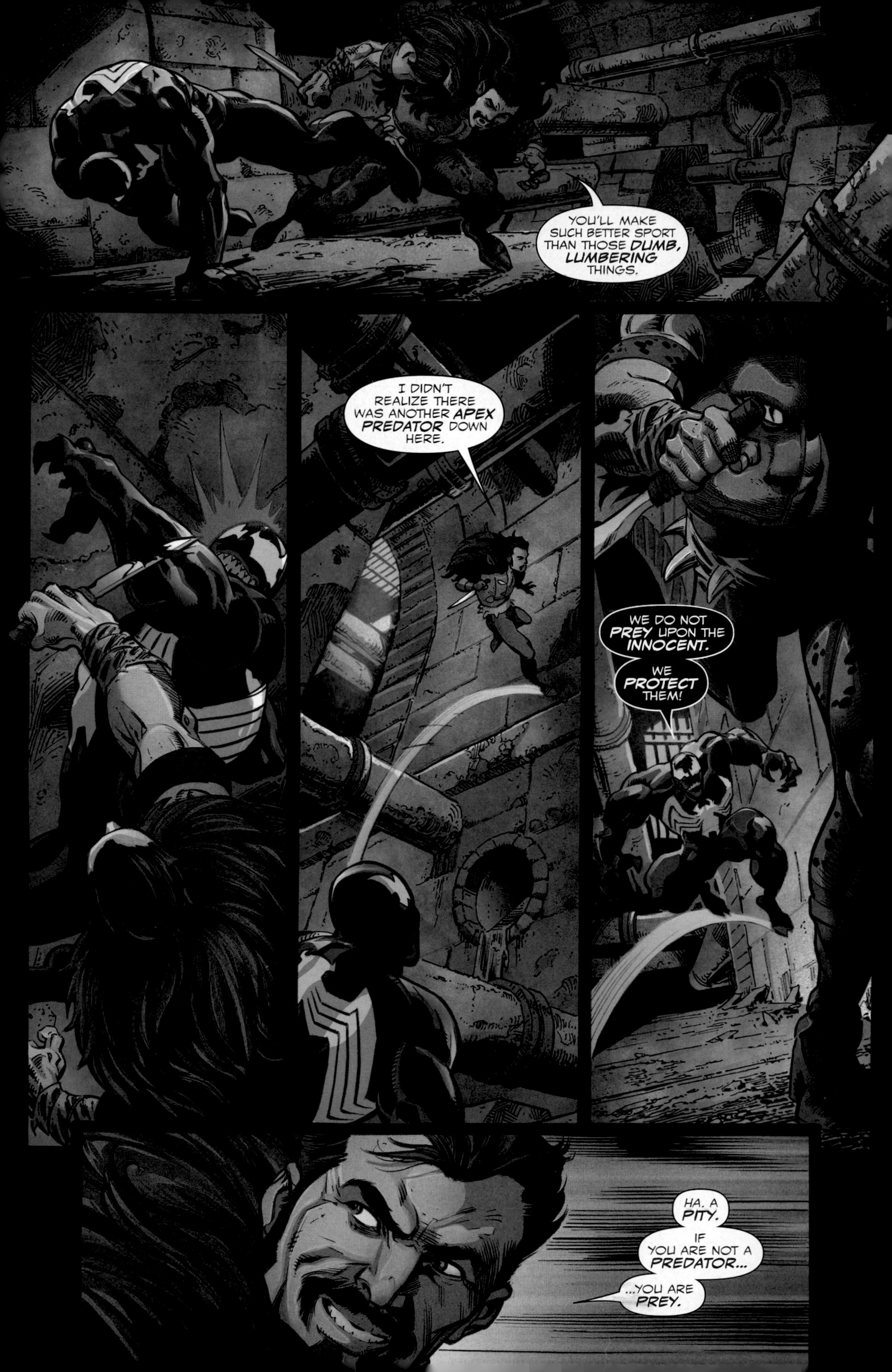
YOU'LL MAKE SUCH BETTER SPORT THAN THOSE DUMB, LUMBERING THINGS.
I DIDN'T REALIZE THERE WAS ANOTHER APEX PREDATOR DOWN HERE.
WE DO NOT PREY UPON THE INNOCENT.
WE PROTECT THEM!
HA. A PITY.
IF YOU ARE NOT A PREDATOR...
...YOU ARE PREY.

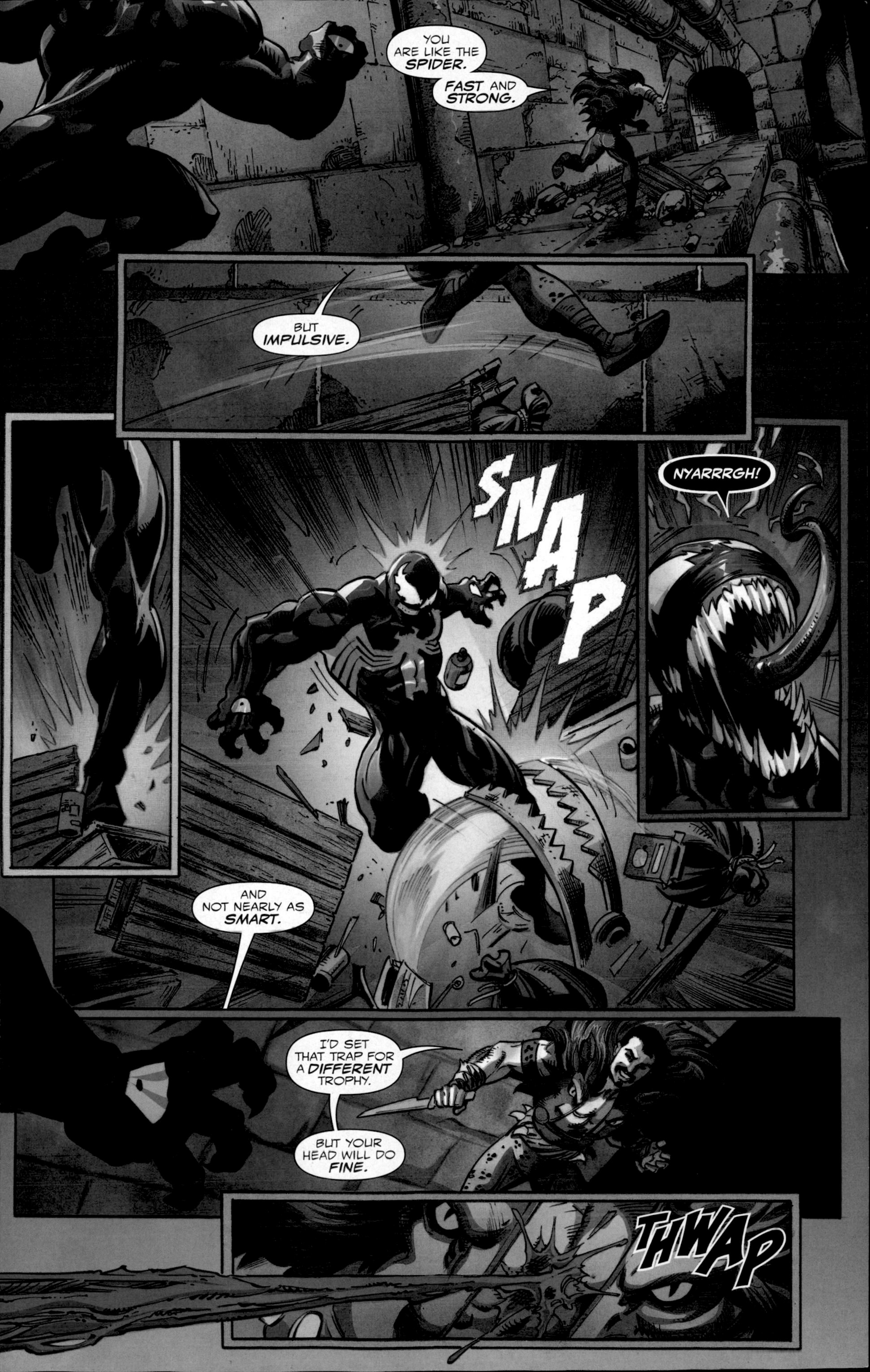
YOU ARE LIKE THE SPIDER.
FAST AND STRONG.
BUT IMPULSIVE.
SNAP
NYARRRGH!
AND NOT NEARLY AS SMART.
I'D SET THAT TRAP FOR A DIFFERENT TROPHY.
BUT YOUR HEAD WILL DO FINE.
THWAP

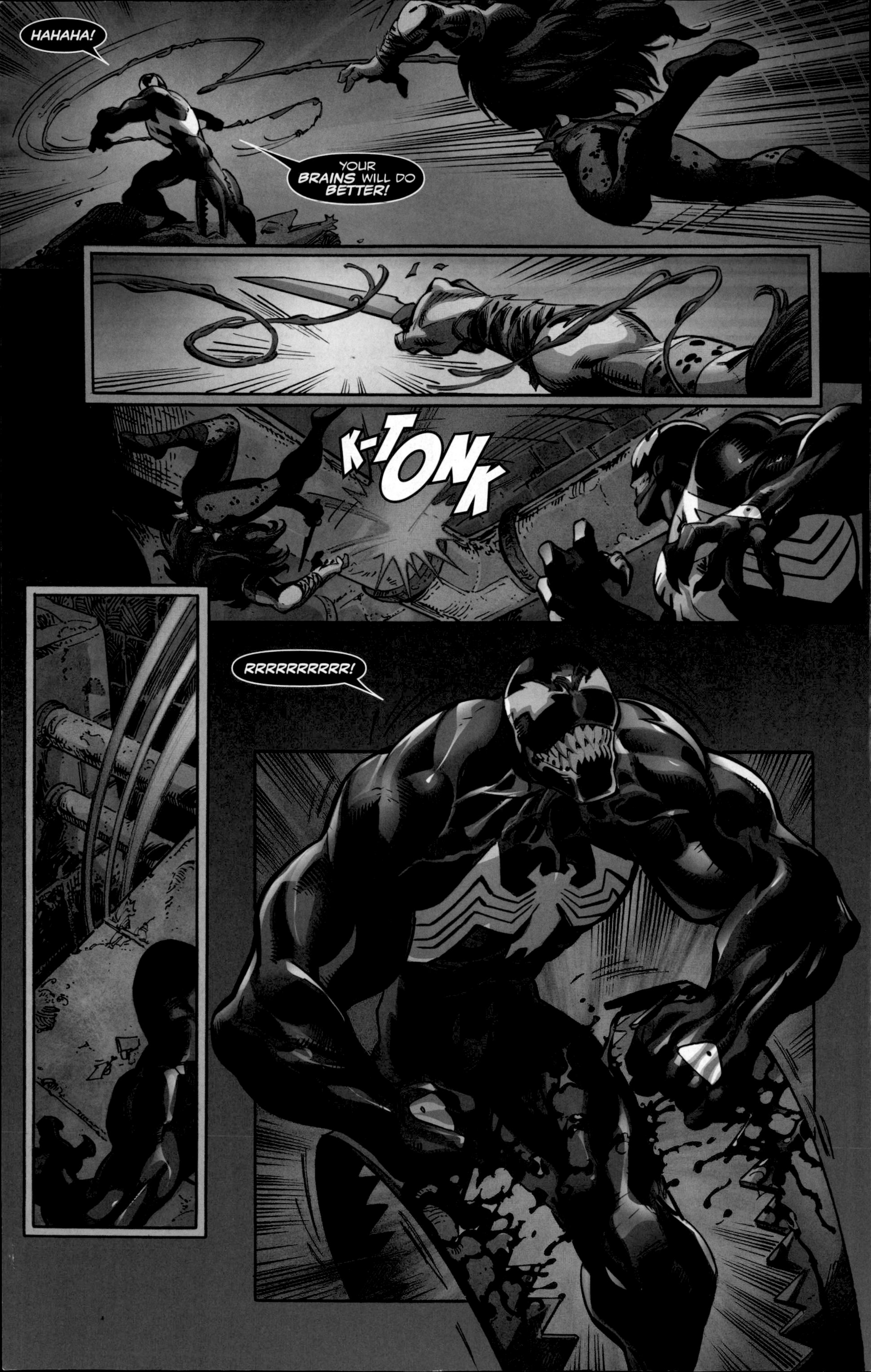
HAHAHA!
YOUR BRAINS WILL DO BETTER!
K-TONK
RRRRRRRRRR!

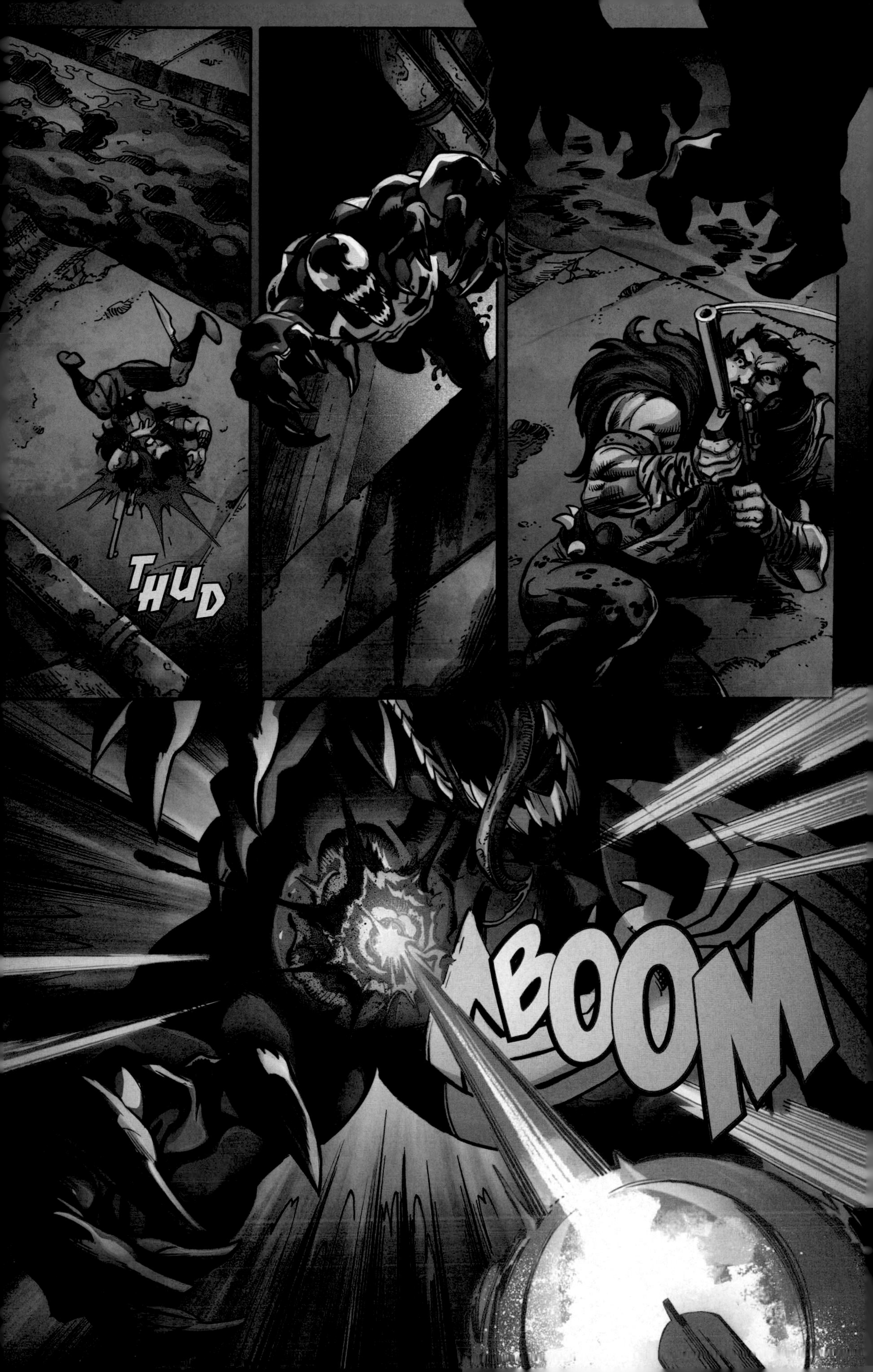
THUD
BOOM

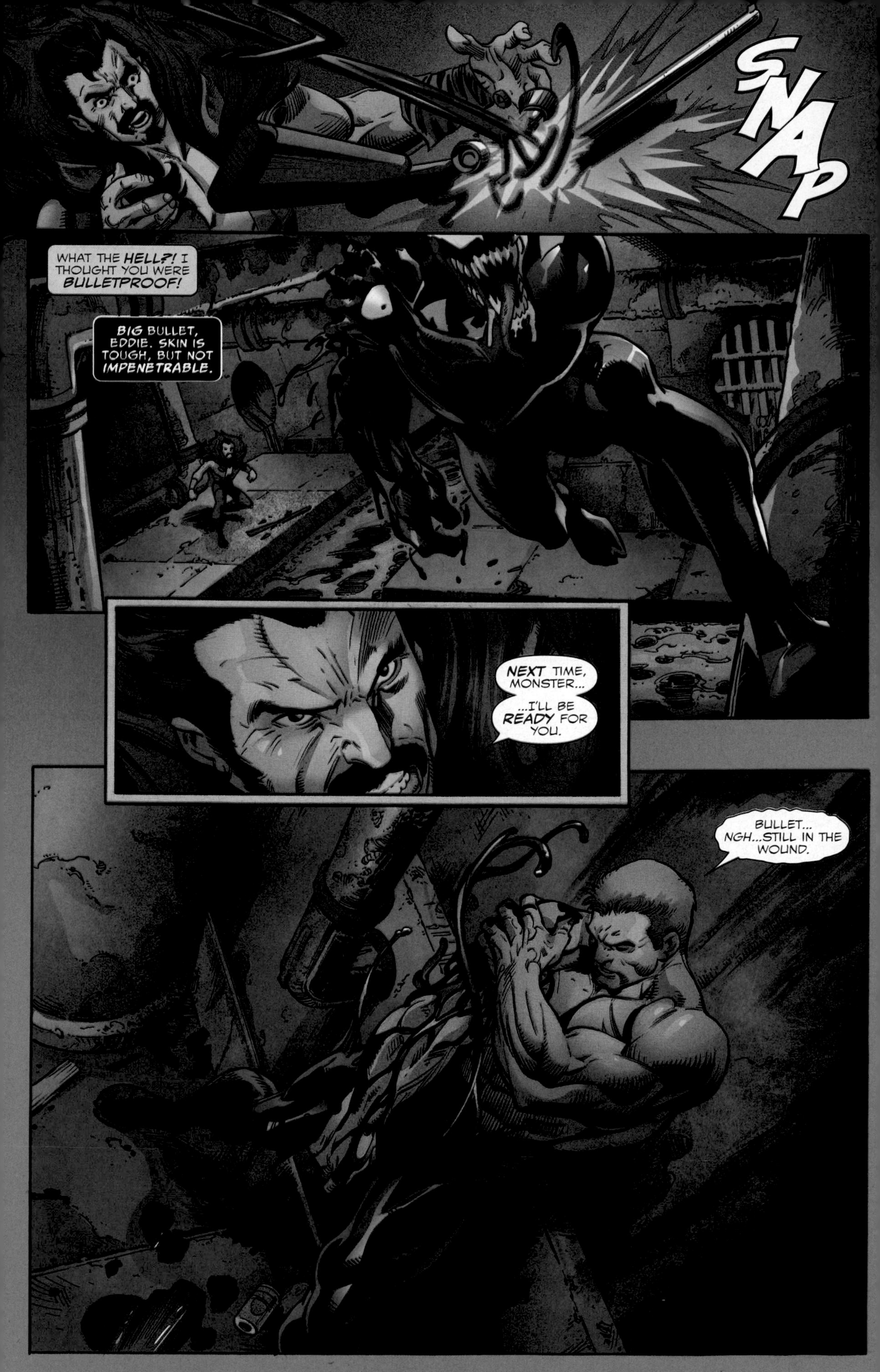
SNAP
WHAT THE HELL?! I THOUGHT YOU WERE BULLETPROOF!
BIG BULLET, EDDIE. SKIN IS TOUGH, BUT NOT IMPENETRABLE.
NEXT TIME, MONSTER...
...I'LL BE READY FOR YOU.
BULLET... NGH...STILL IN THE WOUND.

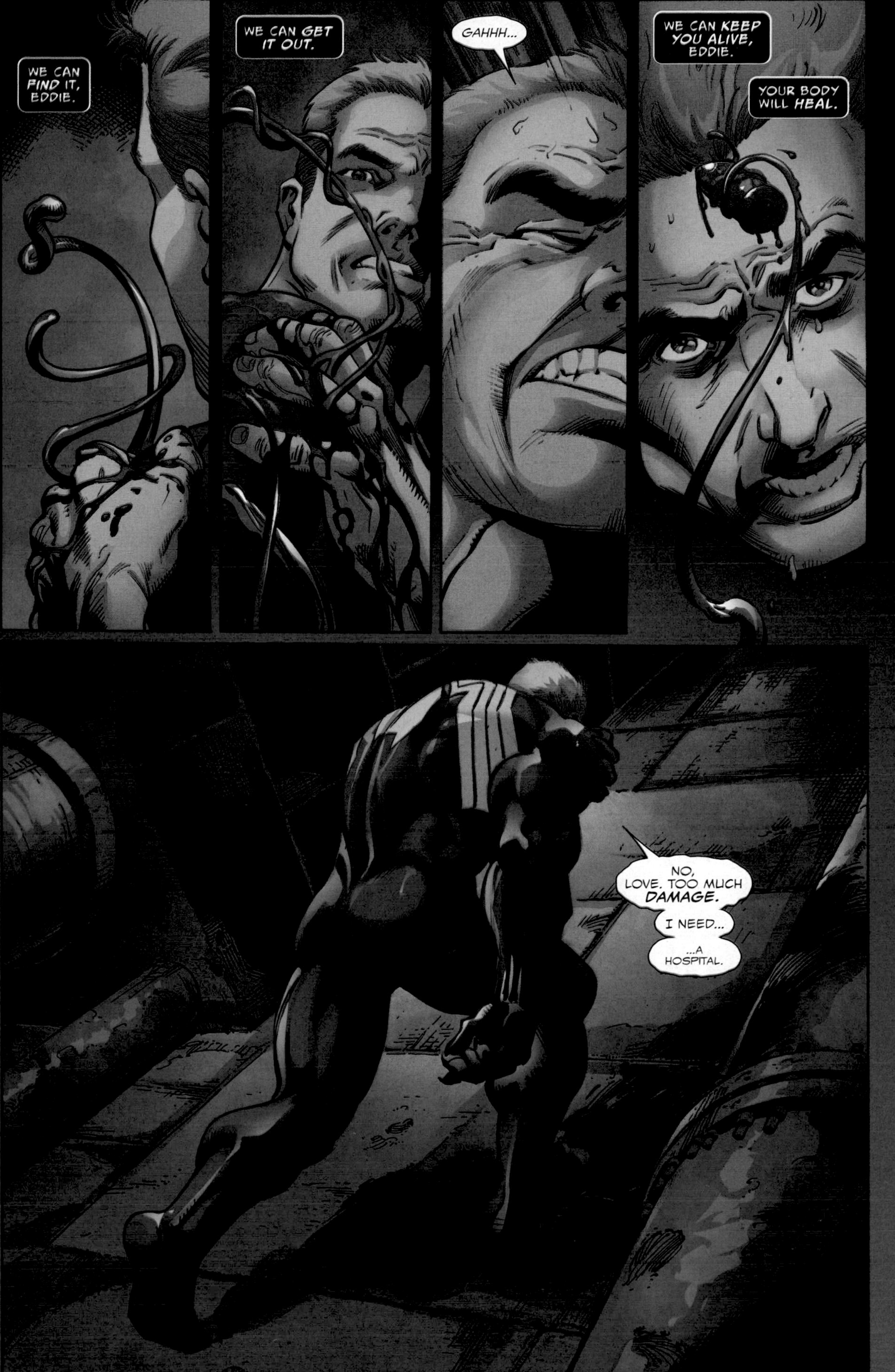
WE CAN FIND IT, EDDIE.
WE CAN GET IT OUT.
GAHHH...
WE CAN KEEP YOU ALIVE, EDDIE.
YOUR BODY WILL HEAL.
NO, LOVE. TOO MUCH DAMAGE.
I NEED...
...A HOSPITAL.

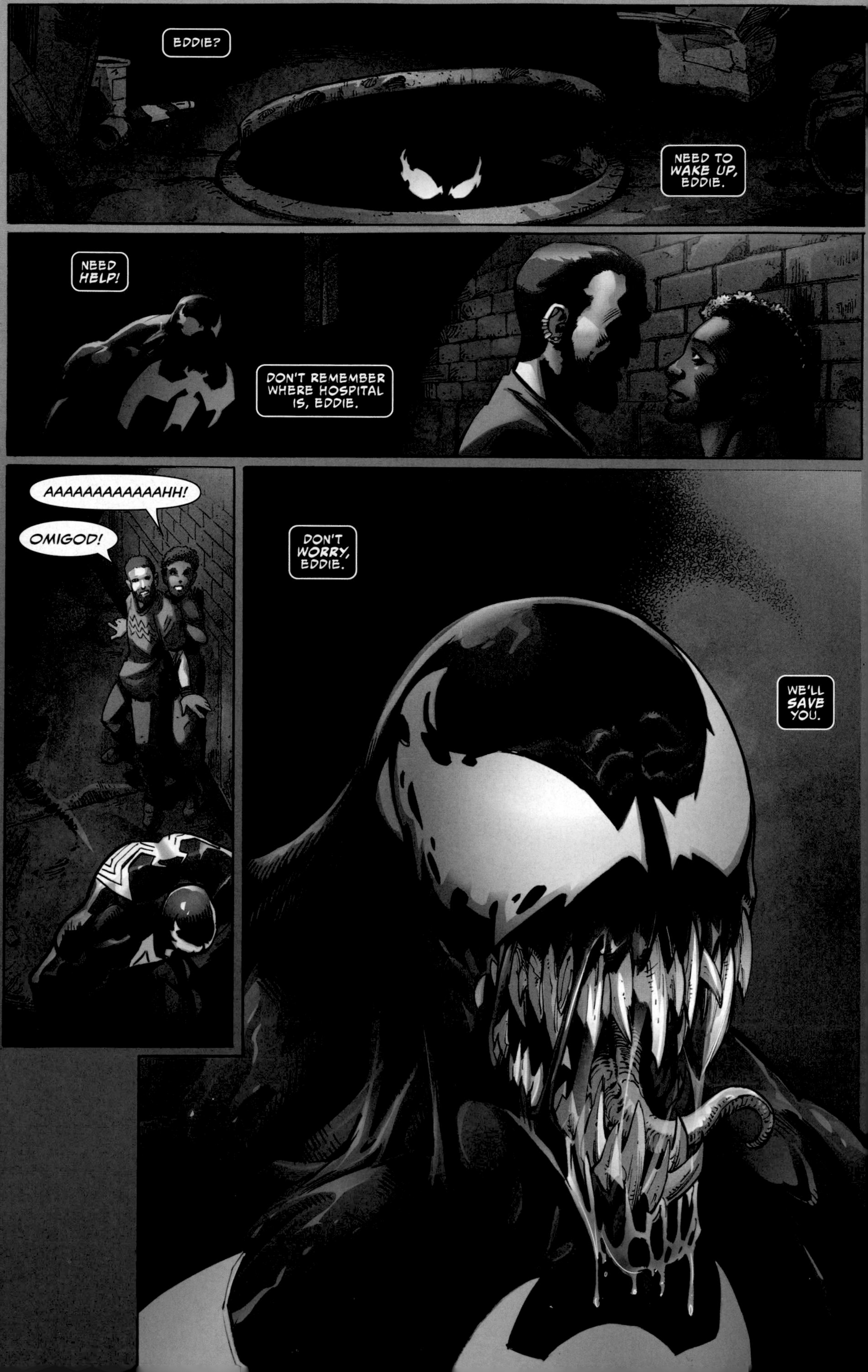
EDDIE?
NEED TO WAKE UP, EDDIE.
NEED HELP!
DON'T REMEMBER WHERE HOSPITAL IS, EDDIE.
AAAAAAAAAAAAAHH!
OMIGOD!
DON'T WORRY, EDDIE.
WE'LL SAVE YOU.

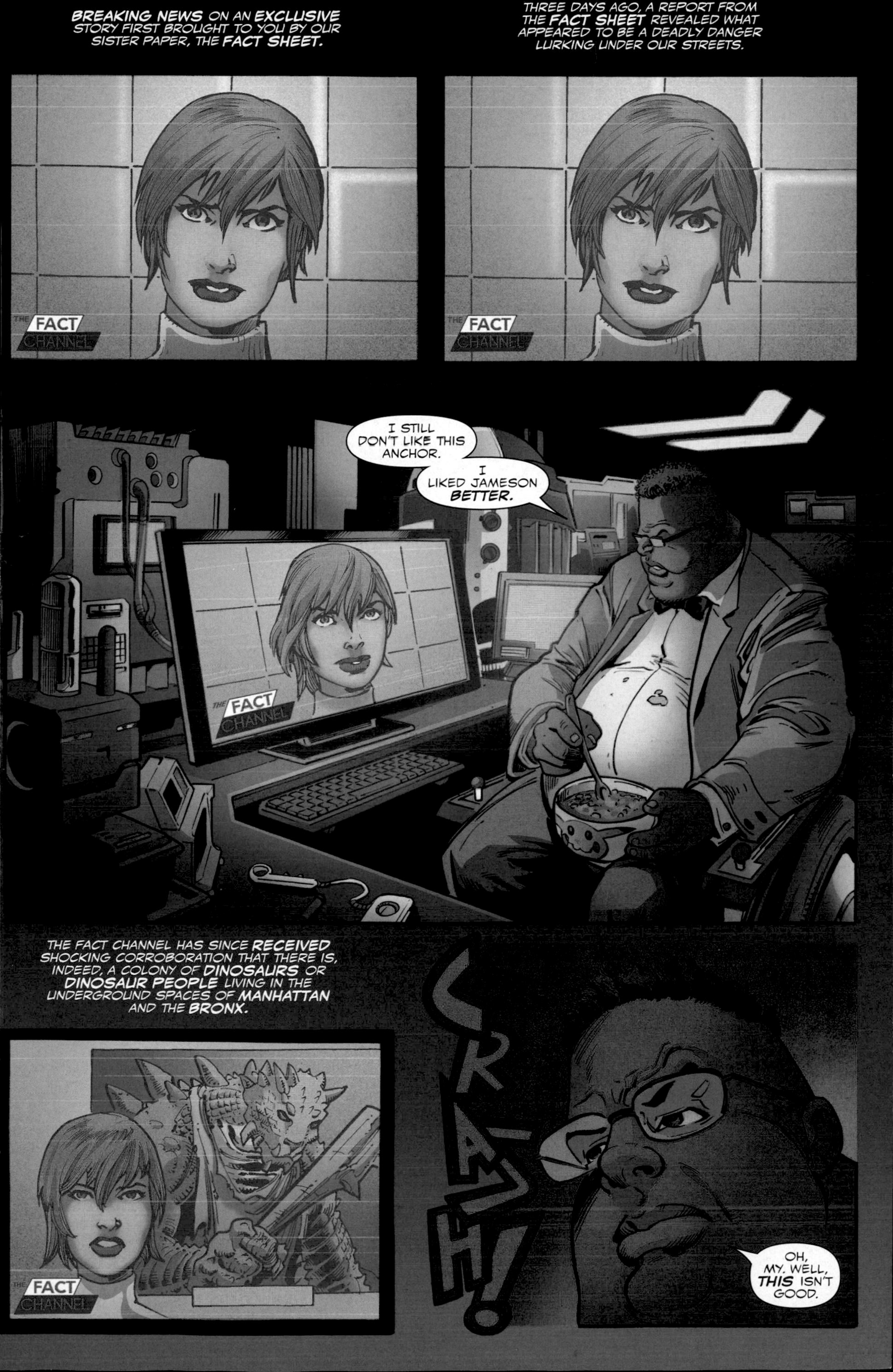
BREAKING NEWS ON AN EXCLUSIVE STORY FIRST BROUGHT TO YOU BY OUR SISTER PAPER, THE FACT SHEET.
THE FACT CHANNEL
THREE DAYS AGO, A REPORT FROM THE FACT SHEET REVEALED WHAT APPEARED TO BE A DEADLY DANGER LURKING UNDER OUR STREETS.
THE FACT CHANNEL
I STILL DON'T LIKE THIS ANCHOR.
I LIKED JAMESON BETTER.
THE FACT CHANNEL
THE FACT CHANNEL HAS SINCE RECEIVED SHOCKING CORROBORATION THAT THERE IS, INDEED, A COLONY OF DINOSAURS OR DINOSAUR PEOPLE LIVING IN THE UNDERGROUND SPACES OF MANHATTAN AND THE BRONX.
THE FACT CHANNEL
CRAASH!
OH, MY. WELL, THIS ISN'T GOOD.

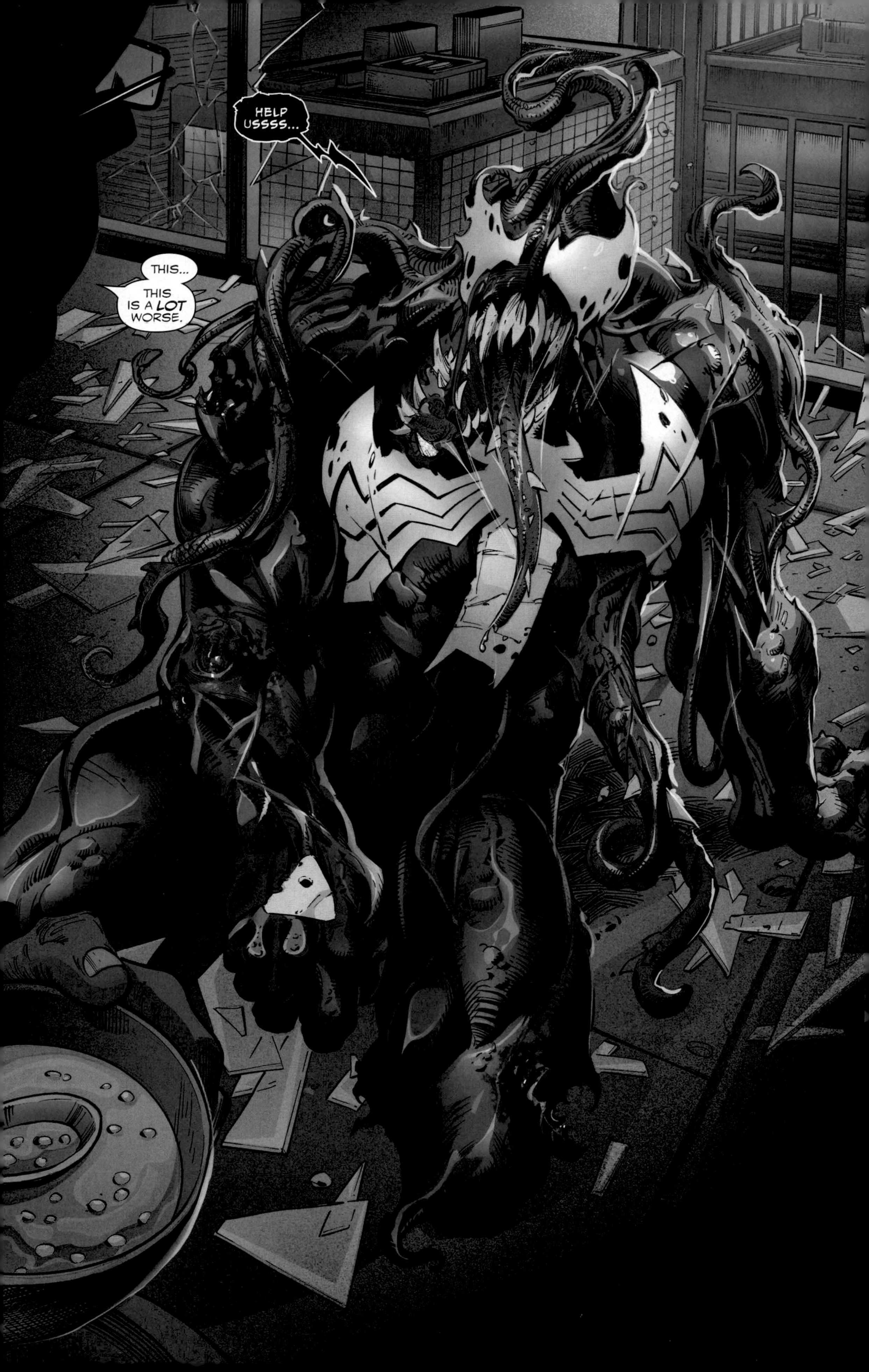
HELP USSSS...
THIS...
THIS IS A LOT WORSE.

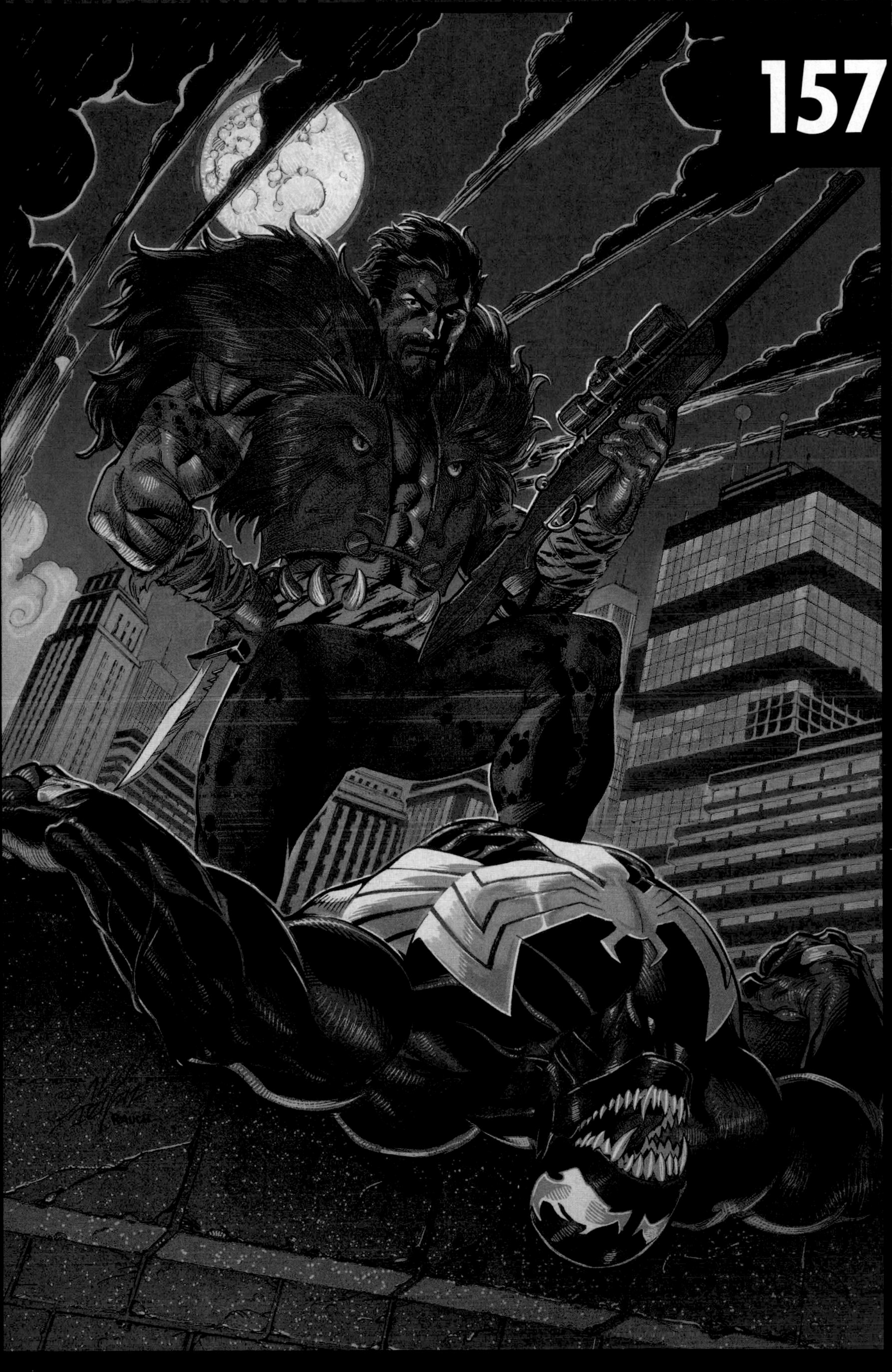
157

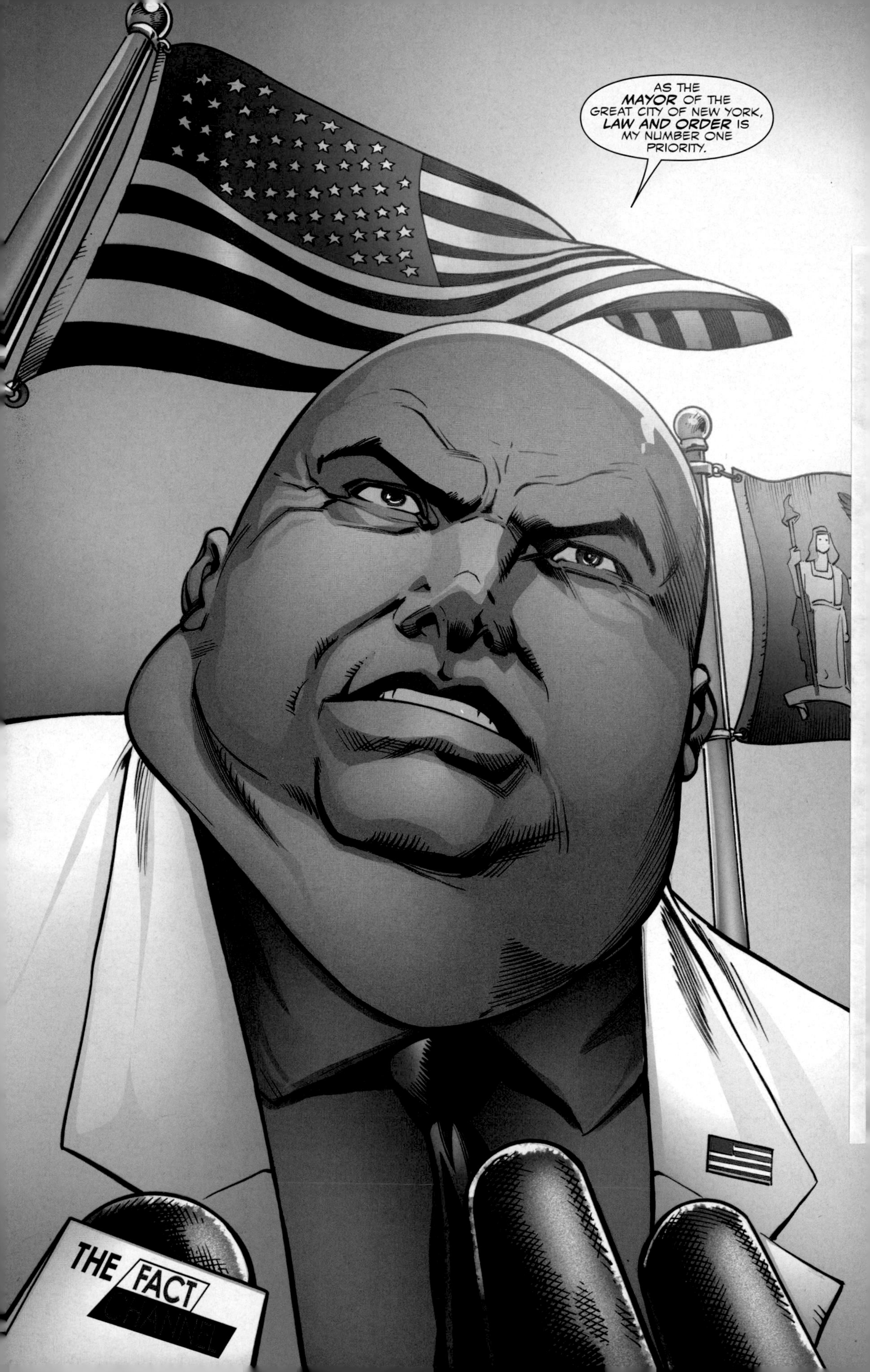
AS THE **MAYOR** OF THE GREAT CITY OF NEW YORK, **LAW AND ORDER** IS MY NUMBER ONE PRIORITY.
THE FACT

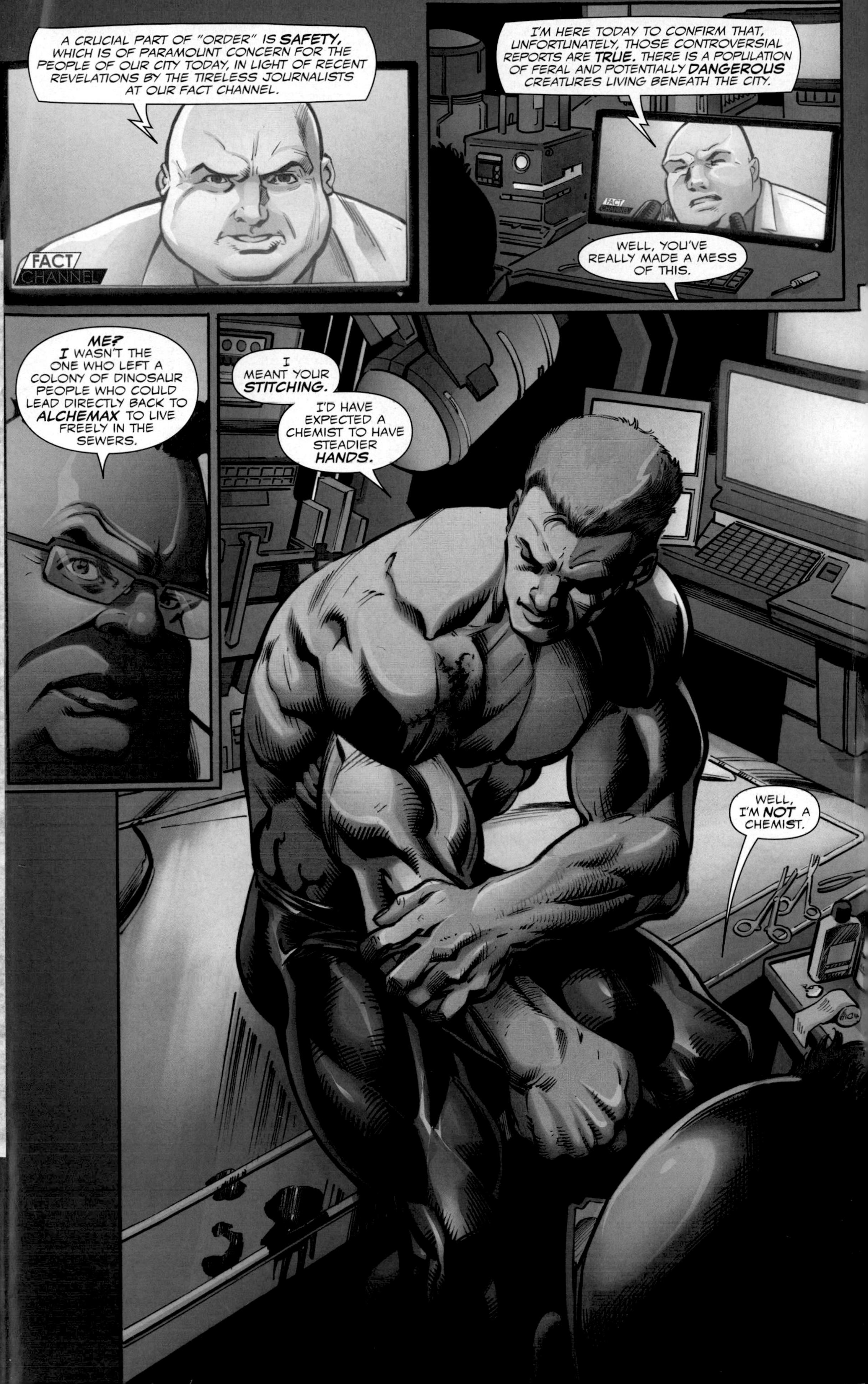
A CRUCIAL PART OF "ORDER" IS SAFETY, WHICH IS OF PARAMOUNT CONCERN FOR THE PEOPLE OF OUR CITY TODAY, IN LIGHT OF RECENT REVELATIONS BY THE TIRELESS JOURNALISTS AT OUR FACT CHANNEL.
FACT CHANNEL
I'M HERE TODAY TO CONFIRM THAT, UNFORTUNATELY, THOSE CONTROVERSIAL REPORTS ARE TRUE. THERE IS A POPULATION OF FERAL AND POTENTIALLY DANGEROUS CREATURES LIVING BENEATH THE CITY.
FACT CHANNEL
WELL, YOU'VE REALLY MADE A MESS OF THIS.
ME? I WASN'T THE ONE WHO LEFT A COLONY OF DINOSAUR PEOPLE WHO COULD LEAD DIRECTLY BACK TO ALCHEMAX TO LIVE FREELY IN THE SEWERS.
I MEANT YOUR STITCHING.
I'D HAVE EXPECTED A CHEMIST TO HAVE STEADIER HANDS.
WELL, I'M NOT A CHEMIST.

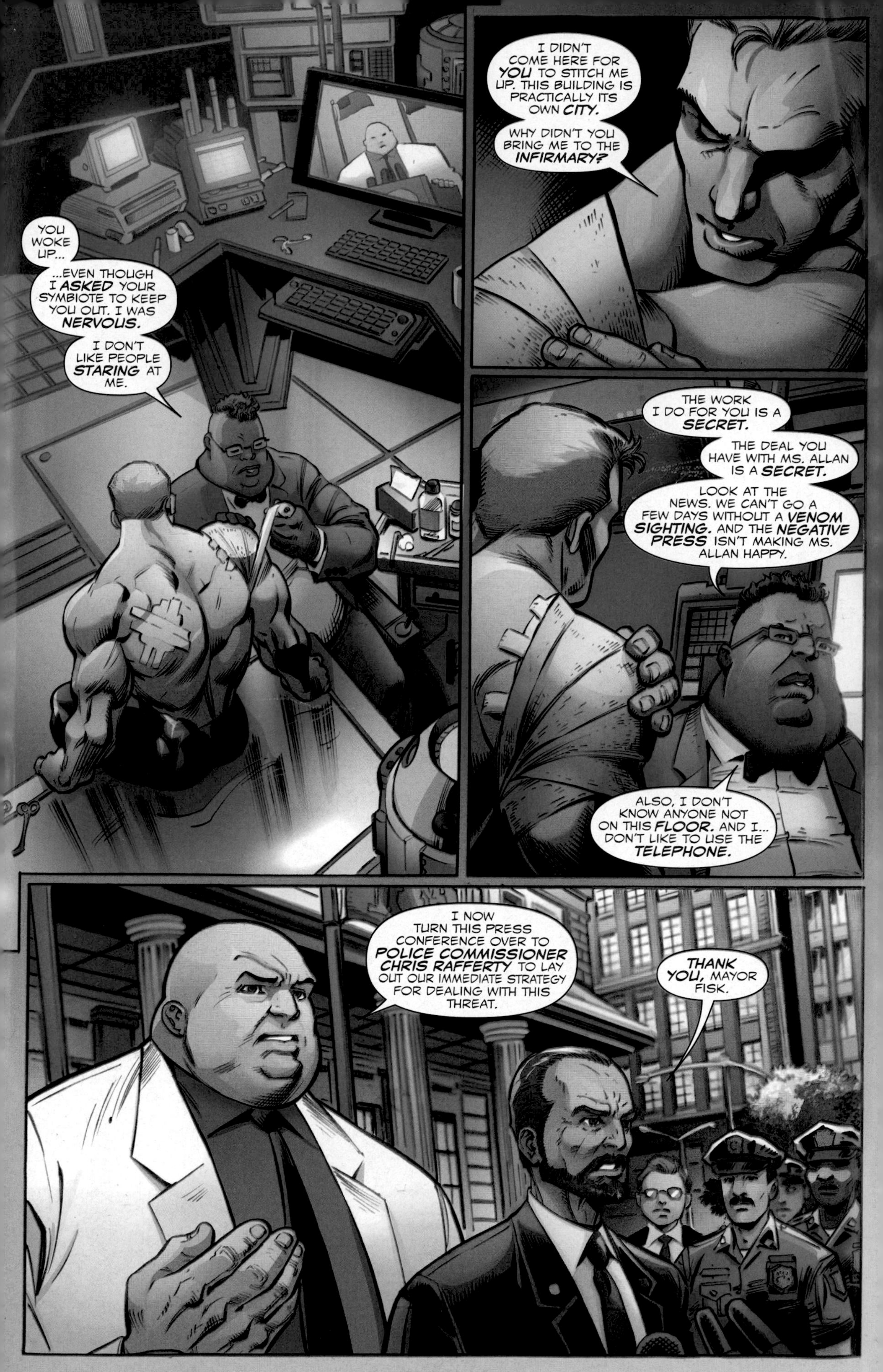
YOU WOKE UP...
...EVEN THOUGH I ASKED YOUR SYMBIOTE TO KEEP YOU OUT. I WAS NERVOUS.
I DON'T LIKE PEOPLE STARING AT ME.
I DIDN'T COME HERE FOR YOU TO STITCH ME UP. THIS BUILDING IS PRACTICALLY ITS OWN CITY.
WHY DIDN'T YOU BRING ME TO THE INFIRMARY?
THE WORK I DO FOR YOU IS A SECRET.
THE DEAL YOU HAVE WITH MS. ALLAN IS A SECRET.
LOOK AT THE NEWS. WE CAN'T GO A FEW DAYS WITHOUT A VENOM SIGHTING. AND THE NEGATIVE PRESS ISN'T MAKING MS. ALLAN HAPPY.
ALSO, I DON'T KNOW ANYONE NOT ON THIS FLOOR. AND I... DON'T LIKE TO USE THE TELEPHONE.
I NOW TURN THIS PRESS CONFERENCE OVER TO POLICE COMMISSIONER CHRIS RAFFERTY TO LAY OUT OUR IMMEDIATE STRATEGY FOR DEALING WITH THIS THREAT.
THANK YOU, MAYOR FISK.

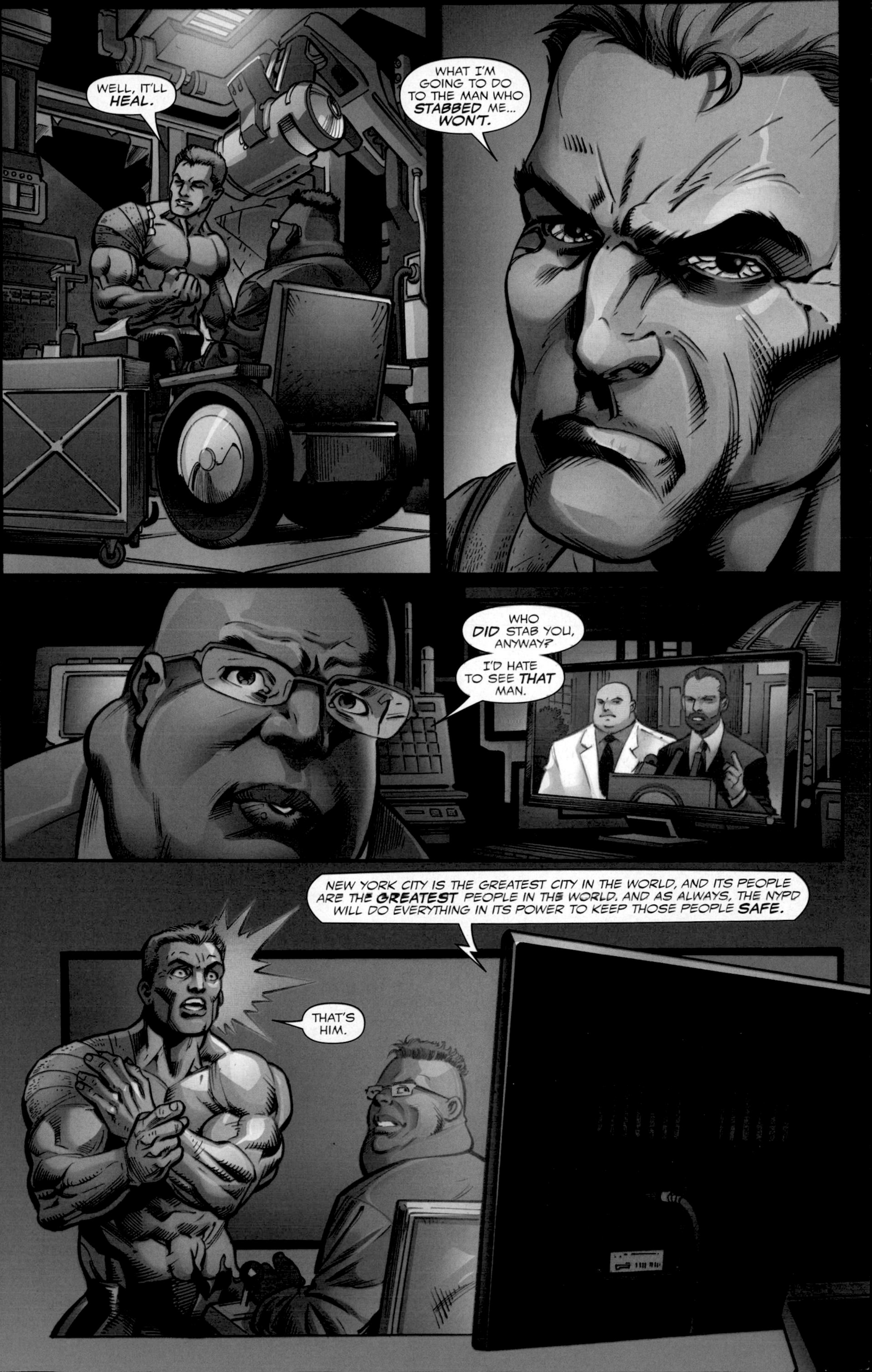
WELL, IT'LL HEAL.
WHAT I'M GOING TO DO TO THE MAN WHO STABBED ME... WON'T.
WHO DID STAB YOU, ANYWAY?
I'D HATE TO SEE THAT MAN.
NEW YORK CITY IS THE GREATEST CITY IN THE WORLD, AND ITS PEOPLE ARE THE GREATEST PEOPLE IN THE WORLD. AND AS ALWAYS, THE NYPD WILL DO EVERYTHING IN ITS POWER TO KEEP THOSE PEOPLE SAFE.
THAT'S HIM.

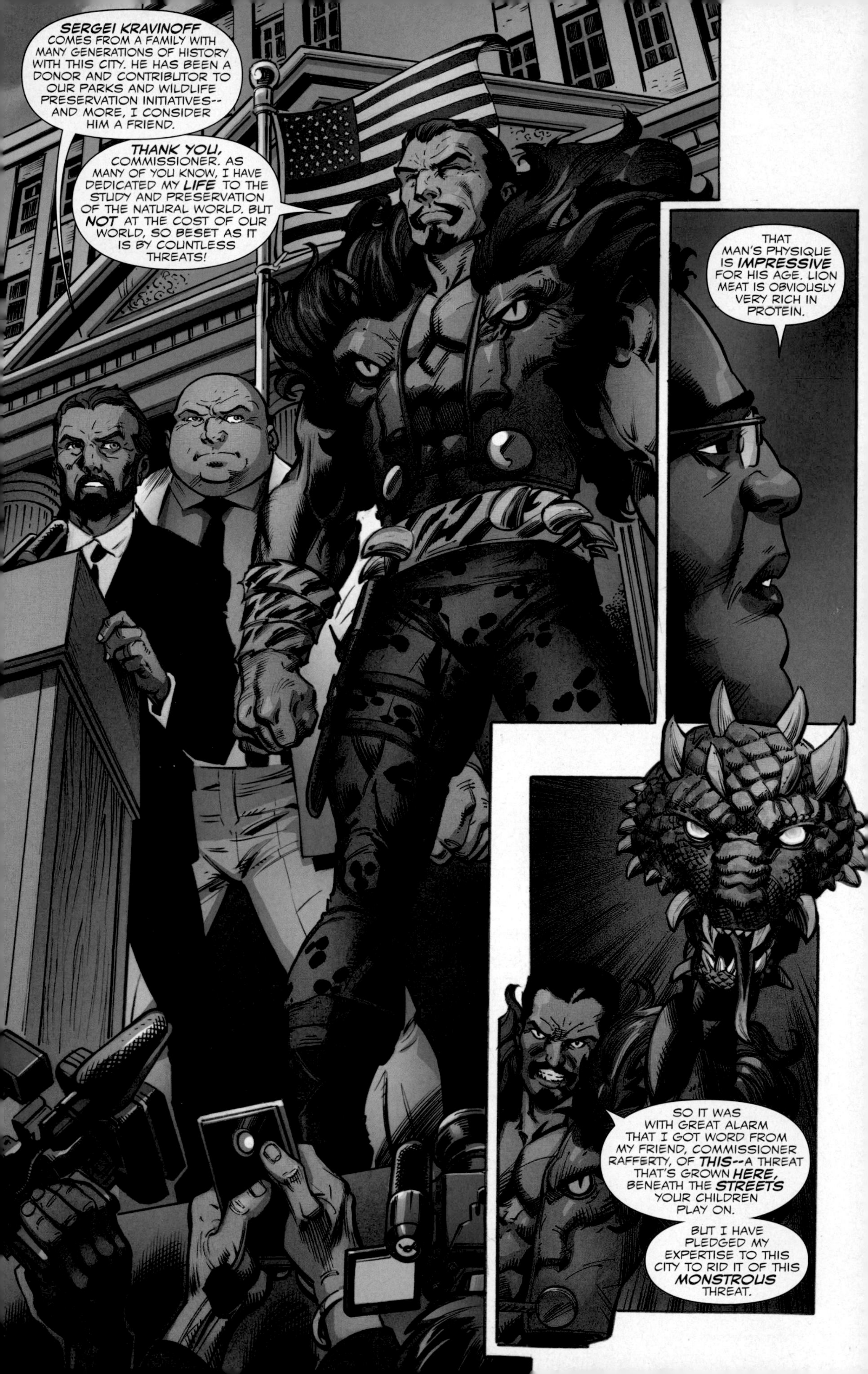
SERGEI KRAVINOFF COMES FROM A FAMILY WITH MANY GENERATIONS OF HISTORY WITH THIS CITY. HE HAS BEEN A DONOR AND CONTRIBUTOR TO OUR PARKS AND WILDLIFE PRESERVATION INITIATIVES-- AND MORE, I CONSIDER HIM A FRIEND.
THANK YOU, COMMISSIONER. AS MANY OF YOU KNOW, I HAVE DEDICATED MY LIFE TO THE STUDY AND PRESERVATION OF THE NATURAL WORLD. BUT NOT AT THE COST OF OUR WORLD, SO BESET AS IT IS BY COUNTLESS THREATS!
THAT MAN'S PHYSIQUE IS IMPRESSIVE FOR HIS AGE. LION MEAT IS OBVIOUSLY VERY RICH IN PROTEIN.
SO IT WAS WITH GREAT ALARM THAT I GOT WORD FROM MY FRIEND, COMMISSIONER RAFFERTY, OF THIS--A THREAT THAT'S GROWN HERE, BENEATH THE STREETS YOUR CHILDREN PLAY ON.
BUT I HAVE PLEDGED MY EXPERTISE TO THIS CITY TO RID IT OF THIS MONSTROUS THREAT.

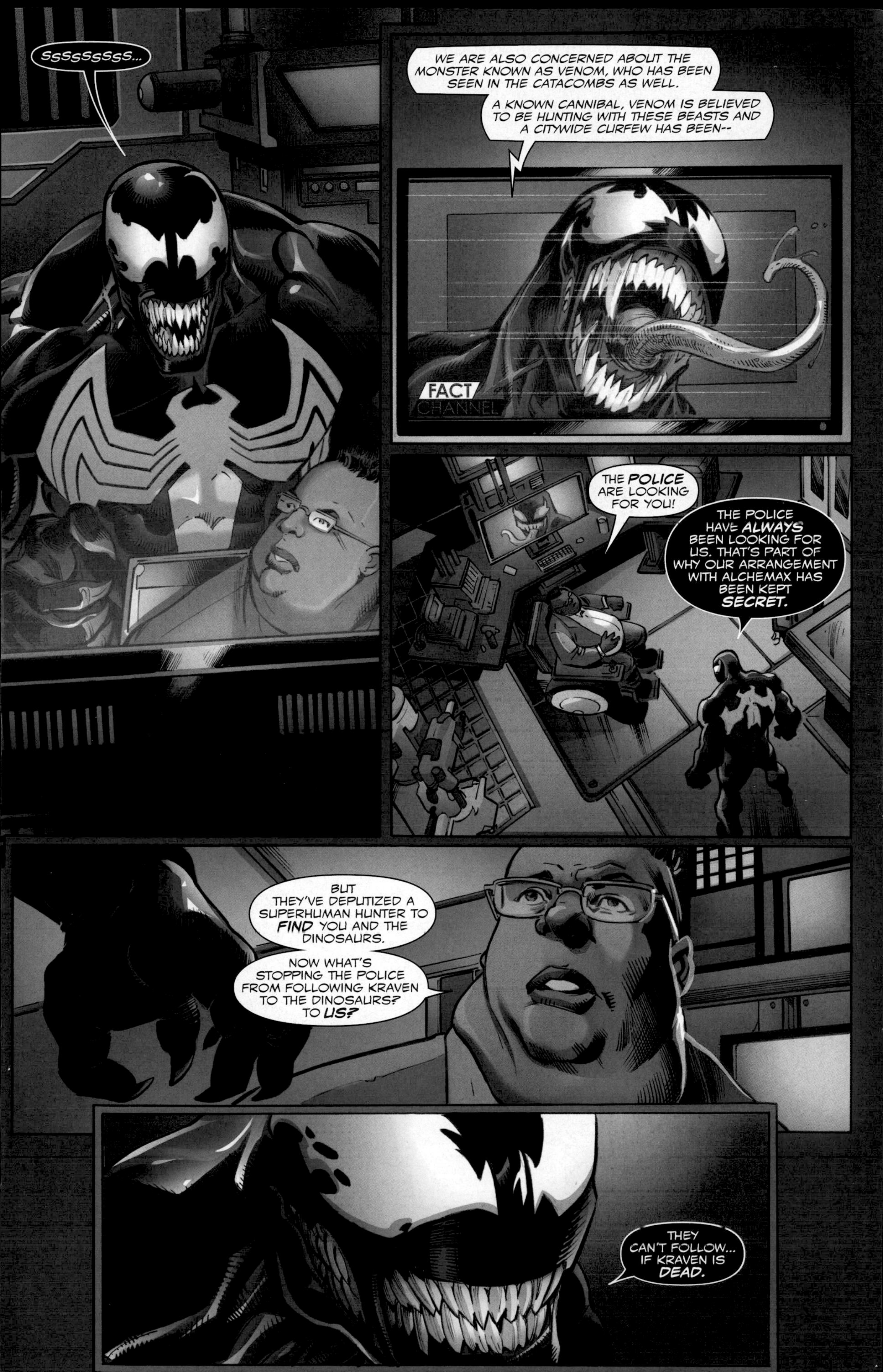
SSSSSSSSS...
WE ARE ALSO CONCERNED ABOUT THE MONSTER KNOWN AS VENOM, WHO HAS BEEN SEEN IN THE CATACOMBS AS WELL.
A KNOWN CANNIBAL, VENOM IS BELIEVED TO BE HUNTING WITH THESE BEASTS AND A CITYWIDE CURFEW HAS BEEN--
FACT CHANNEL
THE POLICE ARE LOOKING FOR YOU!
THE POLICE HAVE ALWAYS BEEN LOOKING FOR US. THAT'S PART OF WHY OUR ARRANGEMENT WITH ALCHEMAX HAS BEEN KEPT SECRET.
BUT THEY'VE DEPUTIZED A SUPERHUMAN HUNTER TO FIND YOU AND THE DINOSAURS.
NOW WHAT'S STOPPING THE POLICE FROM FOLLOWING KRAVEN TO THE DINOSAURS? TO US?
THEY CAN'T FOLLOW... IF KRAVEN IS DEAD.

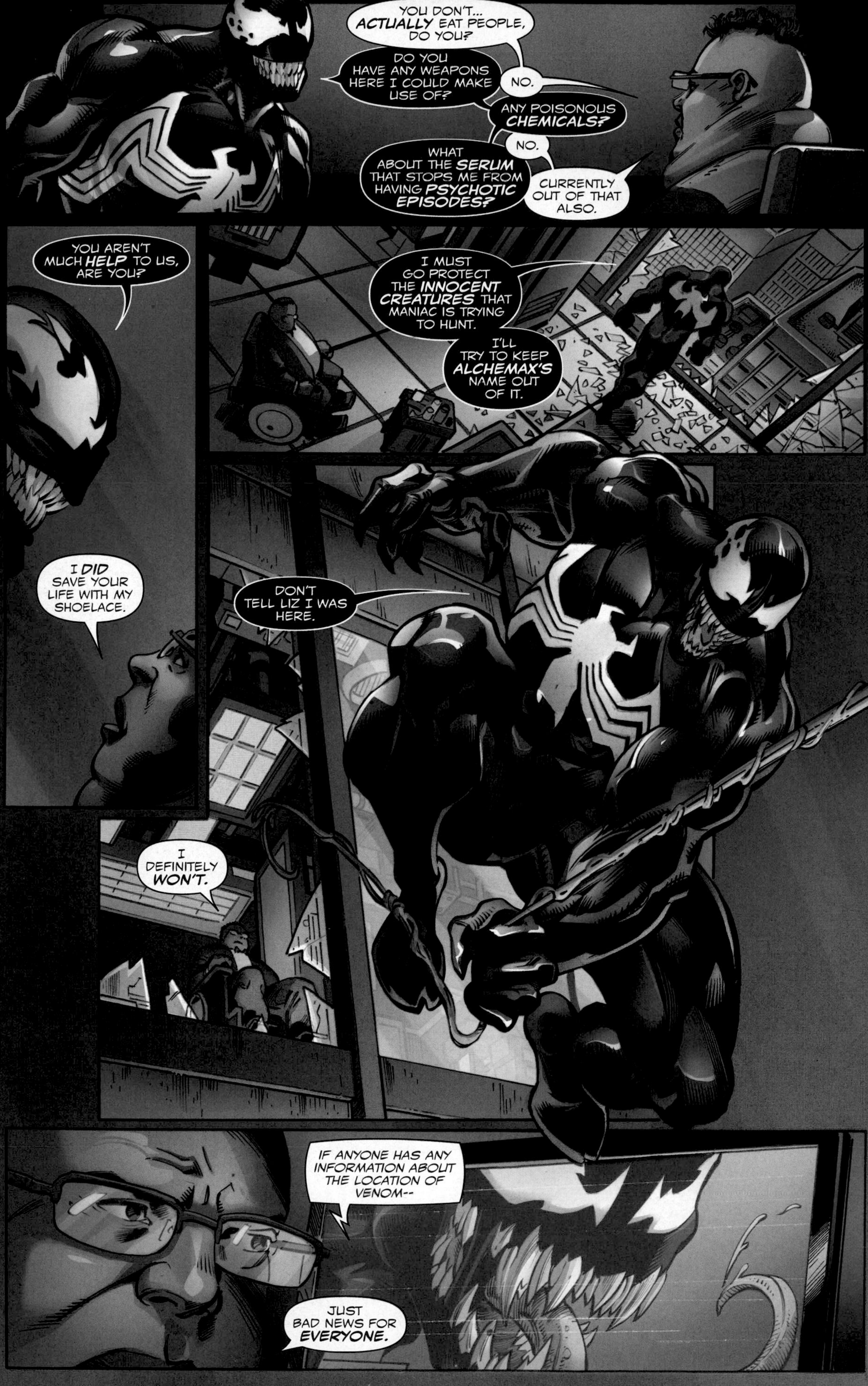
YOU DON'T... ACTUALLY EAT PEOPLE, DO YOU?
NO.
DO YOU HAVE ANY WEAPONS HERE I COULD MAKE USE OF?
NO.
ANY POISONOUS CHEMICALS?
WHAT ABOUT THE SERUM THAT STOPS ME FROM HAVING PSYCHOTIC EPISODES?
CURRENTLY OUT OF THAT ALSO.
YOU AREN'T MUCH HELP TO US, ARE YOU?
I MUST GO PROTECT THE INNOCENT CREATURES THAT MANIAC IS TRYING TO HUNT.
I'LL TRY TO KEEP ALCHEMAX'S NAME OUT OF IT.
I DID SAVE YOUR LIFE WITH MY SHOELACE.
DON'T TELL LIZ I WAS HERE.
I DEFINITELY WON'T.
IF ANYONE HAS ANY INFORMATION ABOUT THE LOCATION OF VENOM--
JUST BAD NEWS FOR EVERYONE.

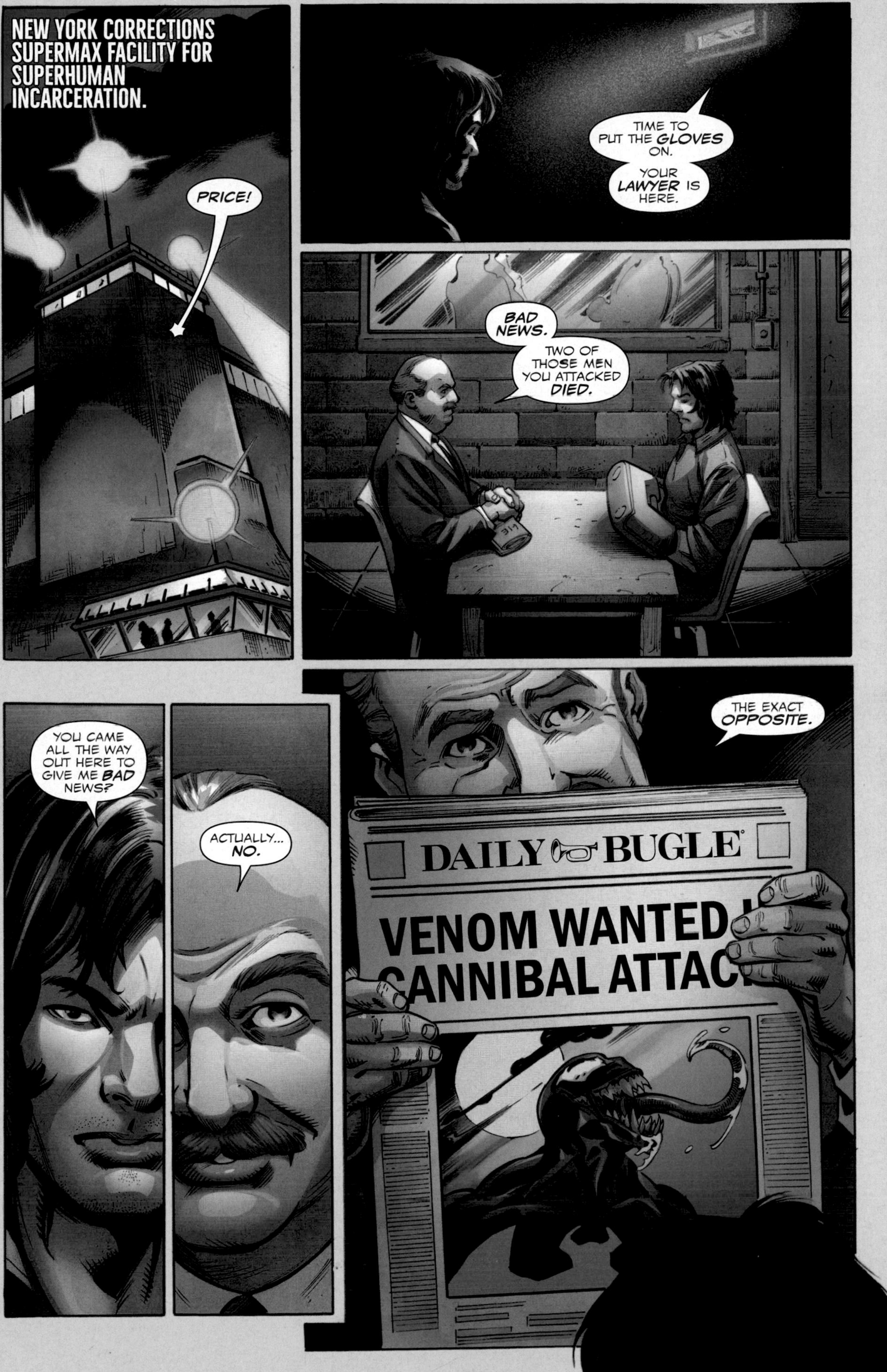
NEW YORK CORRECTIONS SUPERMAX FACILITY FOR SUPERHUMAN INCARCERATION.
PRICE!
TIME TO PUT THE GLOVES ON.
YOUR LAWYER IS HERE.
BAD NEWS.
TWO OF THOSE MEN YOU ATTACKED DIED.
YOU CAME ALL THE WAY OUT HERE TO GIVE ME BAD NEWS?
ACTUALLY... NO.
THE EXACT OPPOSITE.
DAILY BUGLE
VENOM WANTED
CANNIBAL ATTAC

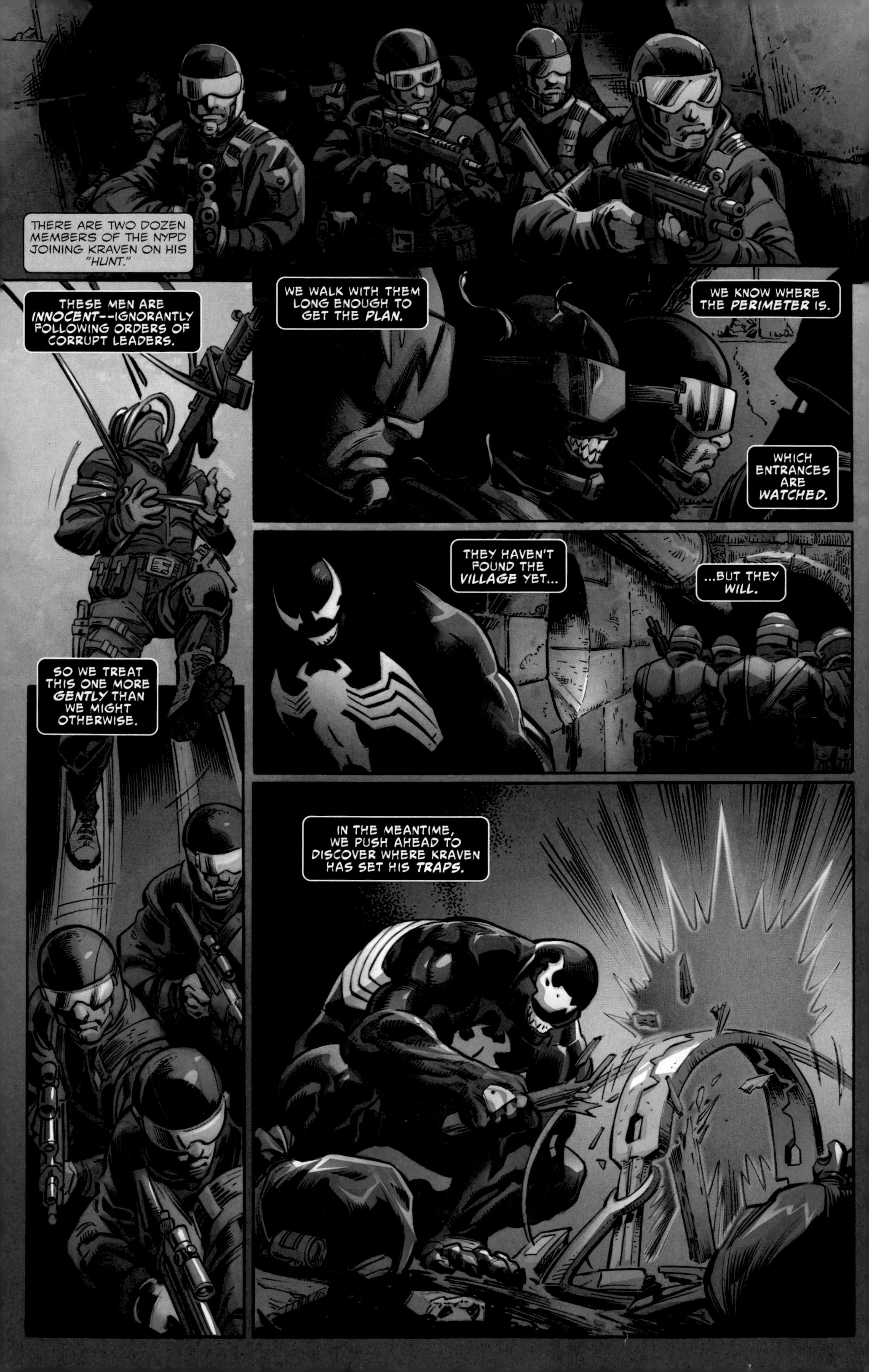
THERE ARE TWO DOZEN MEMBERS OF THE NYPD JOINING KRAVEN ON HIS "HUNT."
THESE MEN ARE INNOCENT--IGNORANTLY FOLLOWING ORDERS OF CORRUPT LEADERS.
SO WE TREAT THIS ONE MORE GENTLY THAN WE MIGHT OTHERWISE.
WE WALK WITH THEM LONG ENOUGH TO GET THE PLAN.
WE KNOW WHERE THE PERIMETER IS.
WHICH ENTRANCES ARE WATCHED.
THEY HAVEN'T FOUND THE VILLAGE YET...
...BUT THEY WILL.
IN THE MEANTIME, WE PUSH AHEAD TO DISCOVER WHERE KRAVEN HAS SET HIS TRAPS.

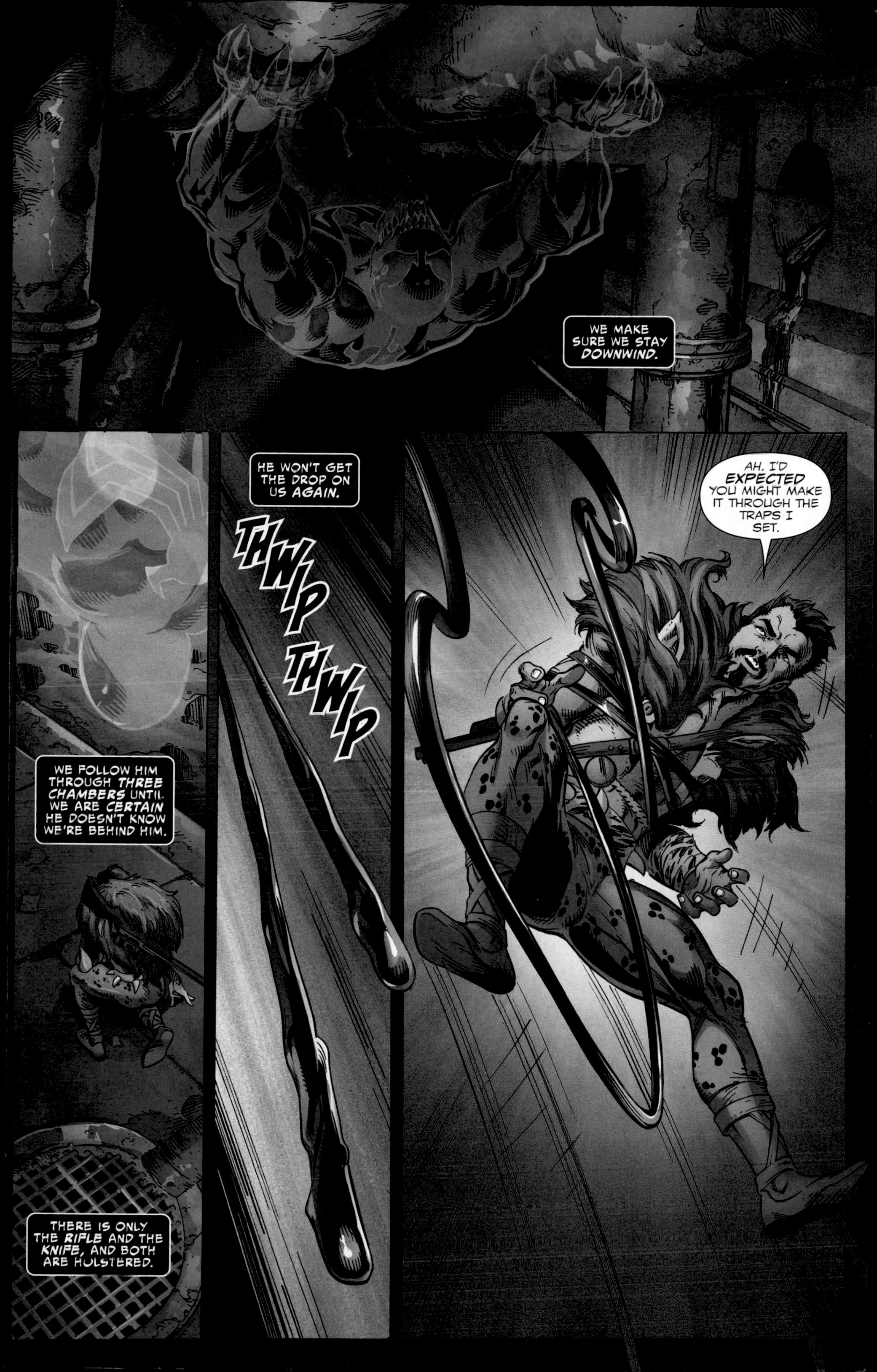
WE MAKE SURE WE STAY DOWNWIND.
HE WON'T GET THE DROP ON US AGAIN.
WE FOLLOW HIM THROUGH THREE CHAMBERS UNTIL WE ARE CERTAIN HE DOESN'T KNOW WE'RE BEHIND HIM.
THERE IS ONLY THE RIFLE AND THE KNIFE, AND BOTH ARE HOLSTERED.
THWIP THWIP
AH. I'D EXPECTED YOU MIGHT MAKE IT THROUGH THE TRAPS I SET.

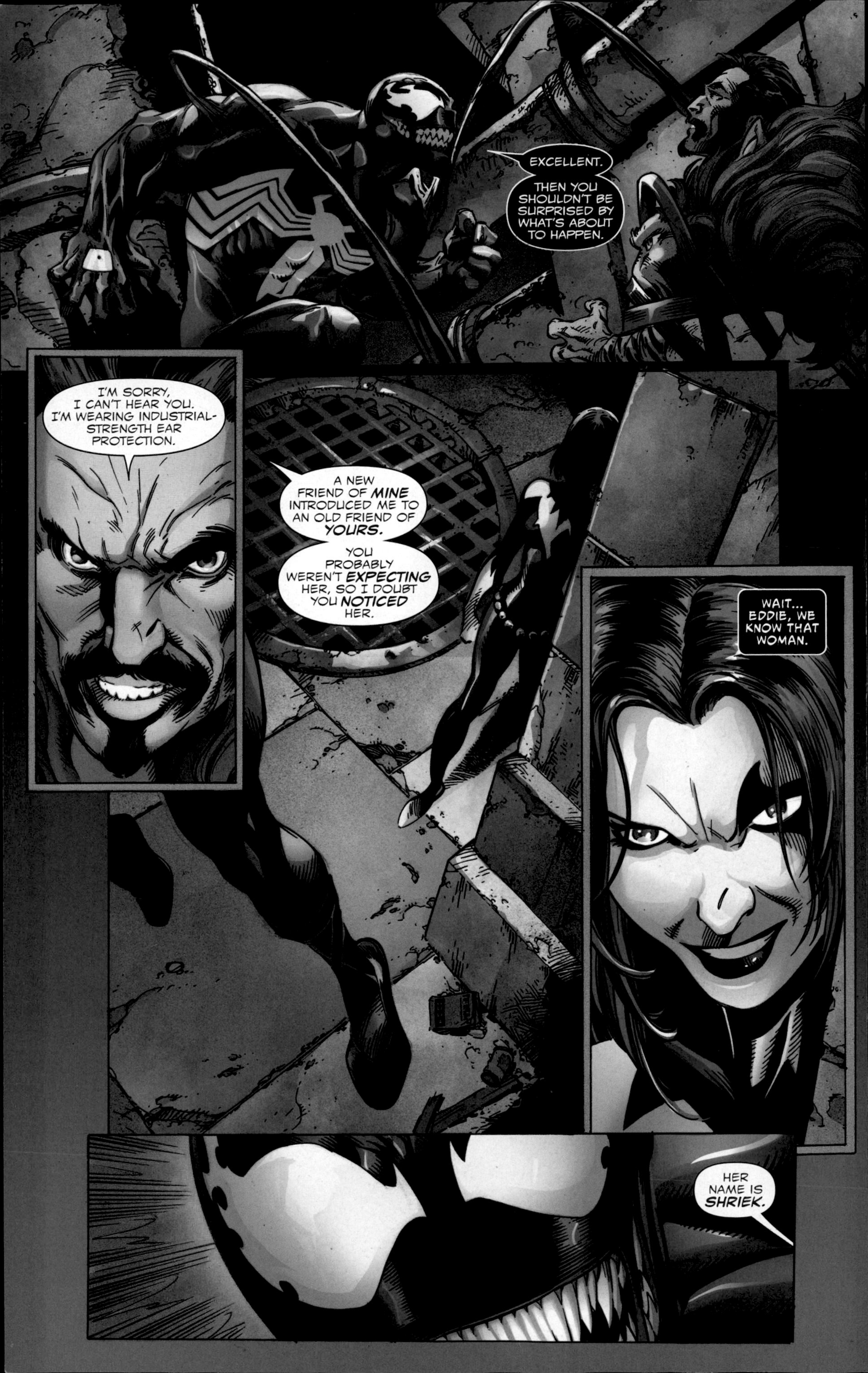
EXCELLENT.
THEN YOU SHOULDN'T BE SURPRISED BY WHAT'S ABOUT TO HAPPEN.
I'M SORRY, I CAN'T HEAR YOU. I'M WEARING INDUSTRIAL-STRENGTH EAR PROTECTION.
A NEW FRIEND OF MINE INTRODUCED ME TO AN OLD FRIEND OF YOURS.
YOU PROBABLY WEREN'T EXPECTING HER, SO I DOUBT YOU NOTICED HER.
WAIT... EDDIE, WE KNOW THAT WOMAN.
HER NAME IS SHRIEK.

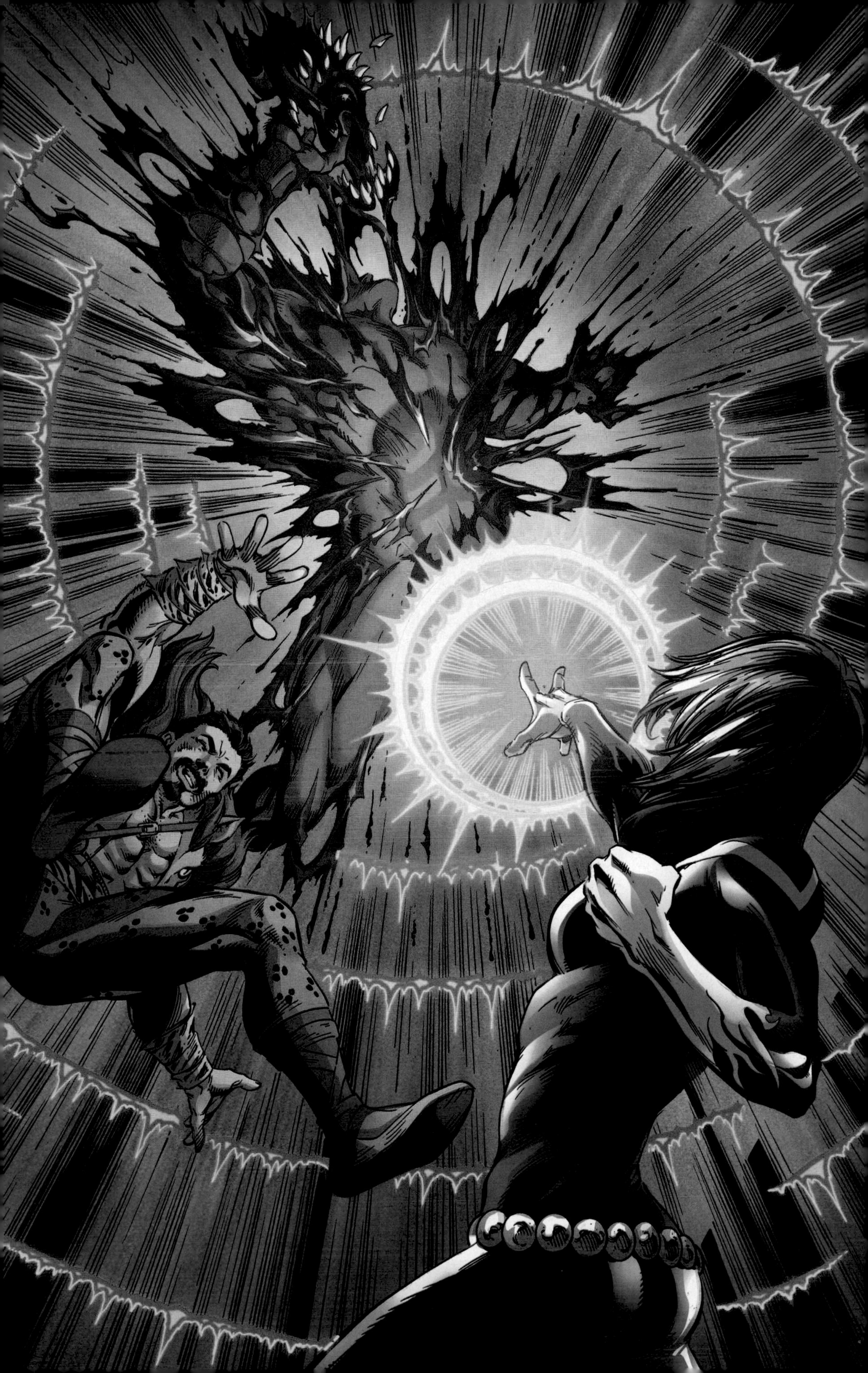

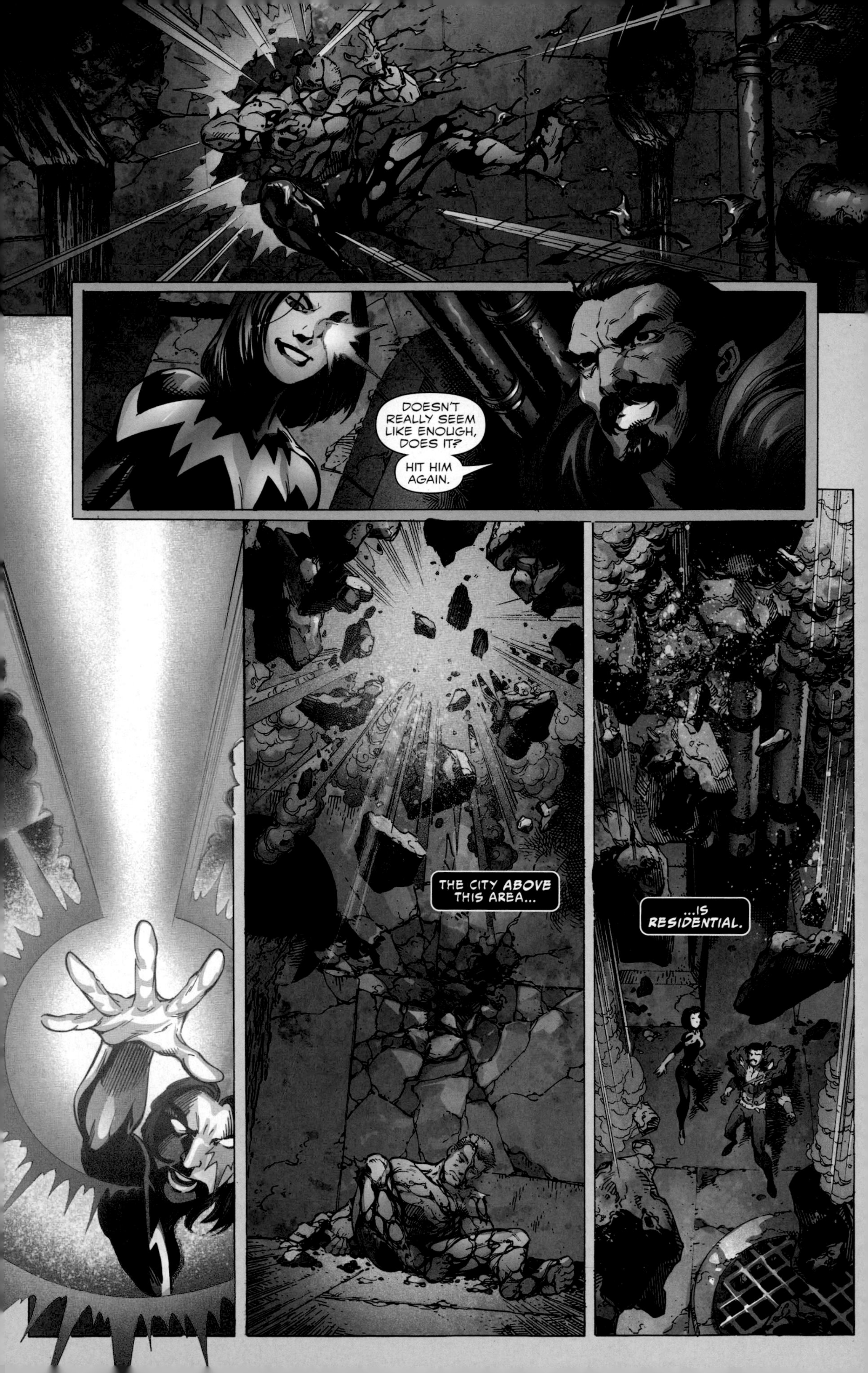
DOESN'T REALLY SEEM LIKE ENOUGH, DOES IT?
HIT HIM AGAIN.
THE CITY ABOVE THIS AREA...
...IS RESIDENTIAL.

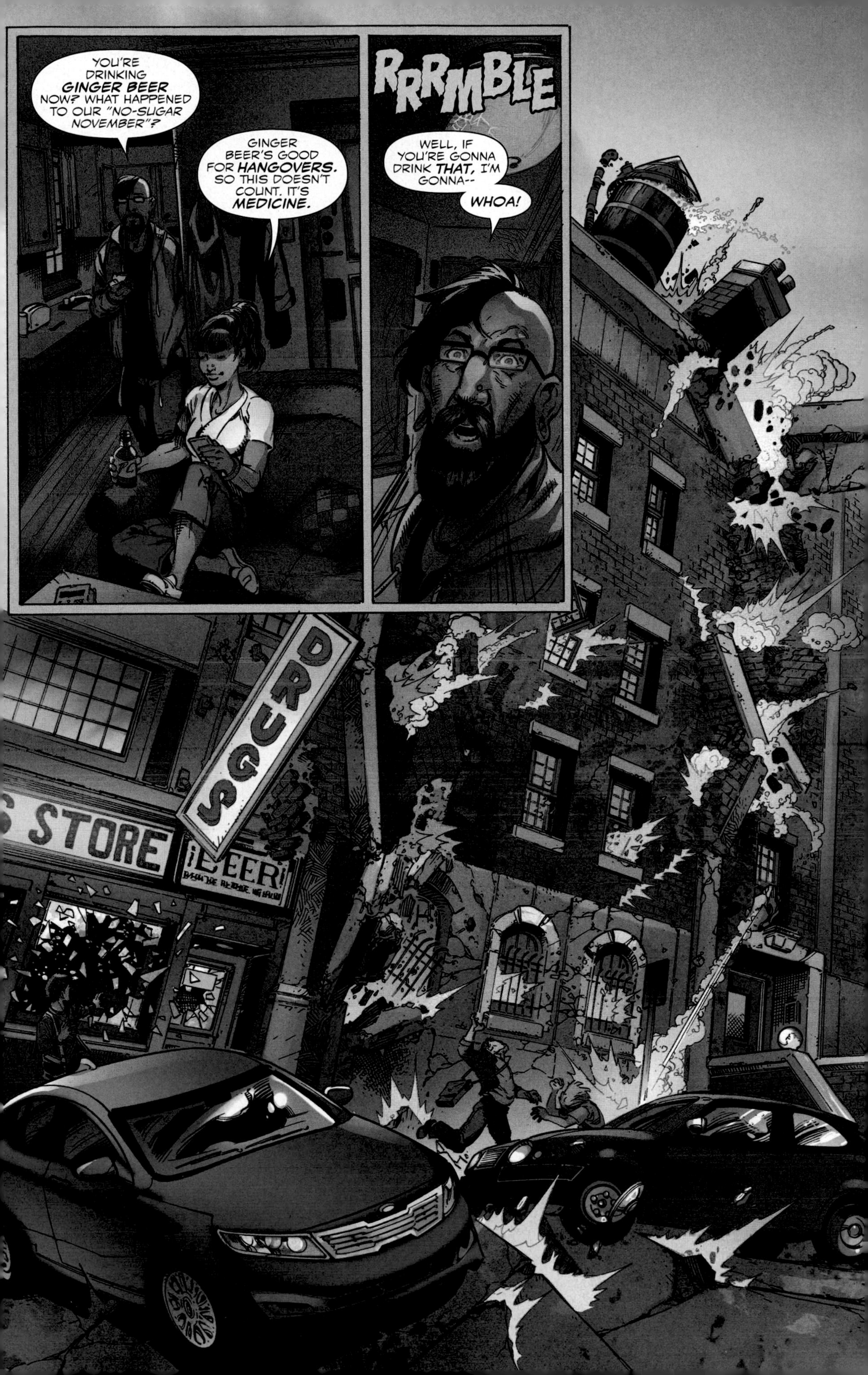
YOU'RE DRINKING GINGER BEER NOW? WHAT HAPPENED TO OUR "NO-SUGAR NOVEMBER"?
GINGER BEER'S GOOD FOR HANGOVERS. SO THIS DOESN'T COUNT. IT'S MEDICINE.
RRRMBLE
WELL, IF YOU'RE GONNA DRINK THAT, I'M GONNA--
WHOA!
DRUGS
STORE
BEER

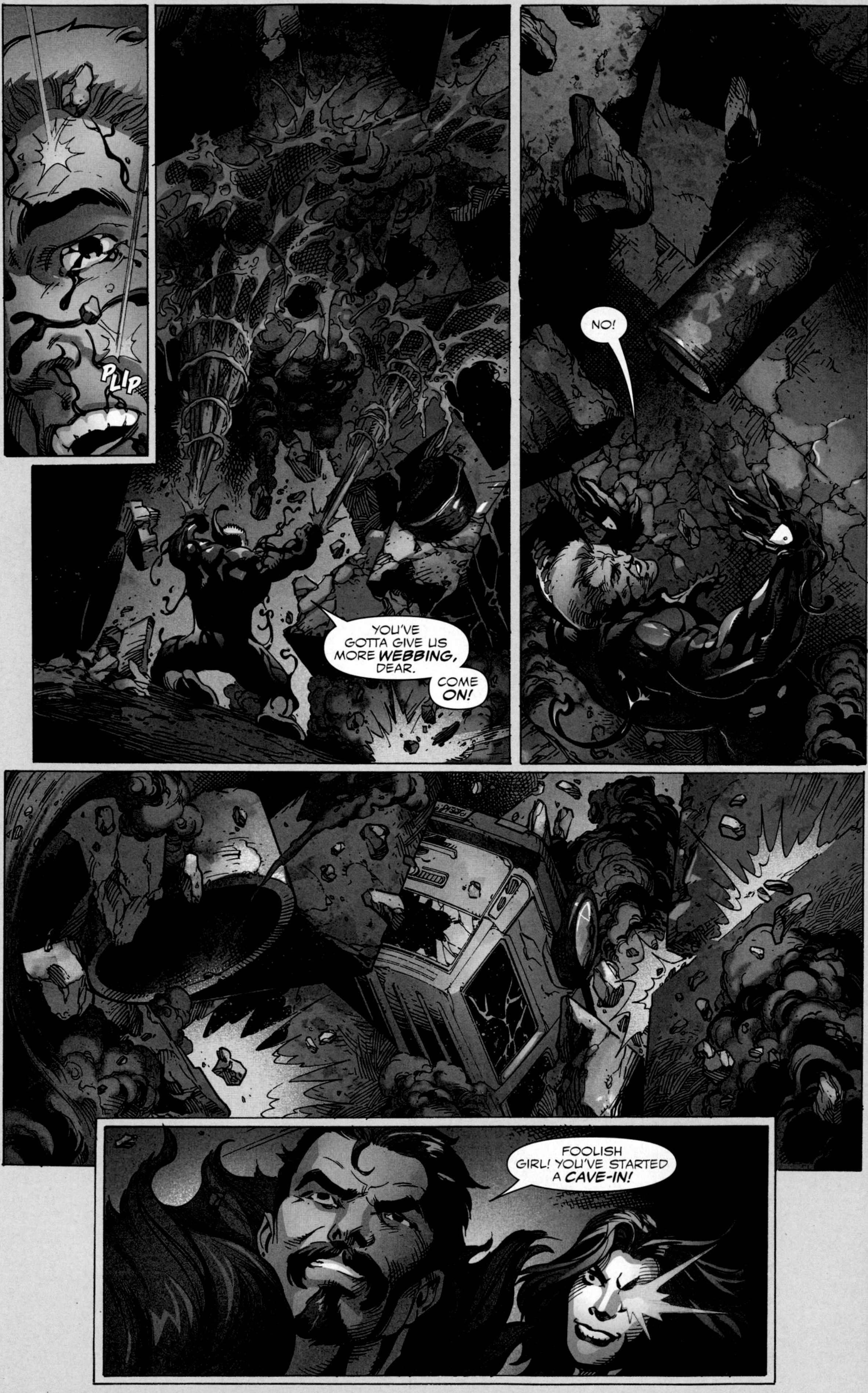
PLIP
YOU'VE GOTTA GIVE US MORE WEBBING, DEAR.
COME ON!
NO!
FOOLISH GIRL! YOU'VE STARTED A CAVE-IN!

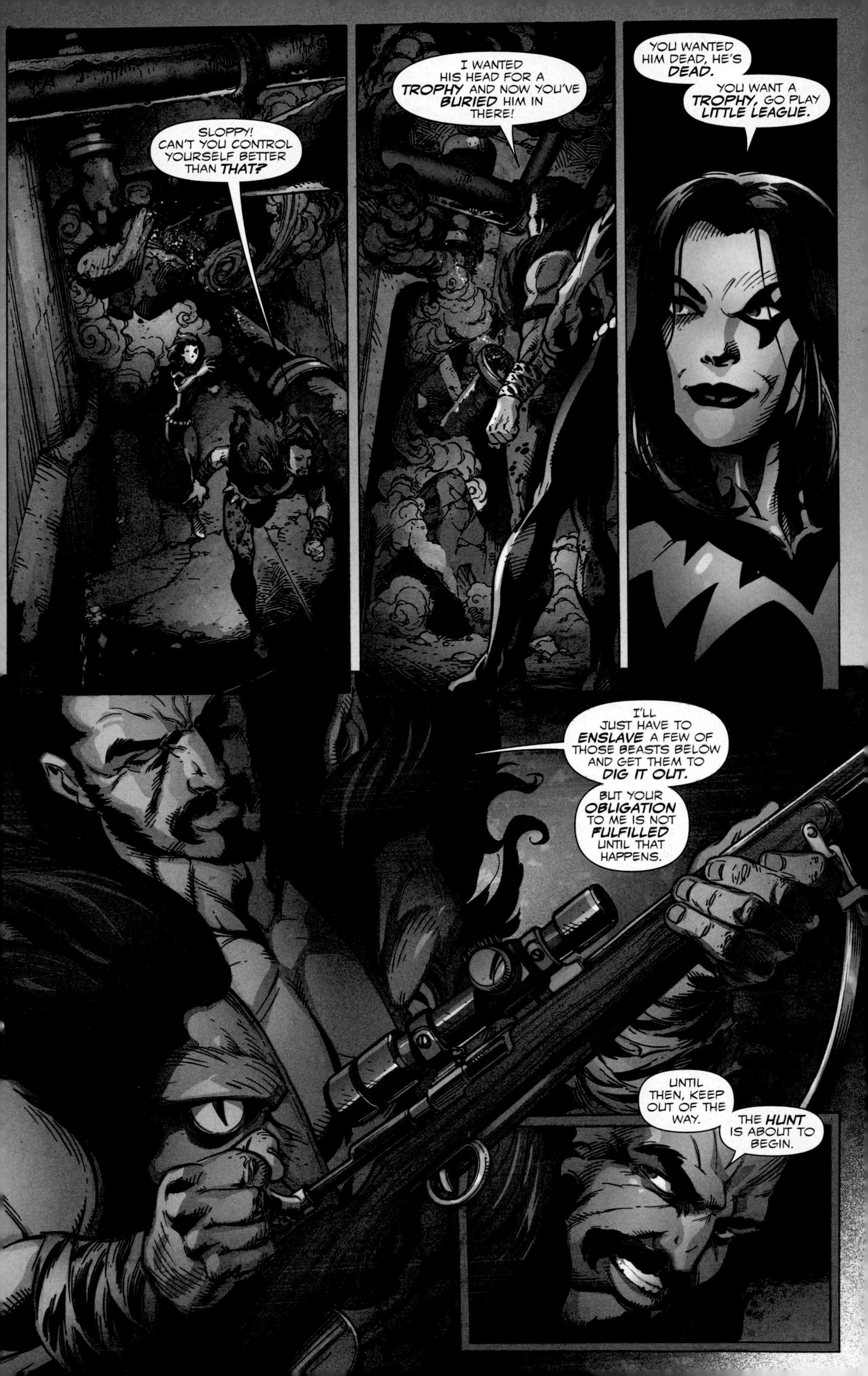
SLOPPY! CAN'T YOU CONTROL YOURSELF BETTER THAN THAT?
I WANTED HIS HEAD FOR A TROPHY AND NOW YOU'VE BURIED HIM IN THERE!
YOU WANTED HIM DEAD, HE'S DEAD.
YOU WANT A TROPHY, GO PLAY LITTLE LEAGUE.
I'LL JUST HAVE TO ENSLAVE A FEW OF THOSE BEASTS BELOW AND GET THEM TO DIG IT OUT.
BUT YOUR OBLIGATION TO ME IS NOT FULFILLED UNTIL THAT HAPPENS.
UNTIL THEN, KEEP OUT OF THE WAY.
THE HUNT IS ABOUT TO BEGIN.

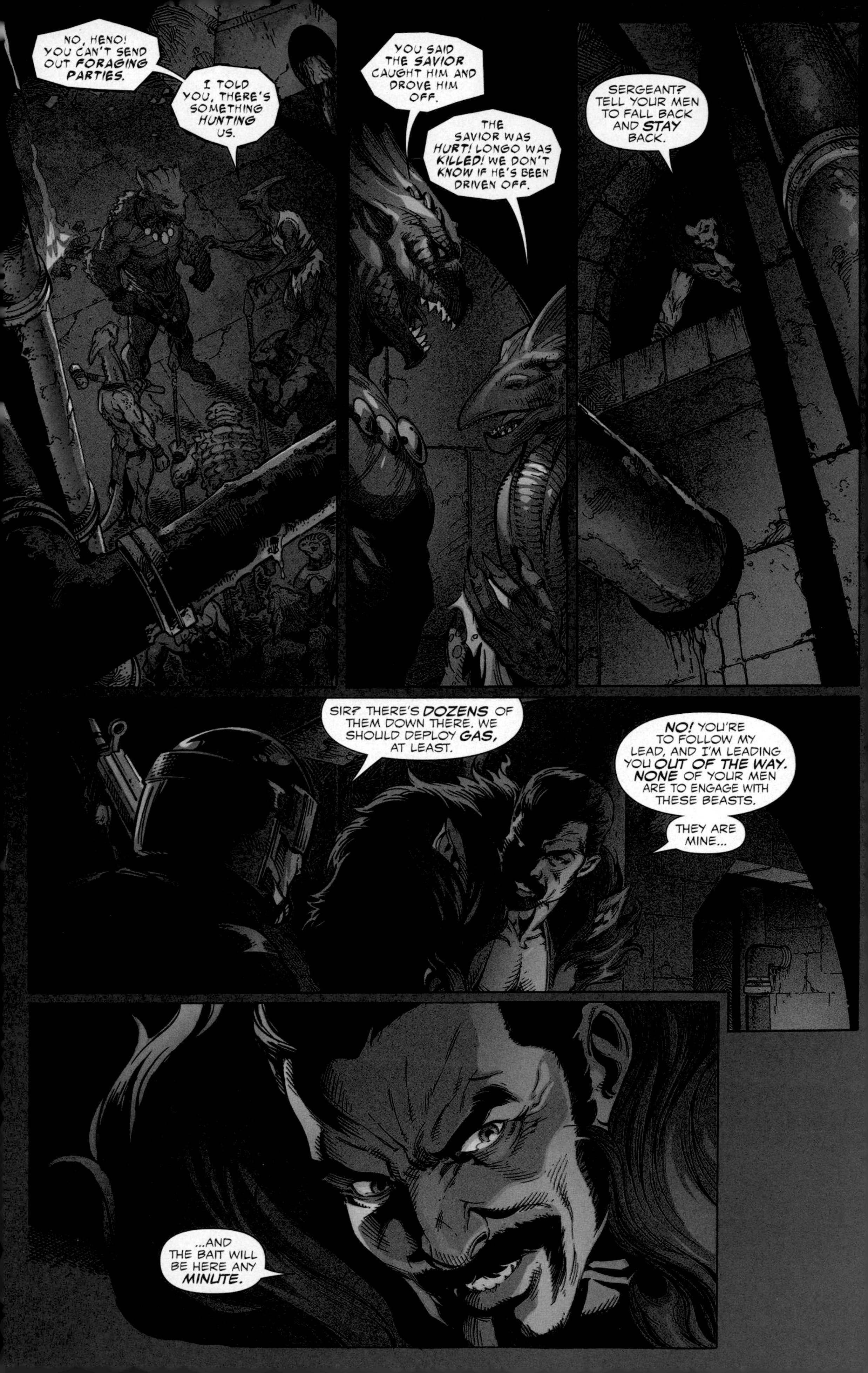
NO, HENO! YOU CAN'T SEND OUT FORAGING PARTIES.
I TOLD YOU, THERE'S SOMETHING HUNTING US.
YOU SAID THE SAVIOR CAUGHT HIM AND DROVE HIM OFF.
THE SAVIOR WAS HURT! LONGO WAS KILLED! WE DON'T KNOW IF HE'S BEEN DRIVEN OFF.
SERGEANT? TELL YOUR MEN TO FALL BACK AND STAY BACK.
SIR? THERE'S DOZENS OF THEM DOWN THERE. WE SHOULD DEPLOY GAS, AT LEAST.
NO! YOU'RE TO FOLLOW MY LEAD, AND I'M LEADING YOU OUT OF THE WAY. NONE OF YOUR MEN ARE TO ENGAGE WITH THESE BEASTS.
THEY ARE MINE...
...AND THE BAIT WILL BE HERE ANY MINUTE.

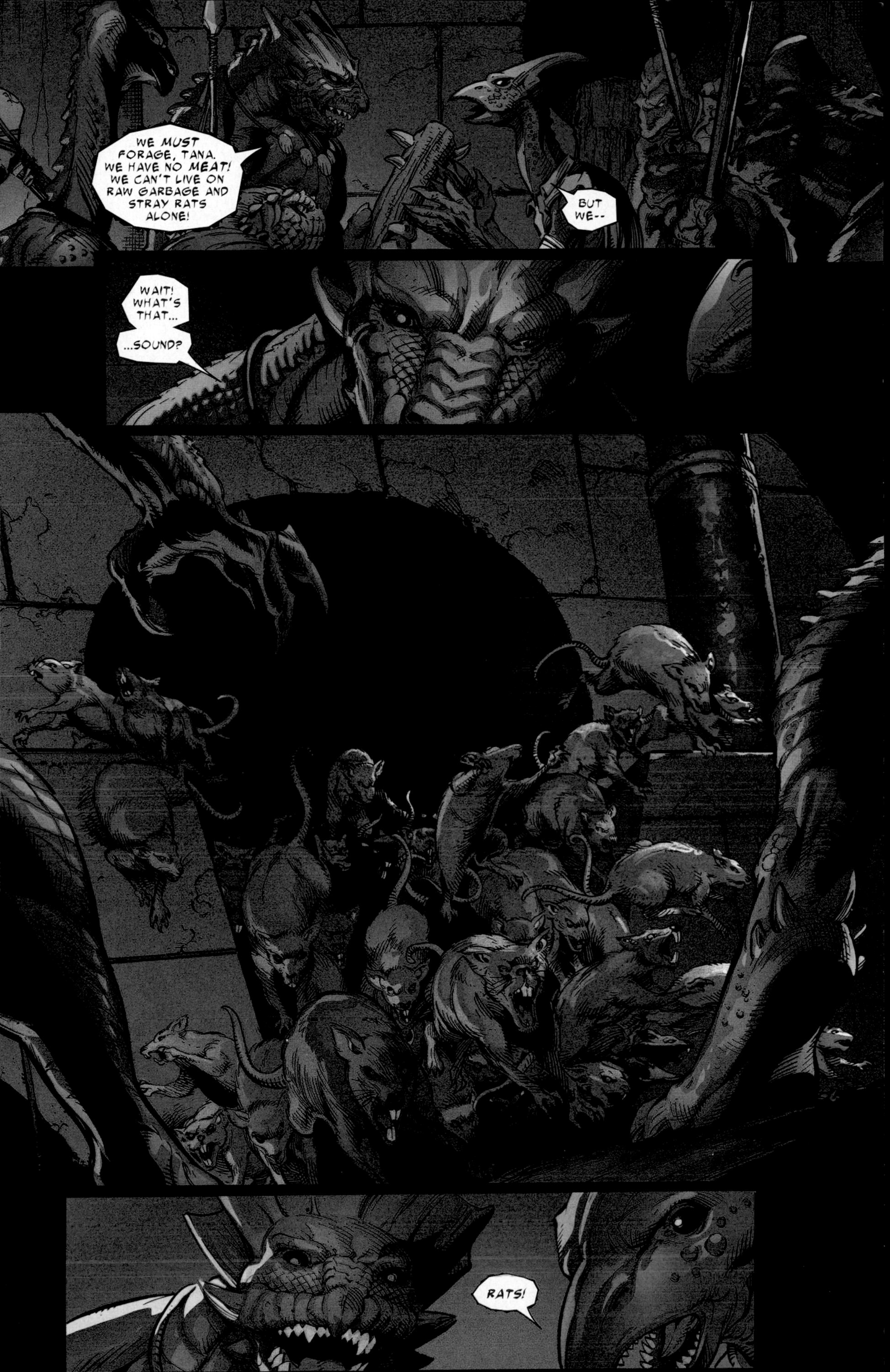
WE MUST FORAGE, TANA. WE HAVE NO MEAT! WE CAN'T LIVE ON RAW GARBAGE AND STRAY RATS ALONE!
BUT WE--
WAIT! WHAT'S THAT...
...SOUND?
RATS!

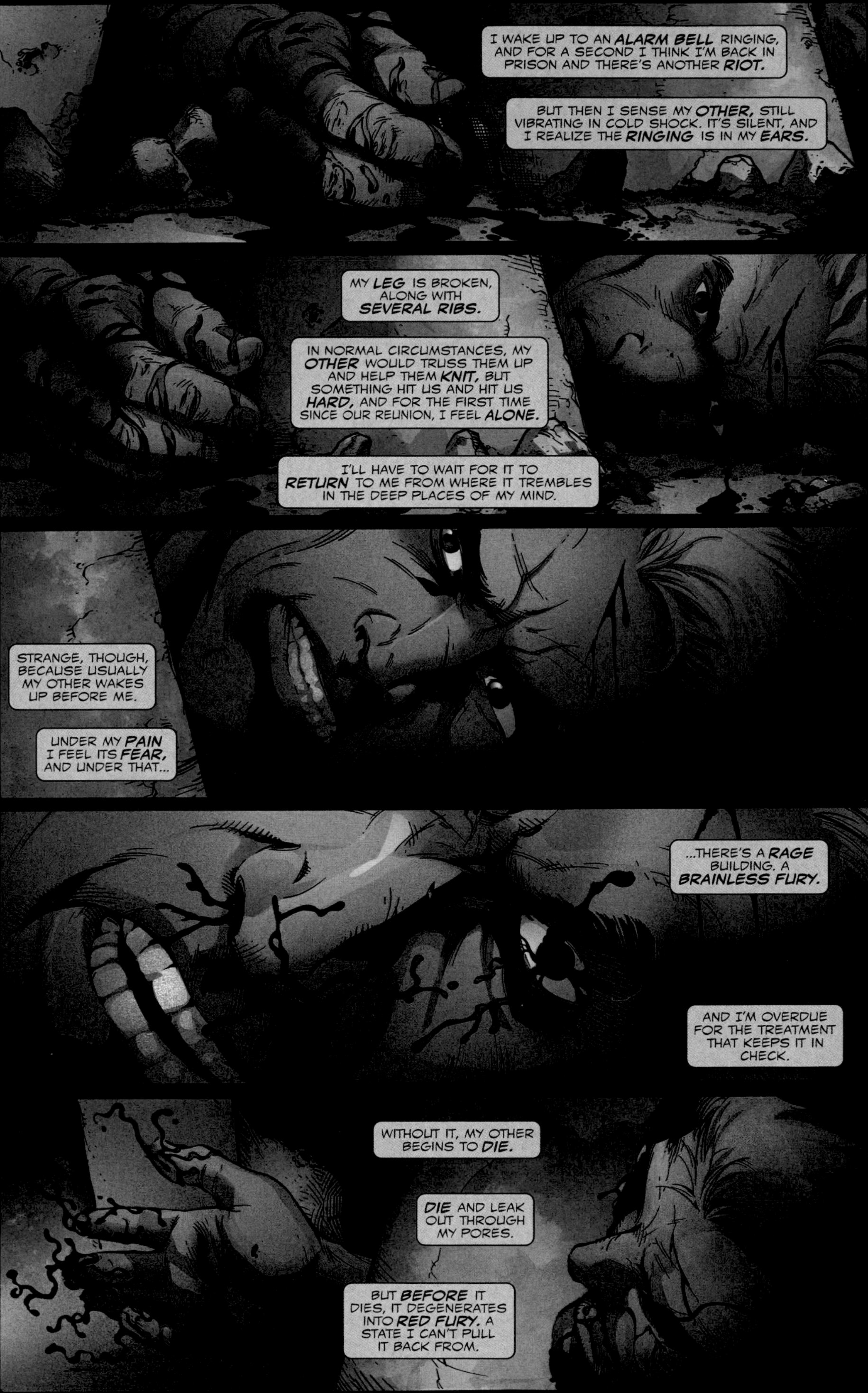
I WAKE UP TO AN ALARM BELL RINGING, AND FOR A SECOND I THINK I'M BACK IN PRISON AND THERE'S ANOTHER RIOT.
BUT THEN I SENSE MY OTHER, STILL VIBRATING IN COLD SHOCK. IT'S SILENT, AND I REALIZE THE RINGING IS IN MY EARS.
MY LEG IS BROKEN, ALONG WITH SEVERAL RIBS.
IN NORMAL CIRCUMSTANCES, MY OTHER WOULD TRUSS THEM UP AND HELP THEM KNIT, BUT SOMETHING HIT US AND HIT US HARD, AND FOR THE FIRST TIME SINCE OUR REUNION, I FEEL ALONE.
I'LL HAVE TO WAIT FOR IT TO RETURN TO ME FROM WHERE IT TREMBLES IN THE DEEP PLACES OF MY MIND.
STRANGE, THOUGH, BECAUSE USUALLY MY OTHER WAKES UP BEFORE ME.
UNDER MY PAIN I FEEL ITS FEAR, AND UNDER THAT...
...THERE'S A RAGE BUILDING. A BRAINLESS FURY.
AND I'M OVERDUE FOR THE TREATMENT THAT KEEPS IT IN CHECK.
WITHOUT IT, MY OTHER BEGINS TO DIE.
DIE AND LEAK OUT THROUGH MY PORES.
BUT BEFORE IT DIES, IT DEGENERATES INTO RED FURY. A STATE I CAN'T PULL IT BACK FROM.

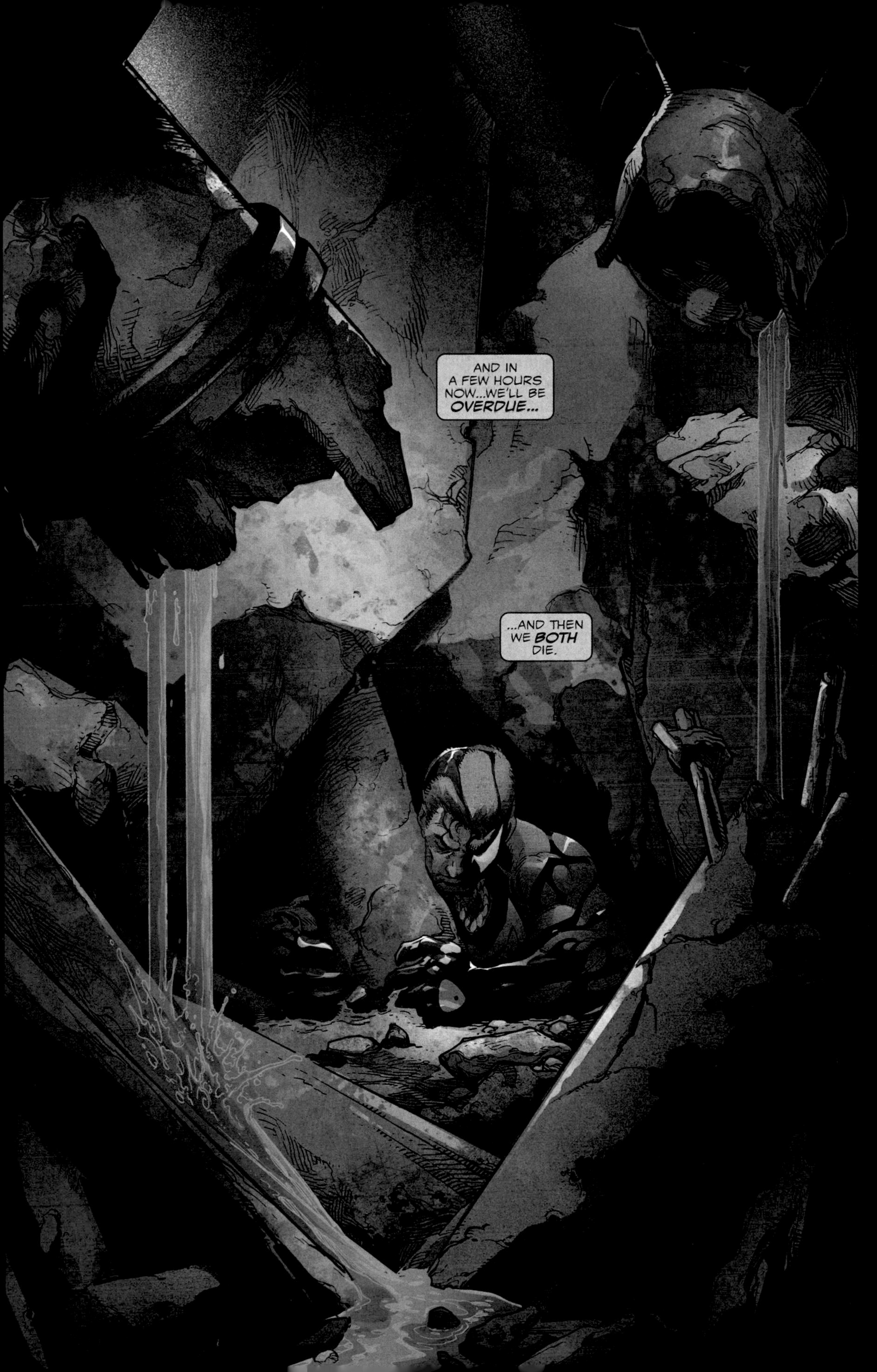
AND IN A FEW HOURS NOW...WE'LL BE OVERDUE...
...AND THEN WE BOTH DIE.

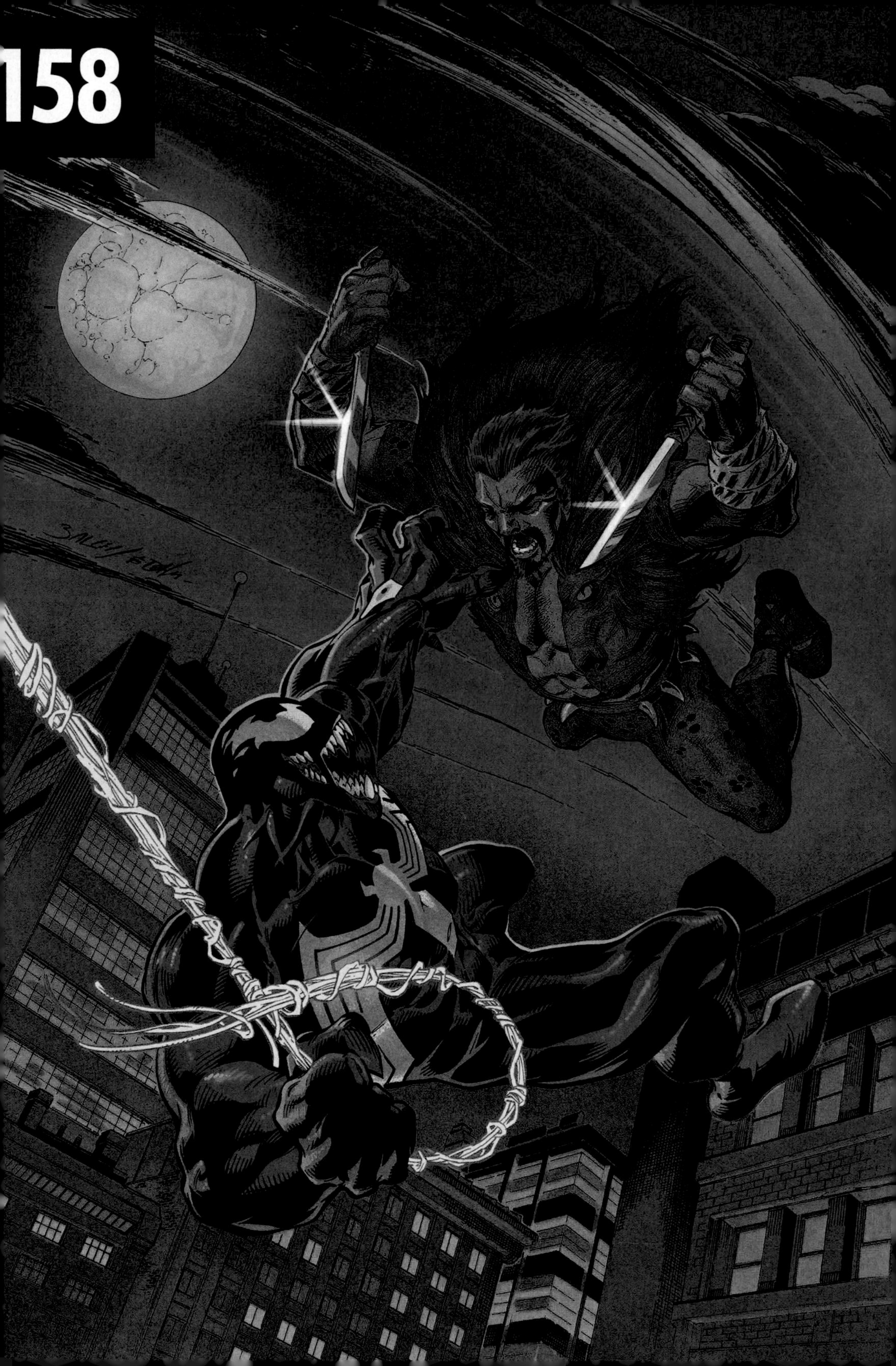

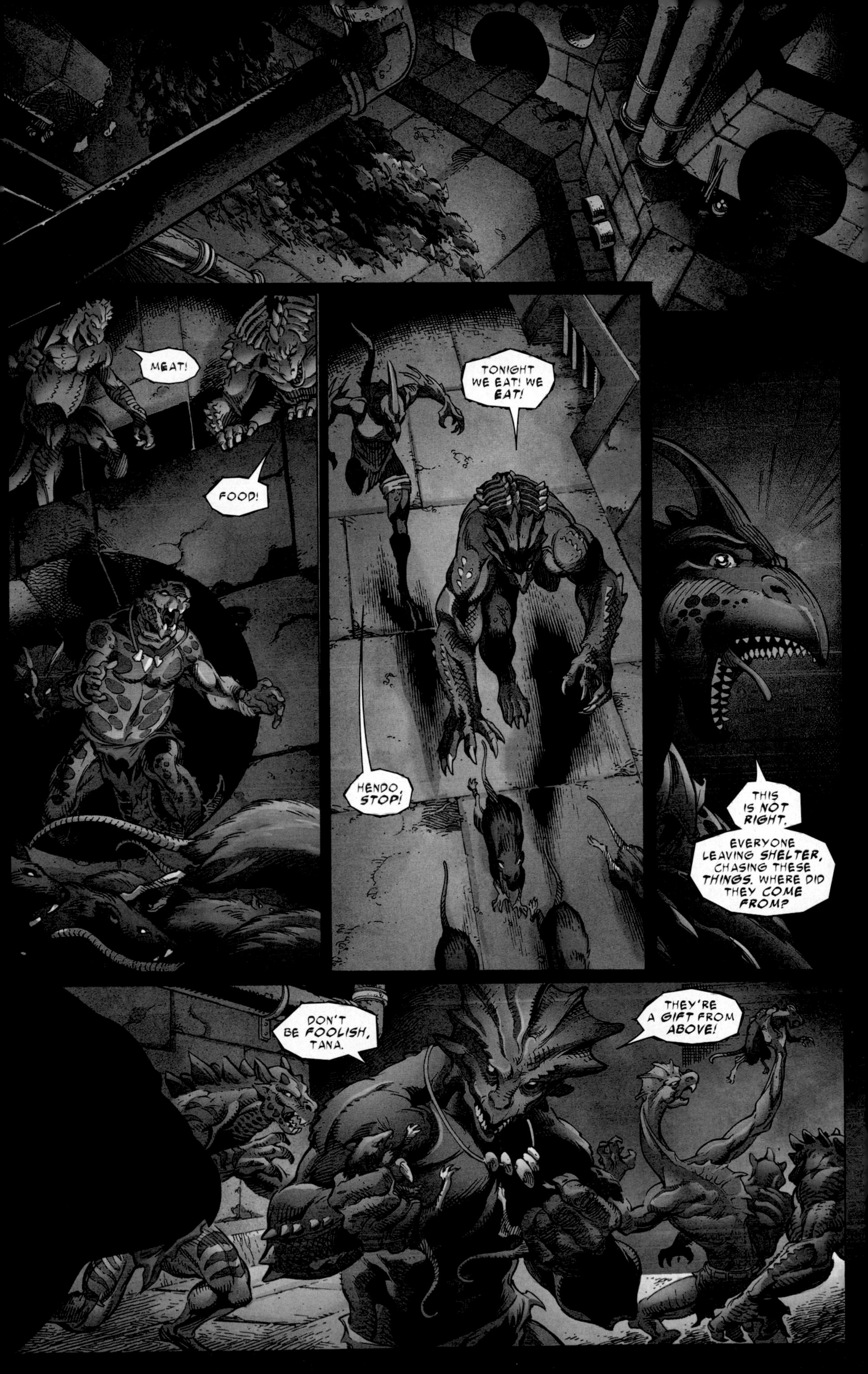
MEAT!
FOOD!
TONIGHT WE EAT! WE EAT!
HENDO, STOP!
THIS IS NOT RIGHT.
EVERYONE LEAVING SHELTER, CHASING THESE THINGS. WHERE DID THEY COME FROM?
DON'T BE FOOLISH, TANA.
THEY'RE A GIFT FROM ABOVE!

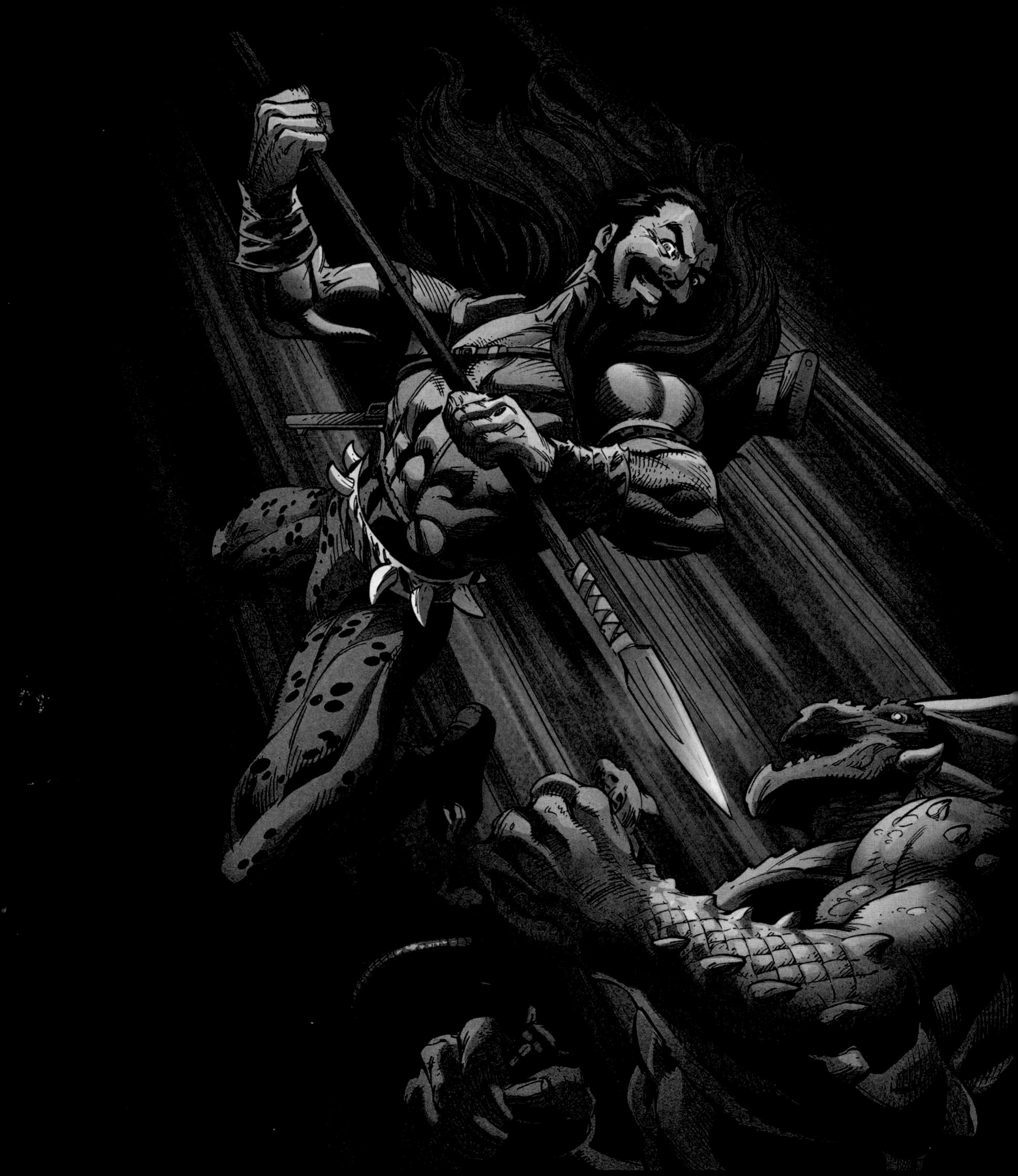

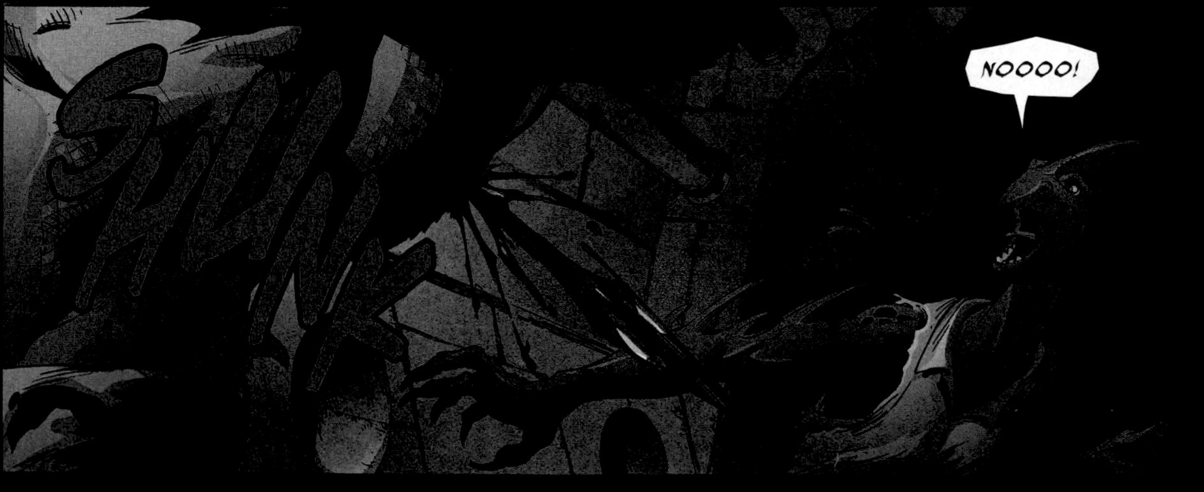
NOOOO!

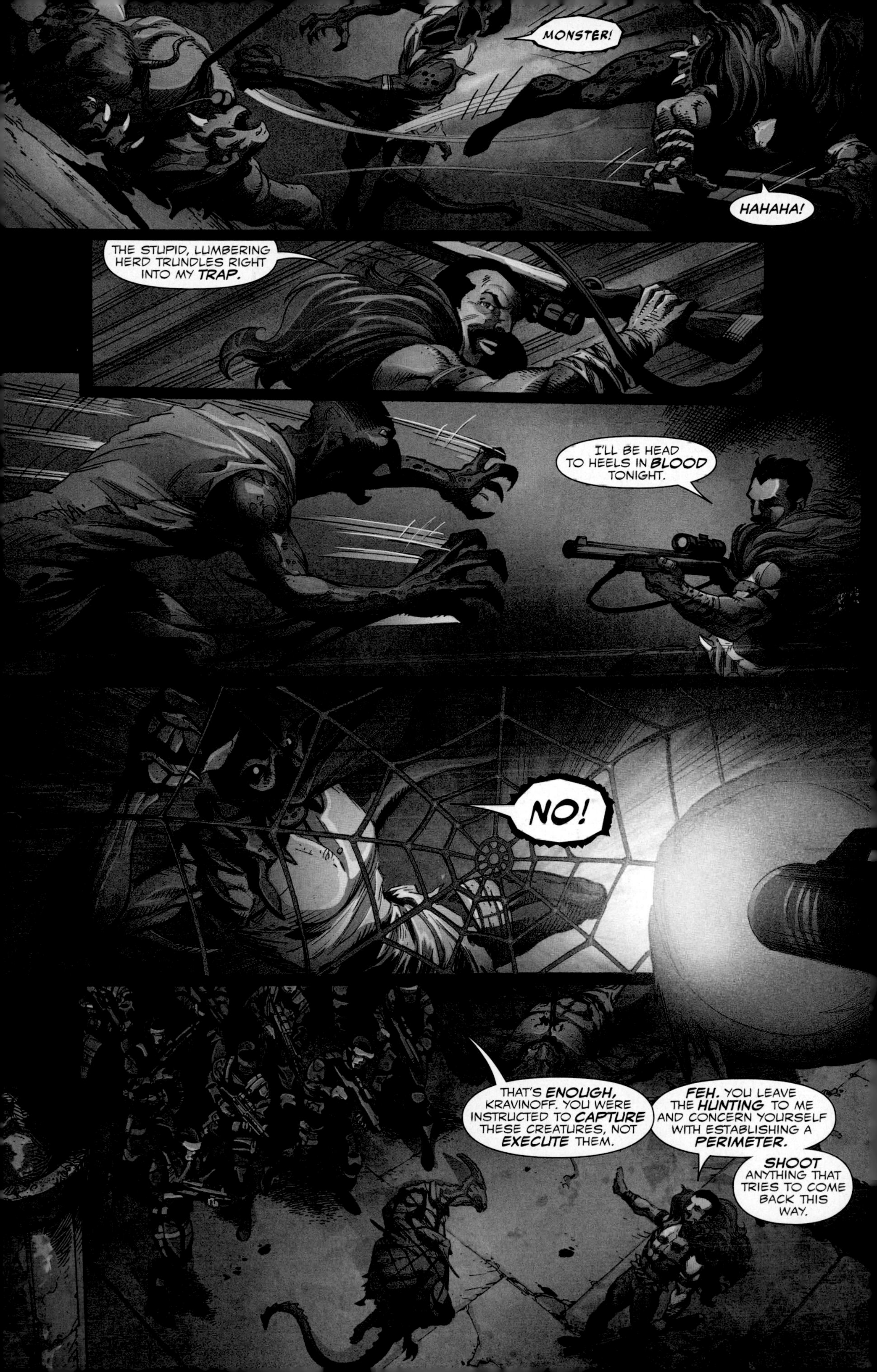
MONSTER!
HAHAHA!
THE STUPID, LUMBERING HERD TRUNDLES RIGHT INTO MY TRAP.
I'LL BE HEAD TO HEELS IN BLOOD TONIGHT.
NO!
THAT'S ENOUGH, KRAVINOFF. YOU WERE INSTRUCTED TO CAPTURE THESE CREATURES, NOT EXECUTE THEM.
FEH. YOU LEAVE THE HUNTING TO ME AND CONCERN YOURSELF WITH ESTABLISHING A PERIMETER.
SHOOT ANYTHING THAT TRIES TO COME BACK THIS WAY.

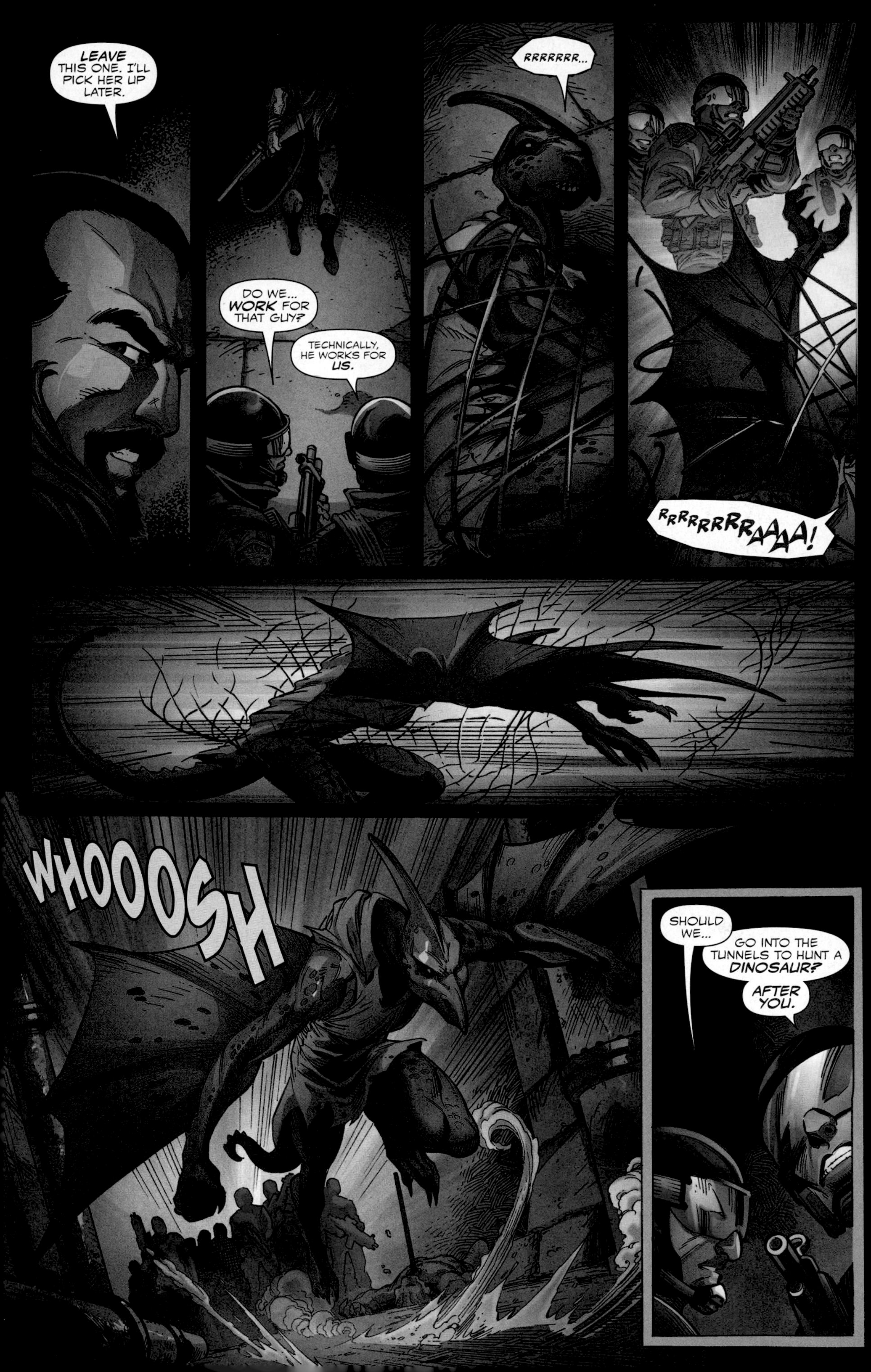
LEAVE THIS ONE. I'LL PICK HER UP LATER.
DO WE... WORK FOR THAT GUY?
TECHNICALLY, HE WORKS FOR US.
RRRRRRR...
RRRRRRRRAAAA!
WHOOOSH
SHOULD WE...
GO INTO THE TUNNELS TO HUNT A DINOSAUR?
AFTER YOU.

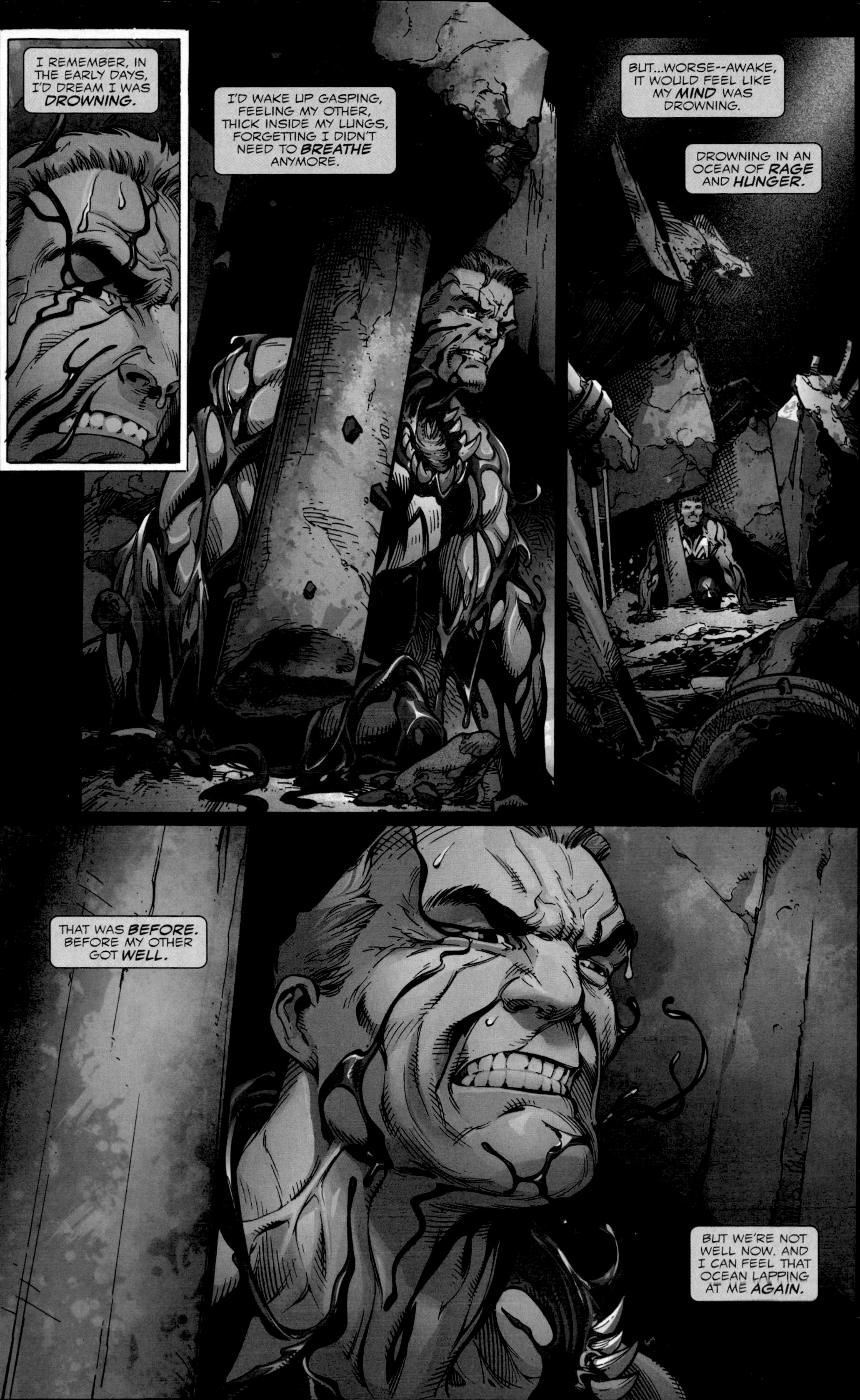
I REMEMBER, IN THE EARLY DAYS, I'D DREAM I WAS DROWNING.
I'D WAKE UP GASPING, FEELING MY OTHER, THICK INSIDE MY LUNGS, FORGETTING I DIDN'T NEED TO BREATHE ANYMORE.
BUT...WORSE--AWAKE, IT WOULD FEEL LIKE MY MIND WAS DROWNING.
DROWNING IN AN OCEAN OF RAGE AND HUNGER.
THAT WAS BEFORE. BEFORE MY OTHER GOT WELL.
BUT WE'RE NOT WELL NOW. AND I CAN FEEL THAT OCEAN LAPPING AT ME AGAIN.

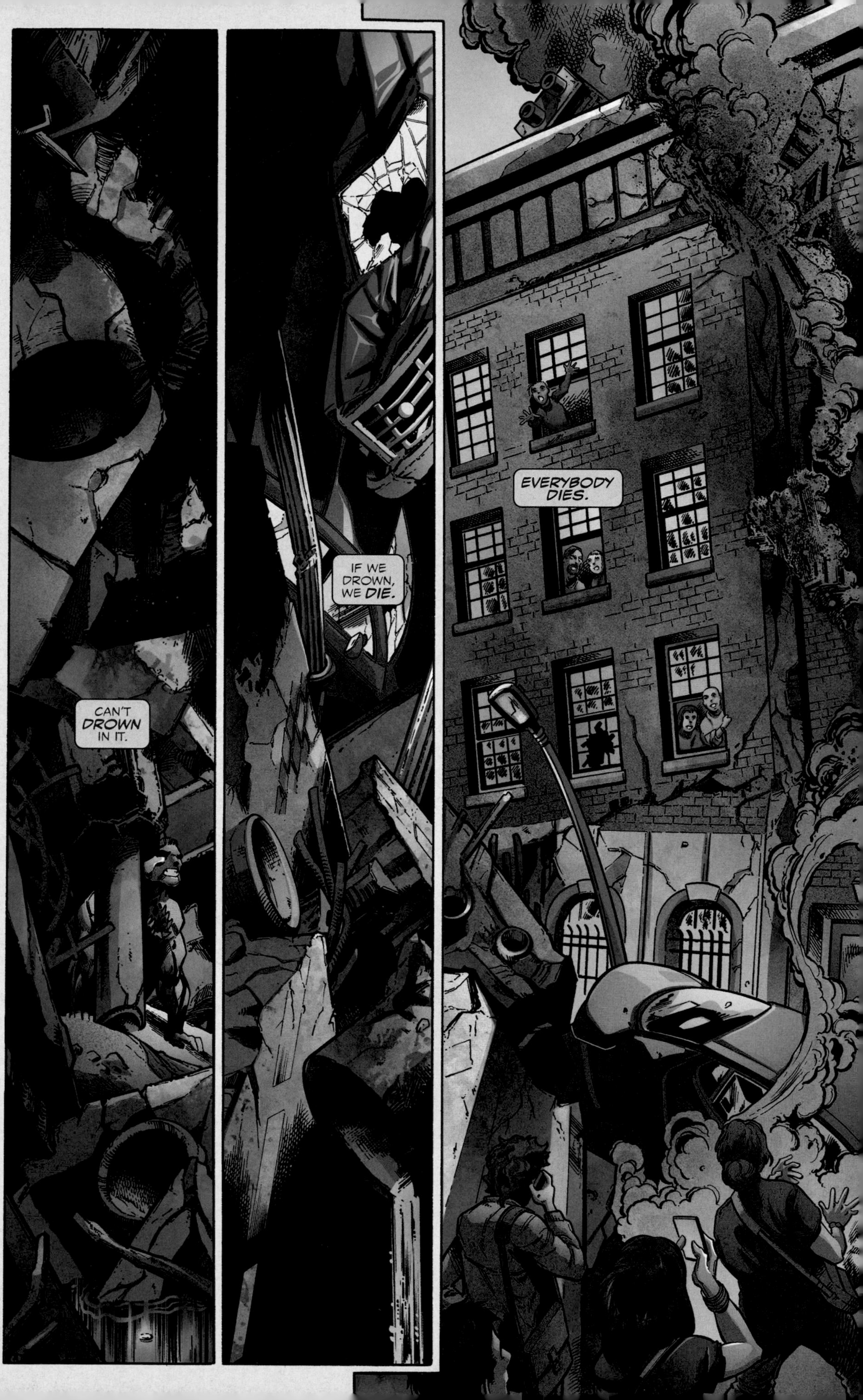
CAN'T DROWN IN IT.
IF WE DROWN, WE DIE.
EVERYBODY DIES.

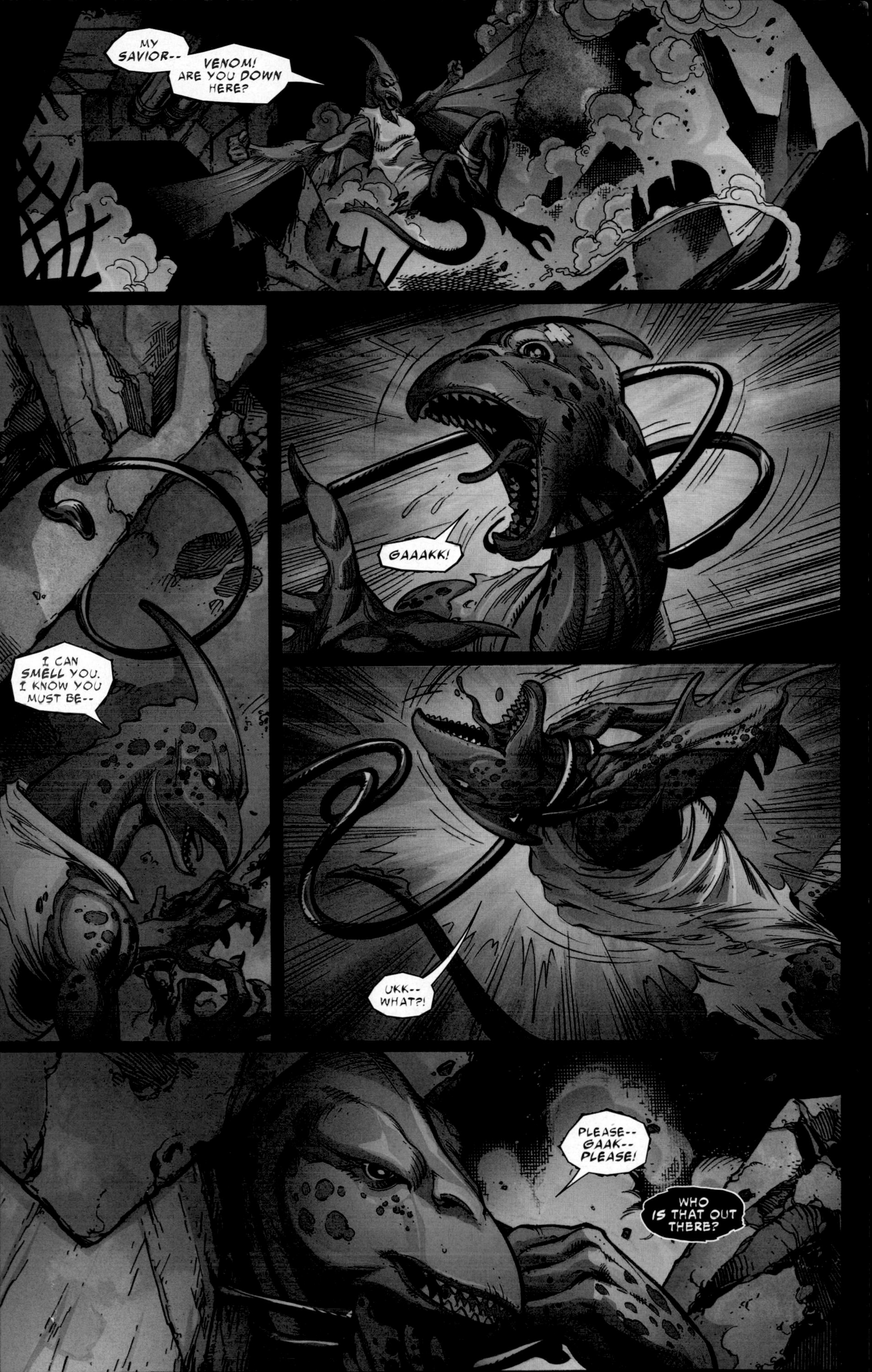

MY SAVIOR--
VENOM! ARE YOU DOWN HERE?
I CAN SMELL YOU. I KNOW YOU MUST BE--
GAAAKK!
UKK-- WHAT?!
PLEASE-- GAAK-- PLEASE!
WHO IS THAT OUT THERE?

TANA?
THE ONE THEY
CALL TANA.

TANA IS A...
FRIEND.

RELEASE...
RELEASE.

SAVIOR, IF
YOU'RE BURIED
IN THERE, I CAN DIG
YOU OUT. MY TALONS
ARE STRONG AND
GOOD FOR--

NO!

IF YOU
DIG US OUT,
THE CHAMBER WILL
COLLAPSE, ALONG
WITH THE STREET
ABOVE IT.

TOO MANY
INNOCENTS...
WE CAN HEAR
THEM...

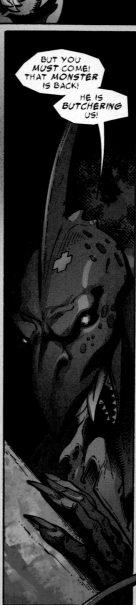

BUT YOU
MUST COME!
THAT MONSTER
IS BACK!

HE IS
BUTCHERING
US!

WE CAN'T
ESCAPE WITHOUT
GETTING INNOCENT
BLOOD ON OUR HANDS...
BUT WE CAN'T LAST
MORE THAN A FEW
MORE HOURS...

...BEFORE
WE LOSE OUR
MINDS.

WE
NEED HELP.
ALLIES.

THAT NOSE
OF YOURS BETTER
BE GOOD FOR MORE
THAN JUST SNIFFING
ME OUT.

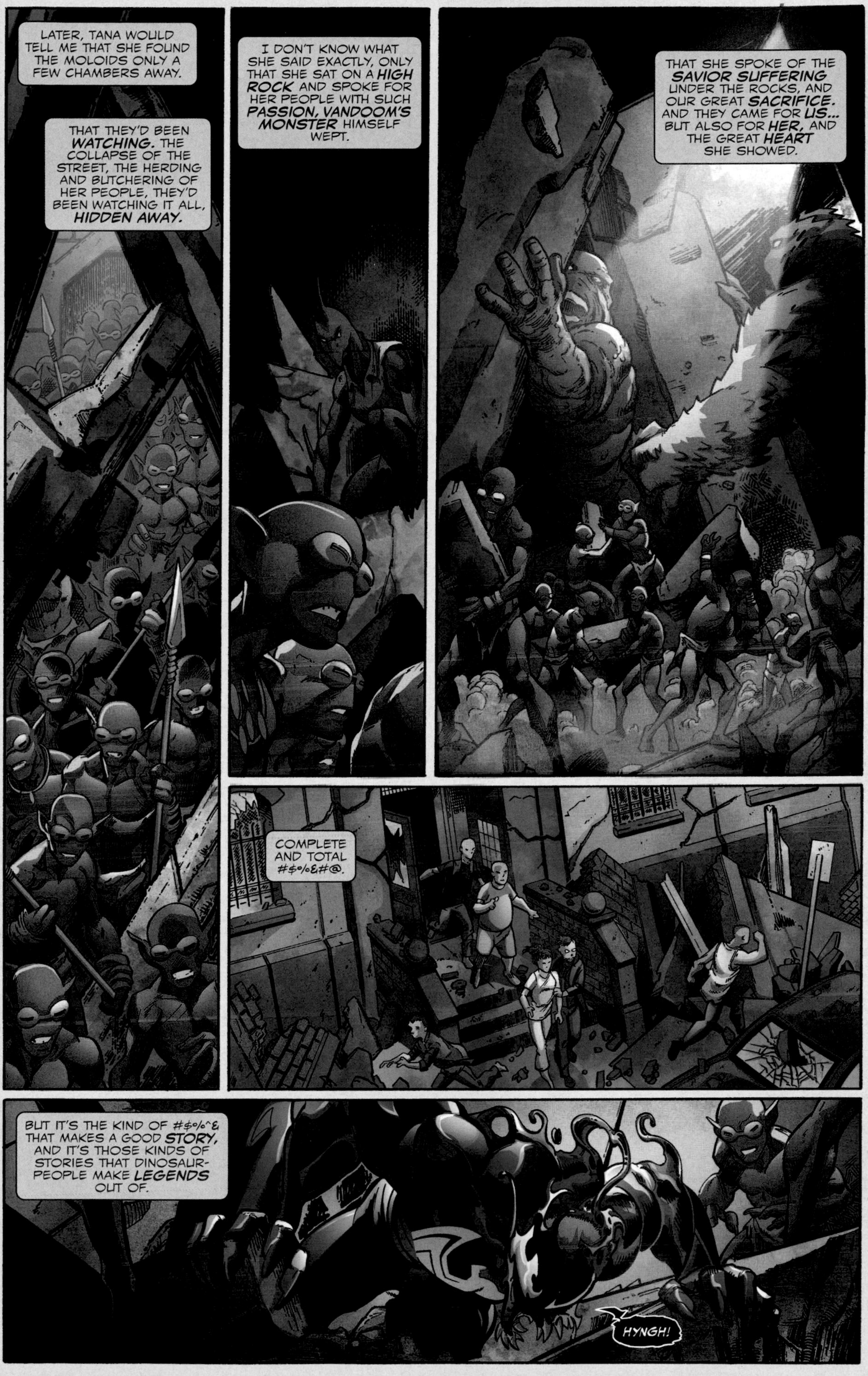
LATER, TANA WOULD TELL ME THAT SHE FOUND THE MOLOIDS ONLY A FEW CHAMBERS AWAY.
THAT THEY'D BEEN WATCHING. THE COLLAPSE OF THE STREET, THE HERDING AND BUTCHERING OF HER PEOPLE, THEY'D BEEN WATCHING IT ALL, HIDDEN AWAY.
I DON'T KNOW WHAT SHE SAID EXACTLY, ONLY THAT SHE SAT ON A HIGH ROCK AND SPOKE FOR HER PEOPLE WITH SUCH PASSION, VANDOOM'S MONSTER HIMSELF WEPT.
THAT SHE SPOKE OF THE SAVIOR SUFFERING UNDER THE ROCKS, AND OUR GREAT SACRIFICE. AND THEY CAME FOR US... BUT ALSO FOR HER, AND THE GREAT HEART SHE SHOWED.
COMPLETE AND TOTAL #$%&#@.
BUT IT'S THE KIND OF #$%^& THAT MAKES A GOOD STORY, AND IT'S THOSE KINDS OF STORIES THAT DINOSAUR-PEOPLE MAKE LEGENDS OUT OF.
HYNGH!

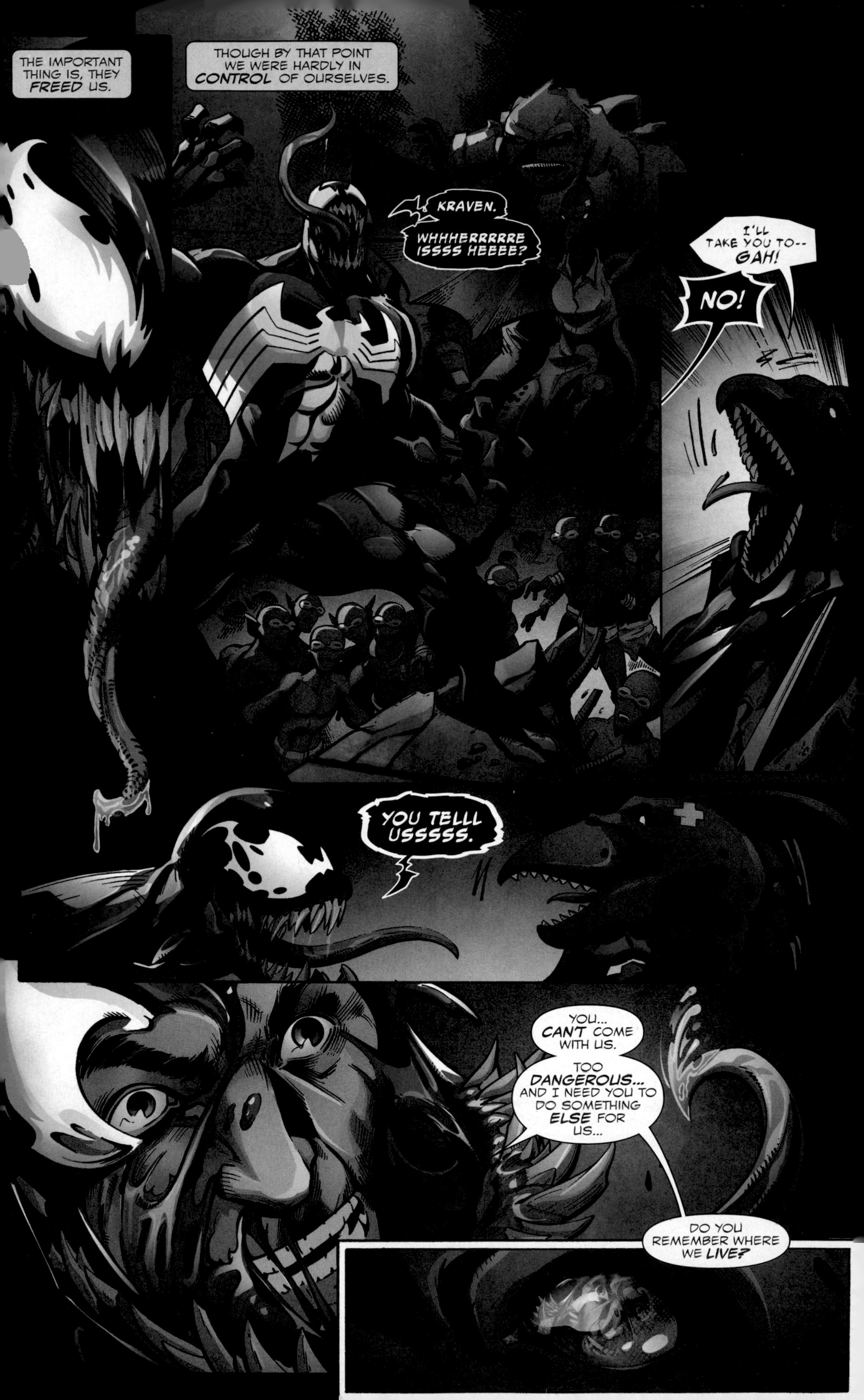
THE IMPORTANT THING IS, THEY FREED US.
THOUGH BY THAT POINT WE WERE HARDLY IN CONTROL OF OURSELVES.
KRAVEN.
WHHHERRRRRE ISSSS HEEEE?
I'LL TAKE YOU TO-- GAH!
NO!
YOU TELLL USSSSS.
YOU... CAN'T COME WITH US.
TOO DANGEROUS... AND I NEED YOU TO DO SOMETHING ELSE FOR US...
DO YOU REMEMBER WHERE WE LIVE?

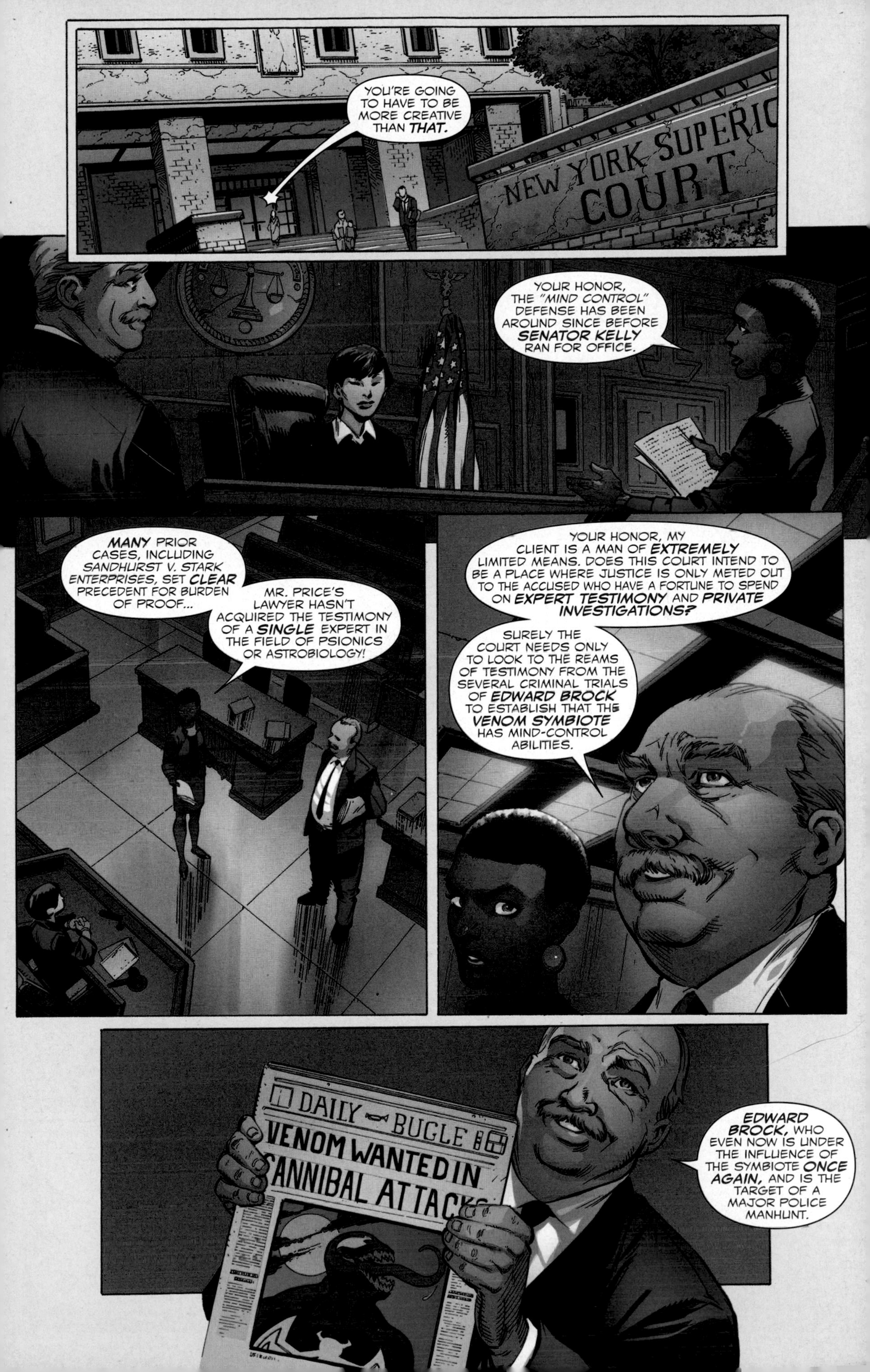
YOU'RE GOING TO HAVE TO BE MORE CREATIVE THAN THAT.
NEW YORK SUPERIO
COURT
YOUR HONOR, THE "MIND CONTROL" DEFENSE HAS BEEN AROUND SINCE BEFORE SENATOR KELLY RAN FOR OFFICE.
MANY PRIOR CASES, INCLUDING SANDHURST V. STARK ENTERPRISES, SET CLEAR PRECEDENT FOR BURDEN OF PROOF...
MR. PRICE'S LAWYER HASN'T ACQUIRED THE TESTIMONY OF A SINGLE EXPERT IN THE FIELD OF PSIONICS OR ASTROBIOLOGY!
YOUR HONOR, MY CLIENT IS A MAN OF EXTREMELY LIMITED MEANS. DOES THIS COURT INTEND TO BE A PLACE WHERE JUSTICE IS ONLY METED OUT TO THE ACCUSED WHO HAVE A FORTUNE TO SPEND ON EXPERT TESTIMONY AND PRIVATE INVESTIGATIONS?
SURELY THE COURT NEEDS ONLY TO LOOK TO THE REAMS OF TESTIMONY FROM THE SEVERAL CRIMINAL TRIALS OF EDWARD BROCK TO ESTABLISH THAT THE VENOM SYMBIOTE HAS MIND-CONTROL ABILITIES.
DAILY BUGLE
VENOM WANTED IN CANNIBAL ATTACKS
EDWARD BROCK, WHO EVEN NOW IS UNDER THE INFLUENCE OF THE SYMBIOTE ONCE AGAIN, AND IS THE TARGET OF A MAJOR POLICE MANHUNT.

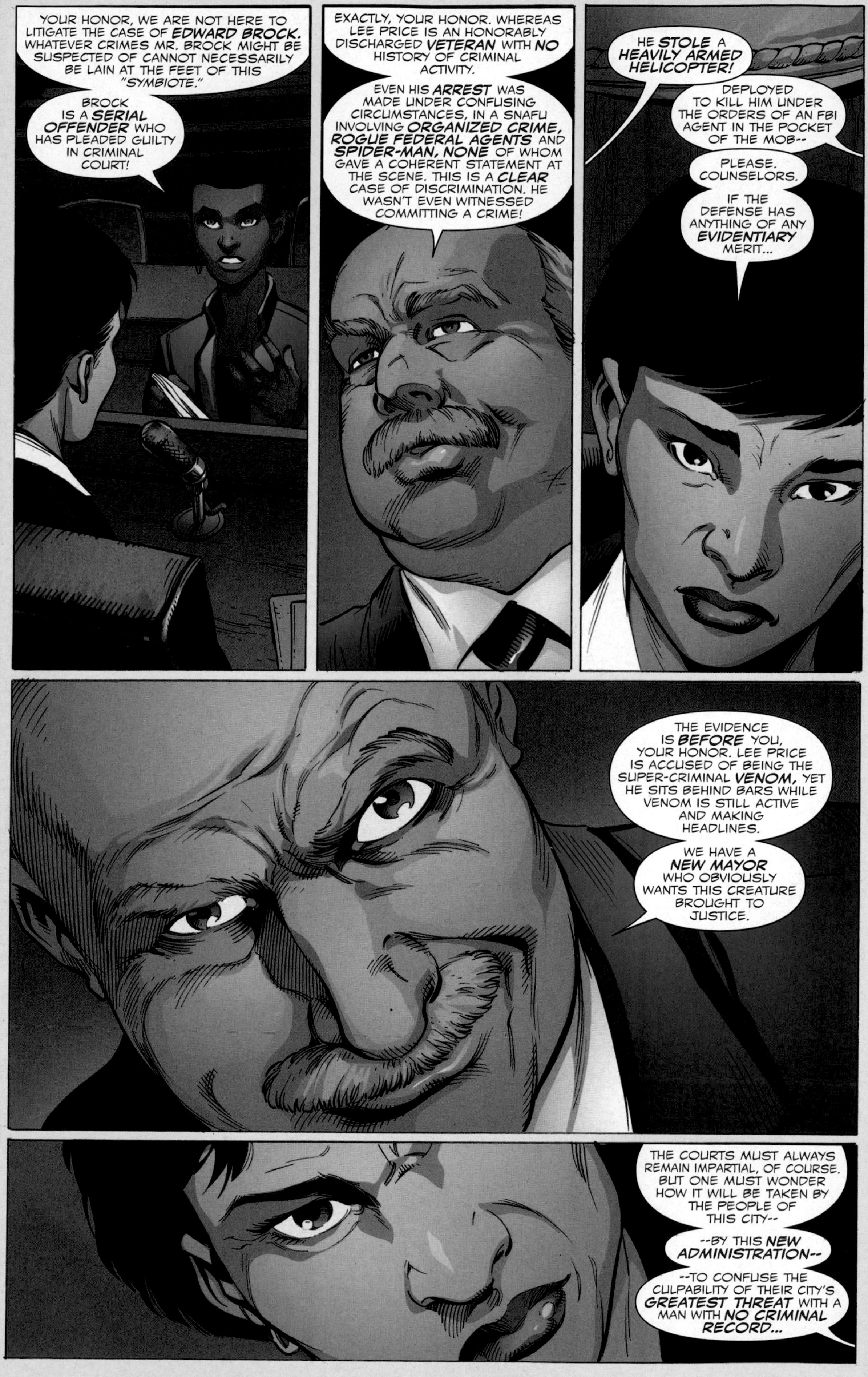
YOUR HONOR, WE ARE NOT HERE TO LITIGATE THE CASE OF EDWARD BROCK. WHATEVER CRIMES MR. BROCK MIGHT BE SUSPECTED OF CANNOT NECESSARILY BE LAIN AT THE FEET OF THIS "SYMBIOTE."
BROCK IS A SERIAL OFFENDER WHO HAS PLEADED GUILTY IN CRIMINAL COURT!
EXACTLY, YOUR HONOR. WHEREAS LEE PRICE IS AN HONORABLY DISCHARGED VETERAN WITH NO HISTORY OF CRIMINAL ACTIVITY.
EVEN HIS ARREST WAS MADE UNDER CONFUSING CIRCUMSTANCES, IN A SNAFU INVOLVING ORGANIZED CRIME, ROGUE FEDERAL AGENTS AND SPIDER-MAN, NONE OF WHOM GAVE A COHERENT STATEMENT AT THE SCENE. THIS IS A CLEAR CASE OF DISCRIMINATION. HE WASN'T EVEN WITNESSED COMMITTING A CRIME!
HE STOLE A HEAVILY ARMED HELICOPTER!
DEPLOYED TO KILL HIM UNDER THE ORDERS OF AN FBI AGENT IN THE POCKET OF THE MOB--
PLEASE. COUNSELORS.
IF THE DEFENSE HAS ANYTHING OF ANY EVIDENTIARY MERIT...
THE EVIDENCE IS BEFORE YOU, YOUR HONOR. LEE PRICE IS ACCUSED OF BEING THE SUPER-CRIMINAL VENOM, YET HE SITS BEHIND BARS WHILE VENOM IS STILL ACTIVE AND MAKING HEADLINES.
WE HAVE A NEW MAYOR WHO OBVIOUSLY WANTS THIS CREATURE BROUGHT TO JUSTICE.
THE COURTS MUST ALWAYS REMAIN IMPARTIAL, OF COURSE. BUT ONE MUST WONDER HOW IT WILL BE TAKEN BY THE PEOPLE OF THIS CITY--
--BY THIS NEW ADMINISTRATION--
--TO CONFUSE THE CULPABILITY OF THEIR CITY'S GREATEST THREAT WITH A MAN WITH NO CRIMINAL RECORD...

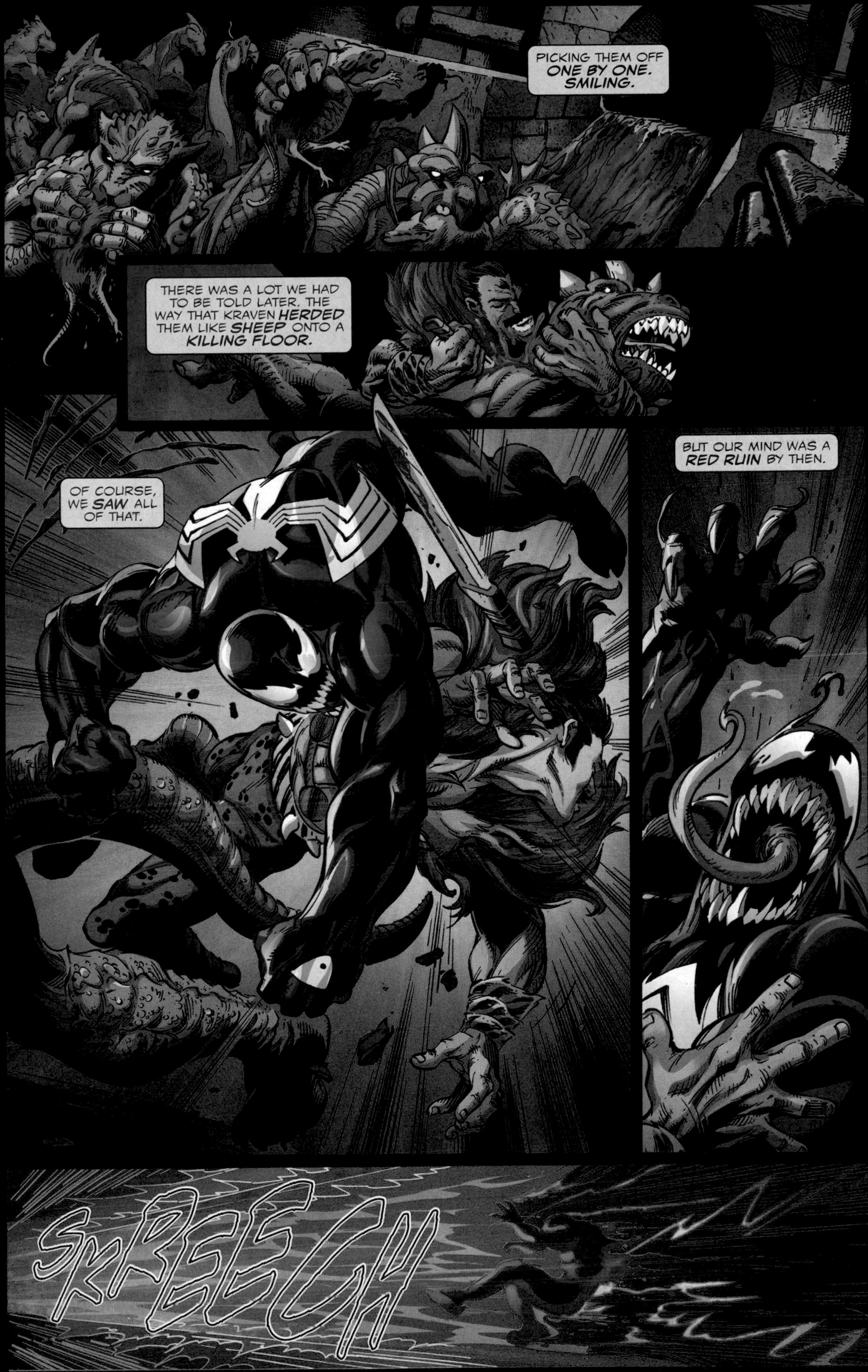
PICKING THEM OFF ONE BY ONE. SMILING.
THERE WAS A LOT WE HAD TO BE TOLD LATER. THE WAY THAT KRAVEN HERDED THEM LIKE SHEEP ONTO A KILLING FLOOR.
OF COURSE, WE SAW ALL OF THAT.
BUT OUR MIND WAS A RED RUIN BY THEN.
SKREEECH

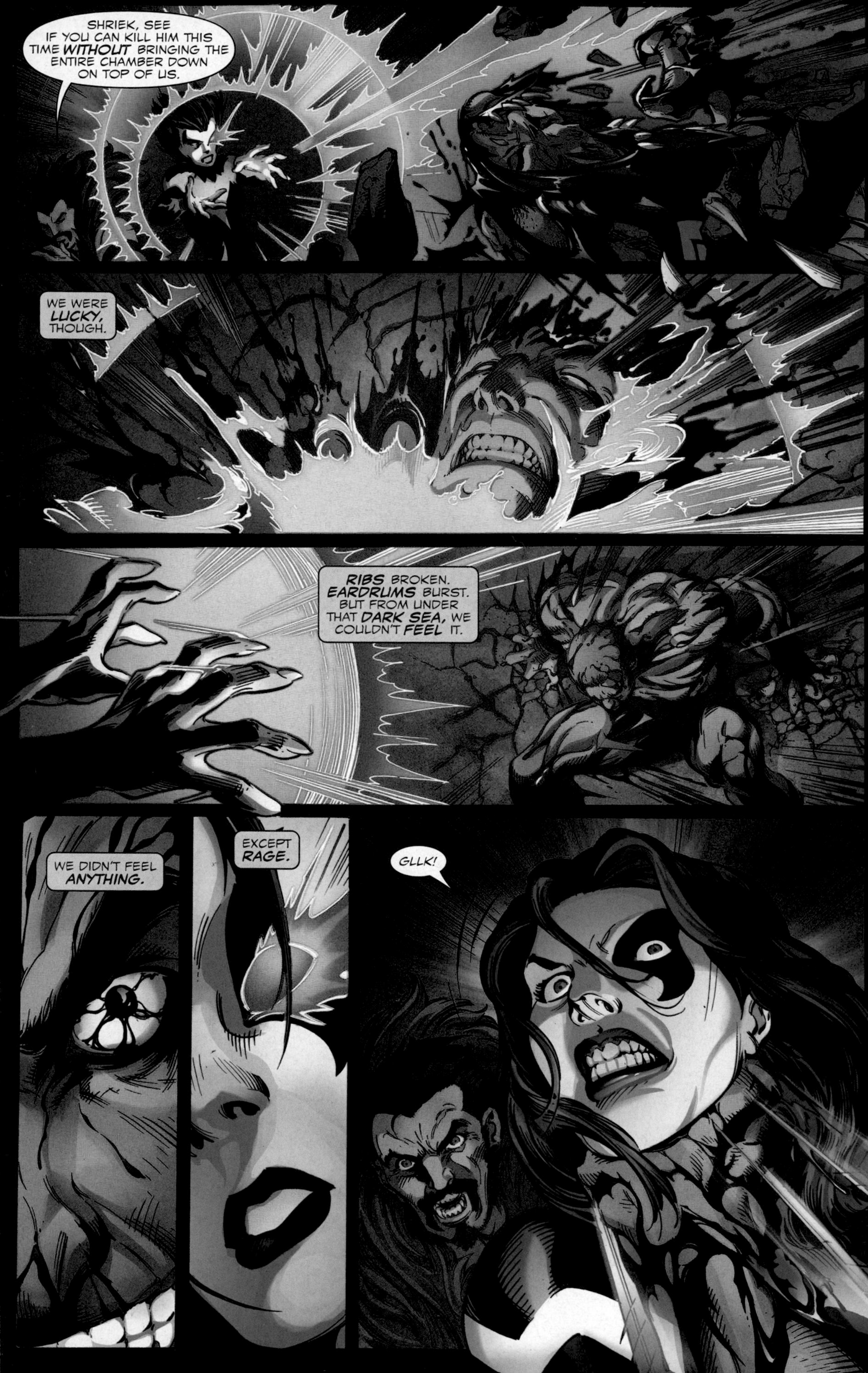
SHRIEK, SEE IF YOU CAN KILL HIM THIS TIME WITHOUT BRINGING THE ENTIRE CHAMBER DOWN ON TOP OF US.
WE WERE LUCKY, THOUGH.
RIBS BROKEN. EARDRUMS BURST. BUT FROM UNDER THAT DARK SEA, WE COULDN'T FEEL IT.
WE DIDN'T FEEL ANYTHING.
EXCEPT RAGE.
GLLK!

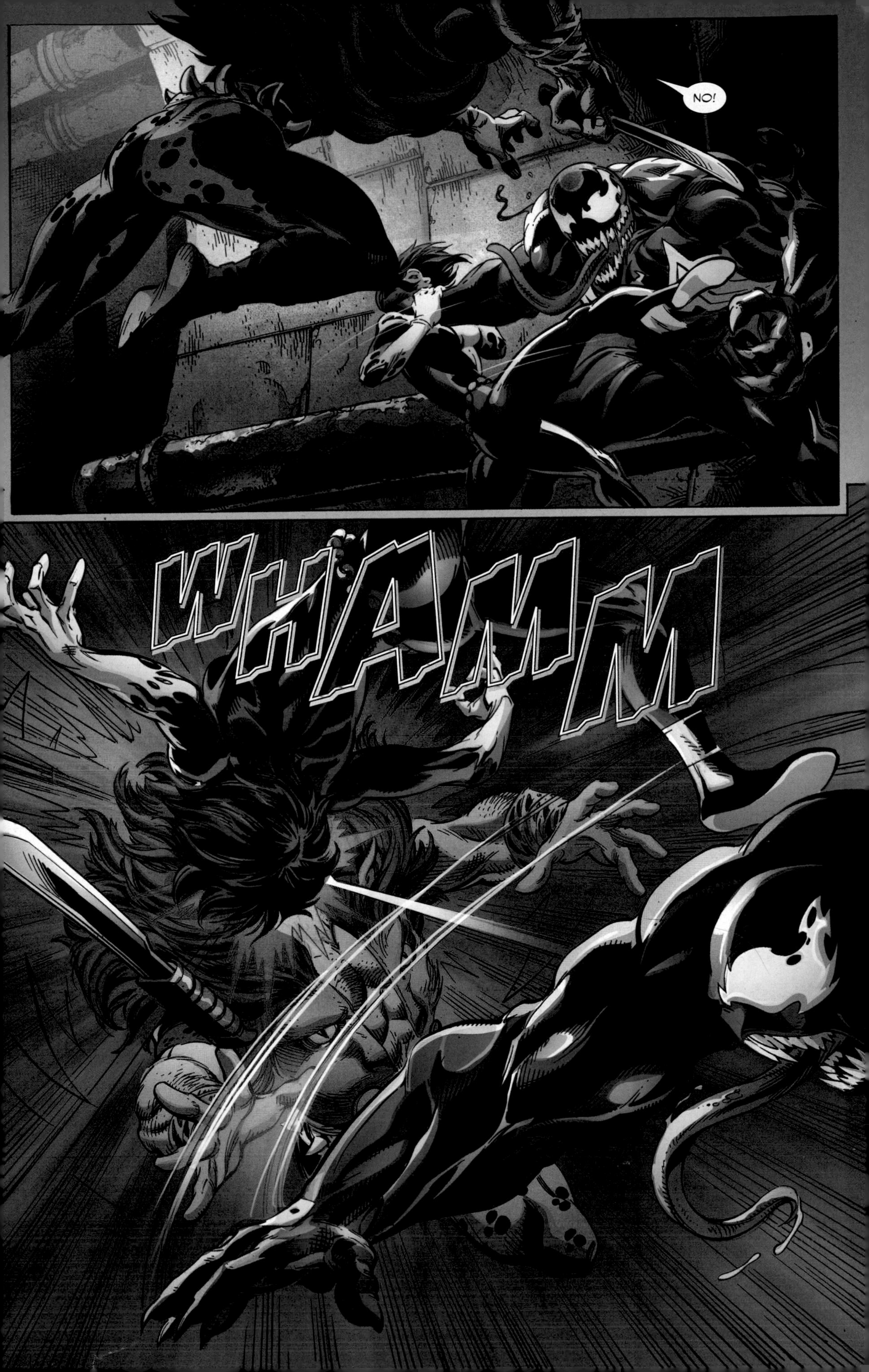
NO!
WHAMM

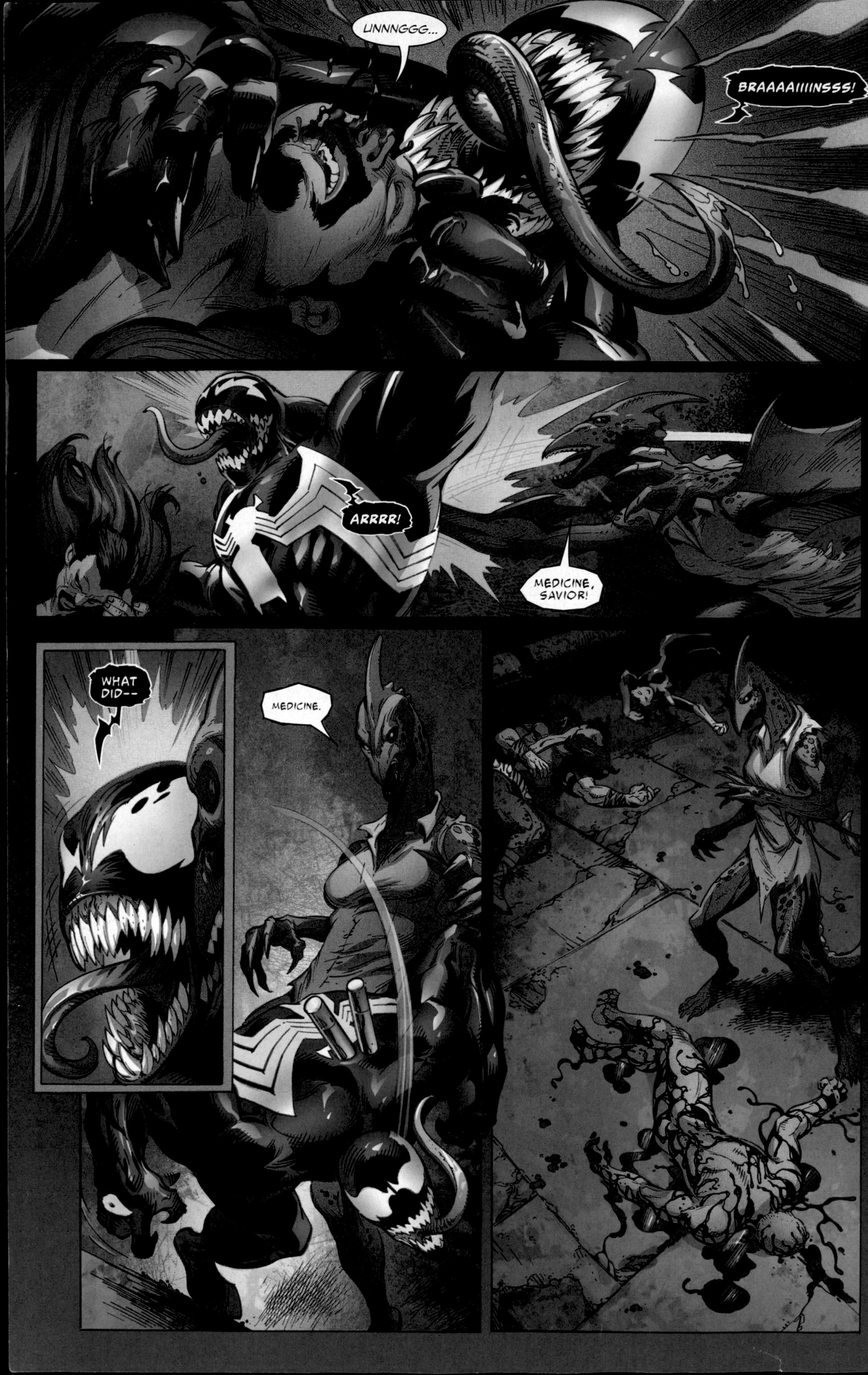
UNNNGGG...
BRAAAAIIIINSSS!
ARRRR!
MEDICINE, SAVIOR!
WHAT DID--
MEDICINE.

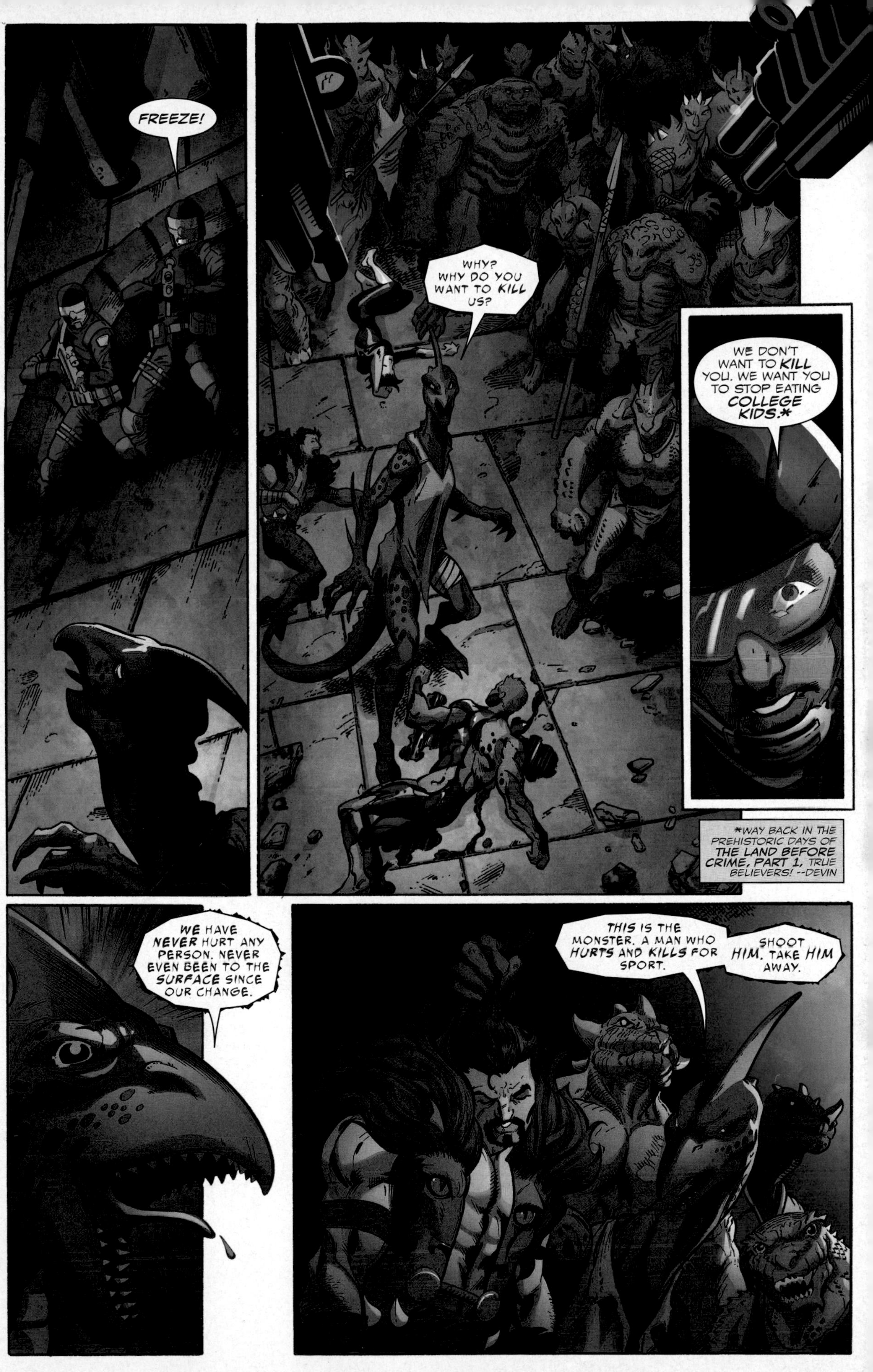

FREEZE!
WHY? WHY DO YOU WANT TO KILL US?
WE DON'T WANT TO KILL YOU. WE WANT YOU TO STOP EATING COLLEGE KIDS.*
*WAY BACK IN THE PREHISTORIC DAYS OF THE LAND BEFORE CRIME, PART 1, TRUE BELIEVERS! --DEVIN
WE HAVE NEVER HURT ANY PERSON. NEVER EVEN BEEN TO THE SURFACE SINCE OUR CHANGE.
THIS IS THE MONSTER. A MAN WHO HURTS AND KILLS FOR SPORT.
SHOOT HIM. TAKE HIM AWAY.

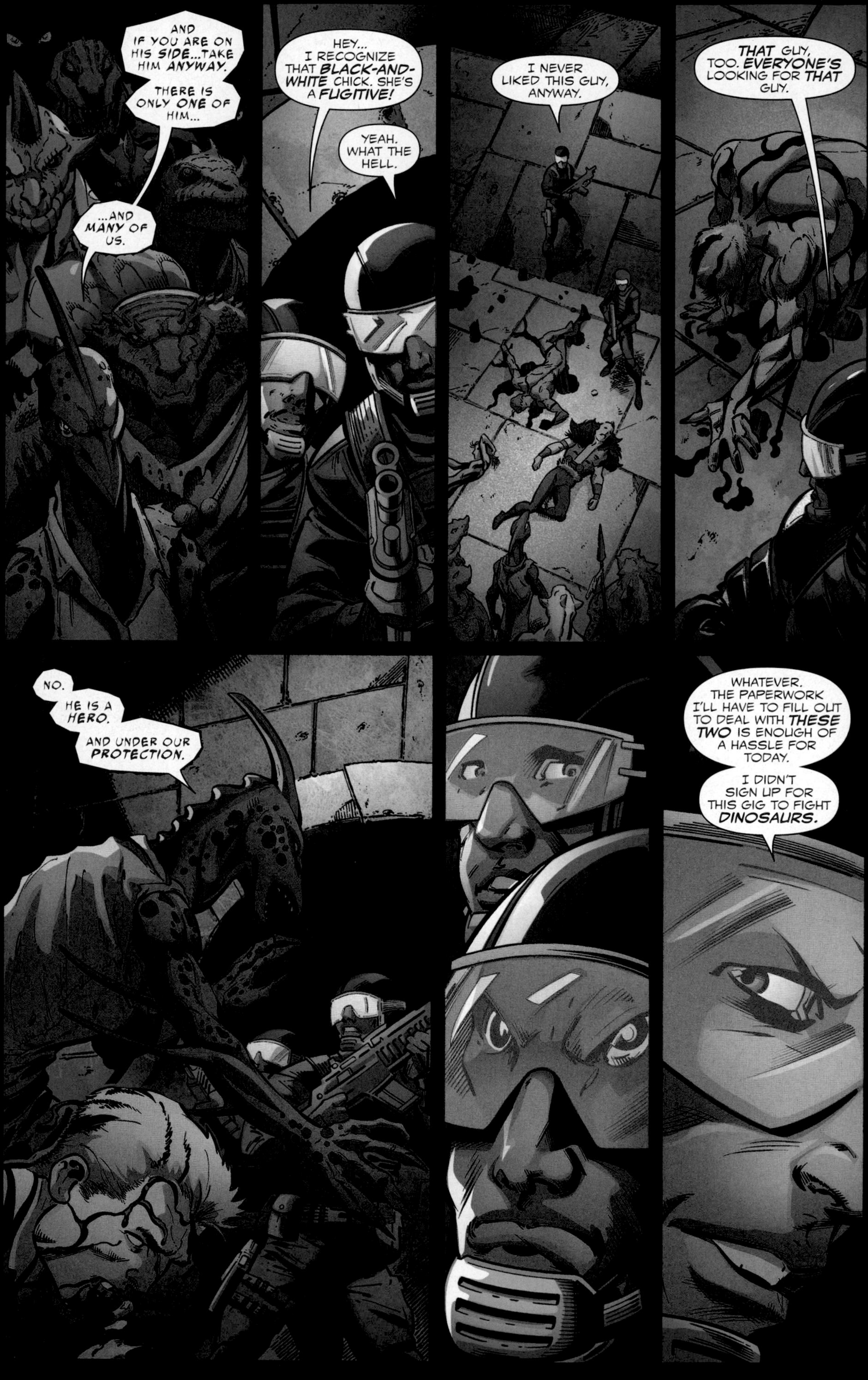
AND IF YOU ARE ON HIS SIDE...TAKE HIM ANYWAY.
THERE IS ONLY ONE OF HIM...
...AND MANY OF US.
HEY... I RECOGNIZE THAT BLACK-AND-WHITE CHICK. SHE'S A FUGITIVE!
YEAH. WHAT THE HELL.
I NEVER LIKED THIS GUY, ANYWAY.
THAT GUY, TOO. EVERYONE'S LOOKING FOR THAT GUY.
NO.
HE IS A HERO.
AND UNDER OUR PROTECTION.
WHATEVER. THE PAPERWORK I'LL HAVE TO FILL OUT TO DEAL WITH THESE TWO IS ENOUGH OF A HASSLE FOR TODAY.
I DIDN'T SIGN UP FOR THIS GIG TO FIGHT DINOSAURS.

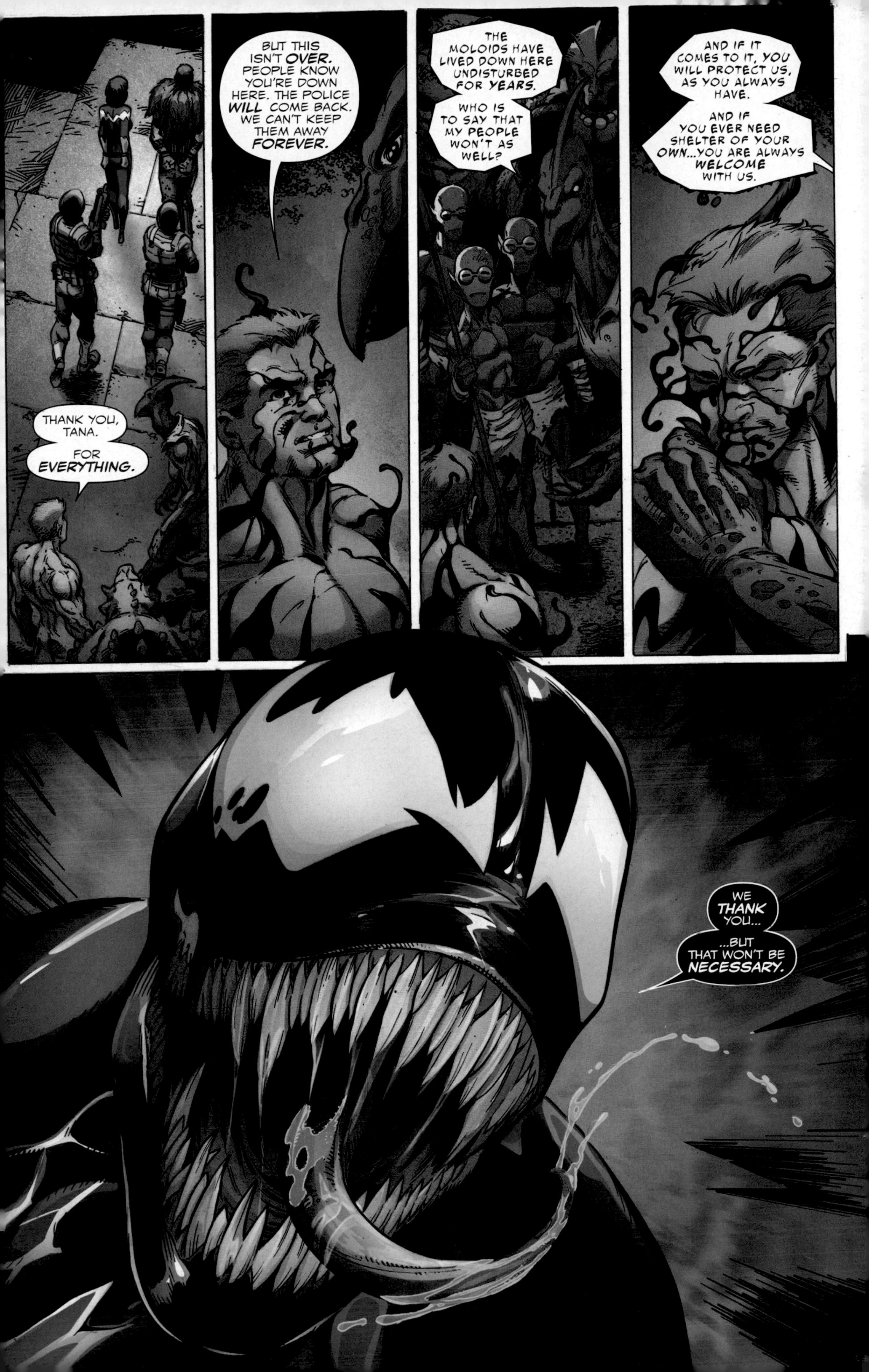

THANK YOU, TANA.
FOR EVERYTHING.
BUT THIS ISN'T OVER. PEOPLE KNOW YOU'RE DOWN HERE. THE POLICE WILL COME BACK. WE CAN'T KEEP THEM AWAY FOREVER.
THE MOLOIDS HAVE LIVED DOWN HERE UNDISTURBED FOR YEARS.
WHO IS TO SAY THAT MY PEOPLE WON'T AS WELL?
AND IF IT COMES TO IT, YOU WILL PROTECT US, AS YOU ALWAYS HAVE.
AND IF YOU EVER NEED SHELTER OF YOUR OWN...YOU ARE ALWAYS WELCOME WITH US.
WE THANK YOU...
...BUT THAT WON'T BE NECESSARY.

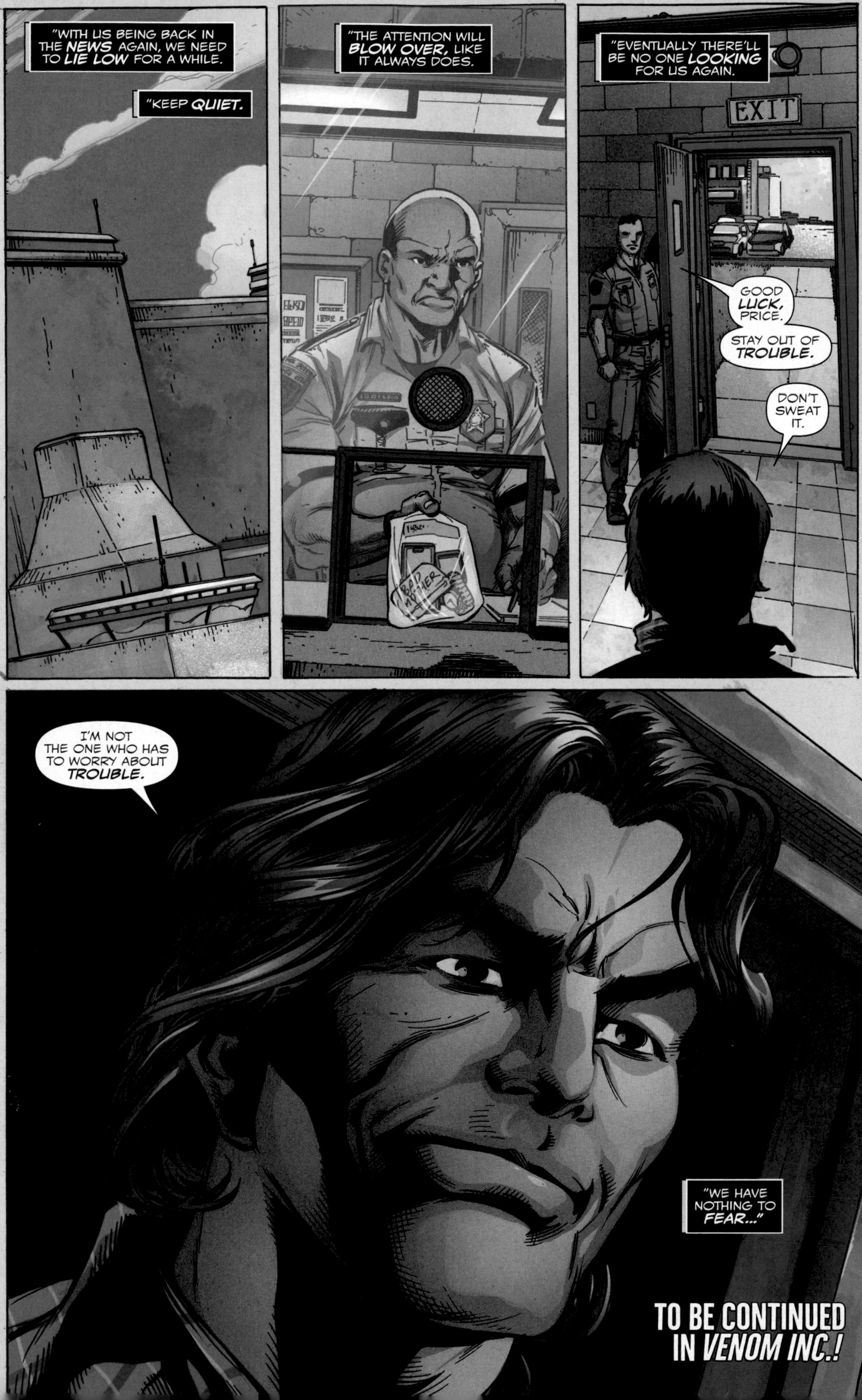
"WITH US BEING BACK IN THE NEWS AGAIN, WE NEED TO LIE LOW FOR A WHILE.
"KEEP QUIET.
"THE ATTENTION WILL BLOW OVER, LIKE IT ALWAYS DOES.
"EVENTUALLY THERE'LL BE NO ONE LOOKING FOR US AGAIN.
EXIT
GOOD LUCK, PRICE.
STAY OUT OF TROUBLE.
DON'T SWEAT IT.
I'M NOT THE ONE WHO HAS TO WORRY ABOUT TROUBLE.
"WE HAVE NOTHING TO FEAR..."
TO BE CONTINUED IN VENOM INC.!

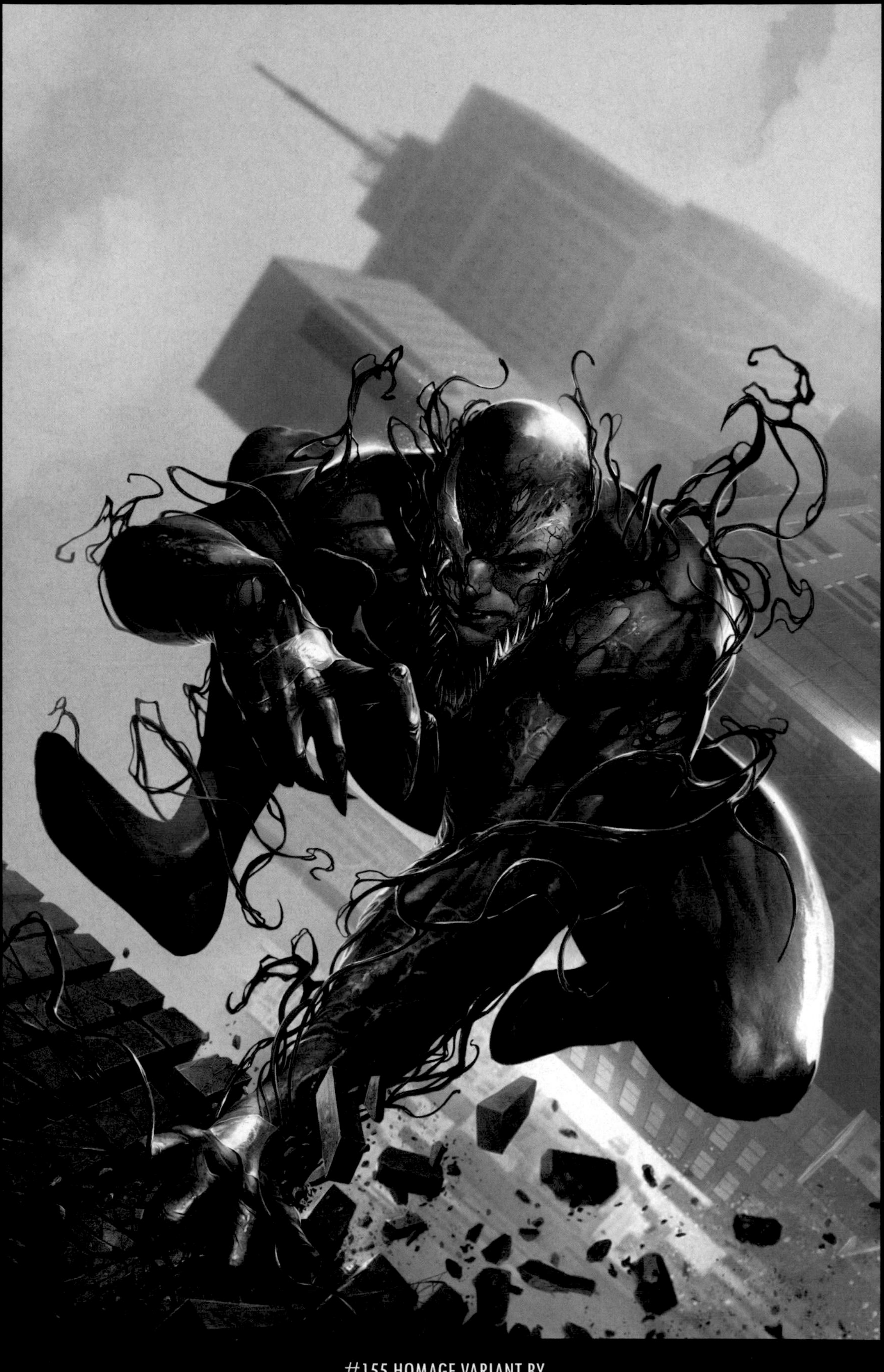

#155 HOMAGE VARIANT BY
FRANCESCO MATTINA

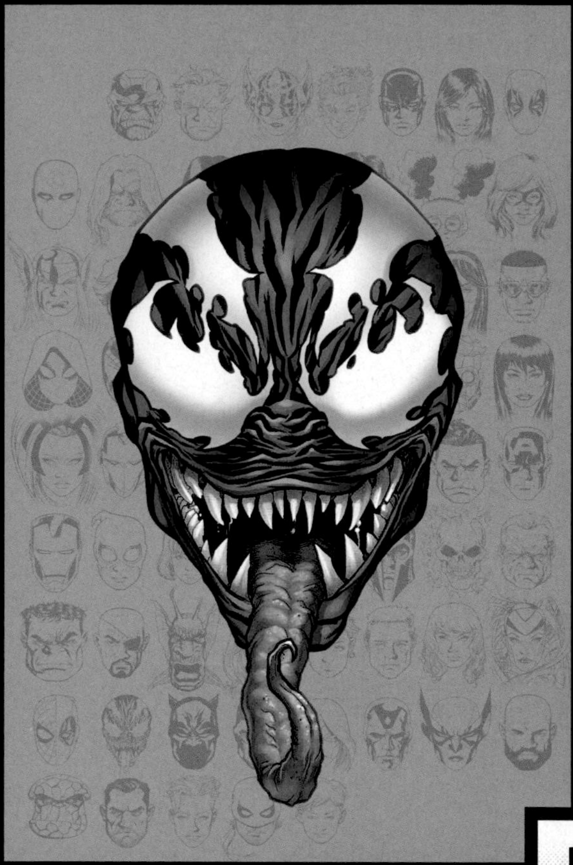

#155 LEGACY HEADSHOT VARIANT BY
MIKE McKONE & RACHELLE ROSENBERG

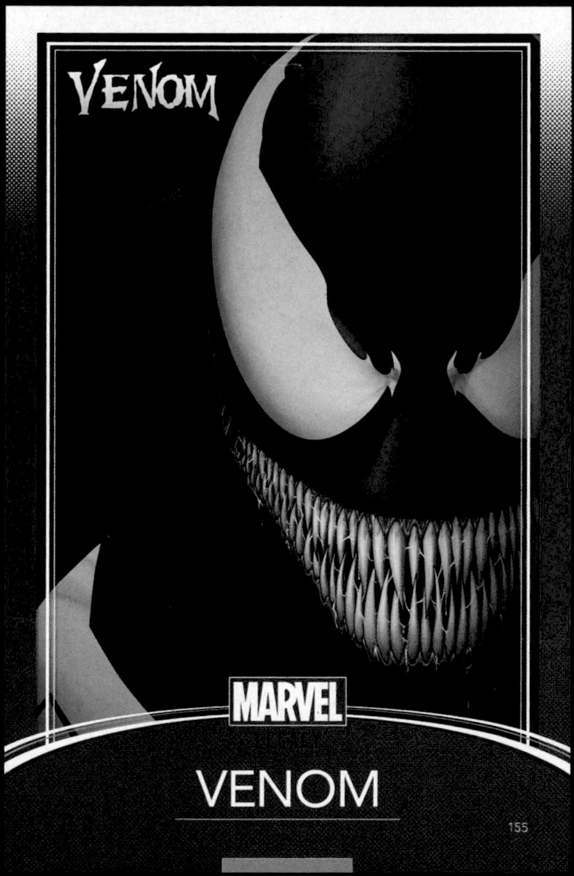
VENOM
MARVEL
VENOM
155

#155 TRADING CARD VARIANT BY
JOHN TYLER CHRISTOPHER

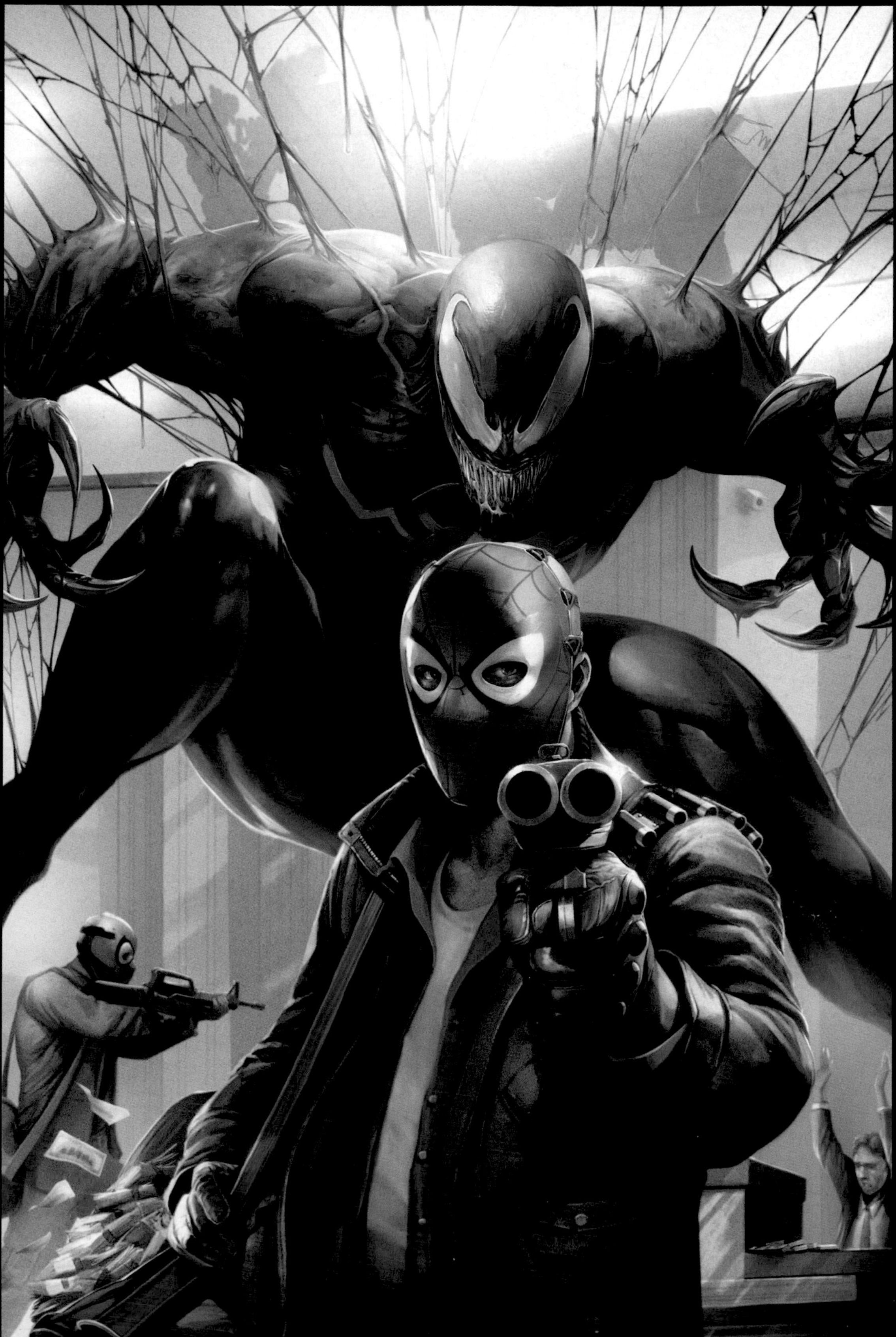

#155 VARIANT BY
FRANCESCO MATTINA

VENOM

HOW TO DRAW VENOM
IN SIX EASY STEPS!
BY CHIP "THE LIVING SUIT" ZDARSKY

Wow! A "sketch variant cover"! And a scary one at that, if "a Spider-Man with teeth" sounds scary to you! Well, to prepare you to draw your very own VENOM, here's a fun and informative step-by-step guide!

1

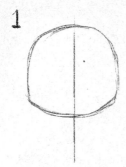

VENOM has a very distinct head shape, so I find it best to start with the top half! It almost looks like half of a pill container! A SCARY one!

2

We want an open-mouthed VENOM here, so the bottom outline should look like a stretched skull's jawbone! Eek!

3

I've described SPIDER-MAN's eyes as looking like two slightly upturned leaves, and these are similar, except the leaves look slightly crunchy and decayed! Ahh!

4

What does VENOM have that SPIDER-MAN doesn't? Teeth! I mean, Spidey has them UNDER his mask, but you get the idea. Draw the bottom of his mouth close to the outside of his jaw bone, and fill that mouth with SPOOKY teeth!

5

Now to render him! I like to keep my black line creaky and conforming to the evil contours of his face! And some light drool in his mouth! SCARY!

6

Ah! I almost forgot the scariest part! His TONGUE! Break out your eraser! Now go and give your friends and family NIGHTMARES with your very own VENOM sketch abilities! Cheers!

#155 HOW TO DRAW VARIANT BY
CHIP ZDARSKY